250
BIGGEST
MISTAKES
3RD YEAR MEDICAL
STUDENTS MAKE
AND HOW TO
AVOID THEM

SAMIR P. DESAI MD
RAJANI KATTA MD

PUBLISHED BY

HOUSTON, TEXAS

250 Biggest Mistakes 3rd Year Medical Students Make and How To Avoid Them is published by MD2B, P.O. Box 300988, Houston, TX 77230-0988.

This title replaces the *101 Biggest Mistakes 3rd year Medical Students Make and How to Avoid Them.* (ISBN 0972556109)

www.MD2B.net

NOTICE: The authors and publisher disclaim any personal liability, either directly or indirectly, for advice or information presented within. The authors and publishers have used care and diligence in the preparation of this book. Every effort has been made to ensure the accuracy and completeness of information contained within this book. The reader should understand, however, that most of the book's subject matter is not rooted in scientific observation. The recommendations made within this book have come from the authors' personal experiences and interactions with other attending physicians, residents, and students over many years. Since expectations vary from medical school to medical school, clerkship to clerkship, attending physician to attending physician, and resident to resident, the recommendations are not universally applicable. No responsibility is assumed for errors, inaccuracies, omissions, or any false or misleading implication that may arise due to the text.

Editorial Note: The pronouns "I" and "he" are used throughout this book for ease of readability

Printed in the United States of America

ISBN # 0-9725561-6-8

Dedication...

To our families who have made it all possible

Contents

About the Authors

Samir P. Desai, M.D.

Dr. Samir Desai serves on the faculty of the Baylor College of Medicine in the Department of Medicine. He has educated and mentored medical students and residents, work for which he has received teaching awards. He is an author and editor, having written ten books that together have sold over 70,000 copies worldwide.

Dr. Desai is the author of the popular *The Residency Match: 101 Biggest Mistakes And How To Avoid Them,* a book that shows applicants how to avoid commonly made mistakes during the residency application process. He is also the editor of the Clerkship Mistakes Series, a series of books developed to help students perform at a high level during clinical rotations and acquire the skills needed for a successful career as a physician.

Dr. Desai conceived of and authored the Clinician's Guide Series, a series of books dedicated to providing clinicians with practical approaches to commonly encountered problems. Now in its third edition, the initial book in this series, the *Clinician's Guide to Laboratory Medicine* has become a popular book for third-year medical students, providing a step-by-step approach to laboratory test interpretation. Other titles in this series include the *Clinician's Guide to Diagnosis* and *Clinician's Guide to Internal Medicine.*

In 2002, he founded www.md2b.net, a website committed to helping today's medical student become tomorrow's doctor. At the site, a variety of tools and resources are available to help students tackle the challenges of medical school.

After completing his residency training in Internal Medicine at Northwestern University in Chicago, Illinois, Dr. Desai had the opportunity of serving as chief medical resident. He received his M.D. degree from Wayne State University School of Medicine in Detroit, Michigan, graduating first in his class.

Rajani Katta, M.D.

Dr. Rajani Katta is an Associate Professor in the Department of Dermatology at Baylor College of Medicine. She has authored over thirty articles published in scientific journals, and lectured extensively both nationally and locally on dermatology and contact dermatitis to students, residents, and physicians. She serves as the course director for dermatology in the basic science years, and has served as the clerkship director for the dermatology rotation. She has seen firsthand the importance of outstanding clinical evaluations in securing a position in a competitive specialty, and her insight in this area has helped students seeking these types of competitive positions. After graduating with honors from Baylor College of Medicine and completing her internship in internal medicine, she completed her dermatology residency at the Northwestern University School of Medicine.

Introduction

"I just can't believe it," said Gary, a third year medical student finishing his first clerkship. "Average? But it seemed like everything was going so well."

Gary had just completed his end-of-clerkship meeting with Dr. Gordon, his attending physician. His overall clinical performance was rated as average. He described his experience.

"During my first few days," he said, "I asked the resident how Dr. Gordon would prefer for me to present patients during rounds. I really took his recommendations to heart. Now I find out that my presentations didn't meet Dr. Gordon's expectations. In attending rounds, I spoke up when my patients were being discussed but I kept quiet otherwise, not wanting to slow things down. Now Dr. Gordon tells me I didn't participate enough. He wasn't sure if I was disinterested or just someone who has a quiet personality. He told me that I needed to be more assertive."

Gary continued, "Even the talk I gave didn't go as well as I thought it had. I spent ten minutes talking about heart failure and gave a comprehensive talk about it. Dr. Gordon said that the talk was too superficial and it would have been better if I had picked a certain aspect of heart failure to talk about. I'm so frustrated. I really wanted to do well. Where did I go wrong?"

Every year, thousands of medical students across the country have similar clerkship experiences. They start their clerkships with tremendous enthusiasm and energy, spend long days in the hospital, and work hard, only to be disappointed in the results. Why? The reason is that many of them overlook a critical step, one that prevents them from reaching their full potential during clerkships. What is that step?

Like Gary, they haven't learned how to make the transition between the basic science and clinical years of medical school.

Many clerkship directors, faculty members, and residents feel that students are not adequately prepared for clerkships.

> **Did you know...**
>
> In a survey of clerkship directors in internal medicine, surgery, pediatrics, family medicine, and obstetrics/gynecology at 32 U.S. medical schools, nearly half reported that students were not adequately prepared in key competency areas prior to beginning their third year of medical school.
>
> From Windish DM, Paulman PM, Goroll AH, Bass EB. Do clerkship directors think medical students are prepared for the clerkship years? *Acad Med* 2004; 79: 56-61.

Times of transition in medical education are particularly stressful, and moving from the classroom to the wards is certainly no exception. When physicians look back on their medical school years, nearly all consider the clinical years to be the highlight of their medical education. However, all will tell you that the transition between the basic science and clinical years was quite difficult. Consider the following statements made by new third year students:

"The third year was a whole new world. When I first started, I felt so lost."

"I felt so confused. You need someone to hold your hand and walk you through it but no one does. I didn't think I would ever catch on."

"It's so easy to start off on the wrong foot."

Why is the transition so difficult? The third year of medical school is like starting a new job. Your new job will be nothing like your old one. The skill set that you developed in order to be a successful basic science student is not the same set you'll need to be successful during the third year. The basic science and clinical years of medical school are fundamentally different, as shown in the following table.

Key differences between the basic science and clinical years of medical school

Basic sciences	Clerkships
Day starts at 8 AM or later	Day often well under way by 8 a.m.
Classes usually over by 5 PM	Day rarely ends at 5 PM
Flexible schedule	Structured schedule
Considerable control over time	Cede control over your time to others
Frequent breaks during the day	Few breaks during the day
Weekends always free	Weekend work responsibilities
Sleeping through the night	Working through the night (i.e., on call)
Few surprises during the day	Expect the unexpected
Expectations clear	Expectations often unclear
Intellectual challenge	People challenge (team members, patients)
Same routine from course to course (attending lecture, reading, studying, taking exam, etc.)	Varying routine from clerkship to clerkship, requiring the ability to adapt
Hearing about patients	Taking care of patients
Primary focus on learning and acquiring knowledge	Expectation to apply this knowledge to patients you are caring for
Lots of time to read and study	Lack of time to read and study
Professors	Bosses (interns, residents, attending physicians)
Individual effort	Team effort
Less initiative required	Lots of initiative required
Can do it your way	Must do it the team's way
Objective grading (tests, etc.)	Subjective grading (evaluations, etc.)

At the heart of the problem is the failure to recognize the "hidden curriculum" of values that exists in clerkships. Too often students are left on their own to figure out just what it takes to do well on the rotation. Just when students have determined which behaviors, actions, and attitudes are valued and rewarded, it's time to move on to the next rotation. This affects the performance of students at the start of the year and impacts their performance at the start of every single new rotation.

Transition is difficult. Every year, however, there are medical students who consistently perform at a high level during their third year. What enables these students to succeed? What limits the success of their colleagues? Is there something that sets these top performers apart from the rest?

These savvy students not only work hard but they also know what it takes to impress attending physicians and residents.

They become familiar with their role and responsibilities quickly and integrate socially and professionally into their teams. They learn to avoid the costly mistakes that their colleagues tend to make. These are the mistakes that prevent students from reaching their full potential during clerkships.

Failure to reach your full potential during clerkships can negatively affect you in many ways. First, the skills, attitudes, behaviors, and habits you develop during this crucial year will shape and impact your future as a physician. In fact, several studies have shown that certain behaviors displayed by third year students have been associated with future disciplinary action by state medical boards.

Did you know...

In 2005, Teherani and colleagues published the results of a study seeking to identify the domains of unprofessional behavior in medical school associated with disciplinary action by a state medical board. Three domains of unprofessional behavior were significantly associated with future disciplinary action: poor reliability and responsibility, poor initiative and motivation, and lack of self-improvement and adaptability.

Teherani A, Hodgson CS, Banach M, and Papadakis MA. Domains of unprofessional behavior during medical school associated with future disciplinary action by a state medical board. *Acad Med* 2005; 80 (10 Suppl): S17-20.

Second, clerkship grades are a major factor used by residency programs when making decisions to interview and rank applicants.

Did you know...

In 1999, Wagoner and Suriano reported the results of a survey of program directors in 14 specialties. In this survey, program directors were asked to rank academic criteria according to level of importance in selecting residents. "Grades in required clerkships" consistently received top ranking from directors in all specialties, including competitive specialties such as orthopedic surgery and ophthalmology. "Number of honors grades" also was highly valued, especially by competitive specialties.

Wagoner NE, Suriano JR. Program directors' responses to a survey on variables used to select residents in a time of change. *Acad Med* 1999; 74 (1): 51-58.

Third, clerkship grades are a major determinant of class rank. How important is class rank in the residency selection process? In the study performed by Wagoner and Suriano, the most competitive specialties cited class rank as one of three factors considered most important in considering a candidate. The other two were grades in required clerkships and total number of honors grades.

Fourth, clerkship grades are a factor used by medical schools in electing students to the Alpha Omega Alpha Honor Medical Society, also known as AOA. According to the AOA constitution, only students "whose scholastic qualifications place them in the upper twenty-five percent of their class shall be considered for election." The most competitive specialties, as well as highly sought residency programs in less competitive specialties, attach considerable importance to AOA membership.

Fifth, comments made on clerkship evaluations by attending physicians and residents are often taken and placed word for word in the medical student performance evaluation (MSPE), formerly known as the Dean's letter. This is an important component of the residency application.

Finally, your clerkship performance is important in securing strong letters of recommendation from faculty, yet another key part of the residency application.

Failure to reach your full potential during clerkships can affect your chances of matching into a particular specialty, a specific residency program, and your future career as a physician.

Starting the clinical years of medical school is a watershed moment in your medical education, one that requires you to have a specific strategy for success. This book focuses on the mistakes that students make during the third year of medical school. Once you are familiar with these mistakes, you can do everything in your power to avoid them. You can then become the savvy student who is poised for clerkship success. You can secure outstanding clinical evaluations, strong letters of recommendation, and have favorable comments added to your MSPE, all of which will maximize your chances of matching with the residency program of your choice. You can build a strong foundation for your career as a physician.

Take charge of your third year, instead of letting it take charge of you.

The Team

During clerkships, you will be part of a team responsible for the care of those patients assigned to the team. The team will usually consist of the following individuals:

- Attending physician
- Resident
- Intern

While all teams will be led by an attending physician, the composition of the rest of your team will often vary from clerkship to clerkship. Your team may have only a resident, only an intern, or both. Some teams have several residents and interns. You may also find yourself working with no interns or residents, reporting directly to the attending physician.

Attending physician

The attending physician is typically a faculty member at the medical school who has been assigned to be the leader of the team. The attending's primary goal is to ensure that the patients assigned to the team receive the best possible care. Providing a solid educational experience for residents, interns, and medical students is also an important goal. The attending physician is responsible for evaluating all team members. The team's contact with the attending varies according to what type of service you are assigned. On an inpatient ward, contact with the attending may be limited to attending rounds. In a clinic or outpatient setting, you may have ongoing contact with the attending physician as each new patient is seen.

Resident

The resident physician is a house officer who, at the minimum, has completed an internship. By definition, internship refers to the first year of residency training that follows medical school graduation. Second in charge, the resident oversees the care of all patients assigned to the team. The resident supervises the work of the interns and medical students, and ensures that the treatment plans for individual patients are implemented. The resident is also responsible for teaching the junior members of the team.

Intern

Next to medical students, the interns are the most junior members of the team. You will probably have the most interaction with the intern, since he or she will also be following patients assigned to you by the resident. When issues arise in the management of your patient, you should first discuss the matter with the intern. Interns have a lot on their plate, which is why they need to function quickly and efficiently to accomplish the day's activities. On a daily basis, some of their responsibilities include scheduling tests and procedures, drawing blood or performing other procedures, checking lab test results, entering orders, writing daily progress notes, and communicating with their patients' families. Although many interns love to teach students, they are often unable to teach as much as they would like because of the many demands placed on their time.

A Typical Day

Here's what a typical clerkship day (inpatient setting) looks like:

6:30 - 7:30 AM	Pre-rounds
7:30 - 9:00 AM	Work rounds
9:00 - 10:00 AM	Time to get your work done or morning report
10:00 - Noon	Attending physician rounds
Noon - 1:00 PM	Noon conference
1:00 -?	Time to get your work done (+ student conferences)

Keep in mind that the day's schedule will vary from clerkship to clerkship. It may also vary within a clerkship when you move from one hospital to another or change teams. Below is a description of pre-rounds, work rounds, and attending physician rounds.

Pre-rounds

The day will typically begin with pre-rounds. During pre-rounds, you will see your patients alone. The goal is to identify any new events that have occurred in your patient's hospital course after you left the hospital on the previous day. The information that you gather will be presented to the resident and intern during work rounds, which immediately follow pre-rounds.

Work rounds

During work rounds, also known as resident rounds, the team (usually without the attending physician) travels from room to room, seeing each of the patients on the service. The most junior member of the team (junior medical student, intern) is required to update the team on the patient's progress. This update will include any significant events that have occurred overnight and the results of any lab/diagnostic testing. The information you present will help the team formulate a diagnostic and therapeutic plan.

Attending physician rounds

Attending physician rounds, generally referred to as attending rounds, is a period of time during which the entire team meets. Your interaction with the attending physician will mainly occur during these rounds. What occurs during attending rounds will vary from day to day. If your team admitted patients the day before, the attending physician will expect to hear about these new patients. Typically, the most junior member of the team following the patient, will present newly admitted patients to the attending. If there are no new patients to present, the attending may ask for updates on previously admitted patients, discuss interesting aspects of patients' illnesses, conduct bedside rounds, or have team members give talks.

Commonly Made Mistakes

With Evaluations

There is a growing body of literature devoted to the study of accurate evaluation. Within medical education, the challenge is to provide an evaluation that accurately summarizes a student's performance in clinical rotations. In the basic sciences, evaluation is completely objective—what score did the student receive on the exam? In clinical rotations, subjective factors become much more important.

Inherent difficulties in subjective evaluations may result in a clerkship grade that doesn't accurately reflect a student's performance level. To increase the likelihood of earning the grade that you deserve, you must understand the problems that exist in the clinical assessment of medical students. In this chapter, the focus is on the evaluation form itself, the factors used by faculty and residents to rate students, and the ways in which you can use this knowledge to increase your chances of clerkship success.

Medical schools utilize a number of methodologies to evaluate students' clinical performance. These include end-of-clerkship written and oral examinations, objective structured clinical exams (OSCE), attendance at mandatory clerkship learning activities (lectures, rounds), review of required assignments (write-ups), and faculty/resident ratings. Of these methodologies, the latter is nearly ubiquitous throughout core clerkships done at U.S. medical schools.

Between 1993 and 1998, the Liaison Committee on Medical Education (LCME) performed full accreditation surveys at 97 medical schools. As part of the survey, the LCME sought to determine how students were evaluated in clinical clerkships. The results showed that almost all clerkships rely on faculty and resident ratings as a method of evaluating student performance.

Percentage of 97 U.S. Medical Schools Using Faculty/Resident Ratings for the Evaluation of Students in the Core Clinical Clerkships

Clerkship	% of medical schools
Family Medicine	96.7
Internal Medicine	98.9
Obstetrics and Gynecology	96.9
Pediatrics	100.0
Psychiatry	96.9
Surgery	96.8

From LCME Medical Education Databases for 97 U.S. medical schools that underwent full accreditation surveys between July 1993 and June 1998. Also from Kassebaum DG, Eaglen RH. Shortcomings in the evaluation of students' clinical skills and behaviors in medical school. *Academic Medicine* 1999; 74 (7): 841-849.

Faculty and resident ratings usually account for a large percentage of a student's clerkship grade. Typically, 50 to 70 percent of a student's grade is based on these ratings. Since clerkship grades are an important component of the residency application, students are naturally interested in learning how they can ensure outstanding clerkship evaluations. Short of filling out the evaluation yourself, there is no way to ensure an outstanding evaluation. However, if you heed the advice of this book, you will maximize your chances of securing an outstanding evaluation.

Mistake # 1

Beginning the rotation without a clear sense of what your evaluators are seeking

In a broad sense, you will be assessed in two areas: your clinical skills and your professional behavior. Evaluators will observe your day-to-day performance during patient care in order to draw conclusions about your abilities in these two areas. In particular, faculty members and residents will take note of your ability to take histories, perform physical examinations, present patient information, create patient write-ups, and interact with team members and patients.

From their observations of your work, your evaluators will rate you on these competencies. While all evaluators in a particular clerkship will be asked to complete the same evaluation form, the emphasis placed on the different competencies will vary, as shown in the following box.

Did you know...

In an analysis of physician ratings of student clinical performance, residents and faculty were found to use different criteria to evaluate students (Metheny). Residents tended to place more value on a student's work ethic, teamwork, motivation, punctuality, interest in the specialty, and patient involvement. Faculty, on the other hand, placed more emphasis on a student's knowledge base and interest level.

Even among evaluators at the same training level, there are differences in the standards used to evaluate clinical performance. The following study highlighted these differences.

Did you know...

In a study of over 200 faculty internists, participants watched a videotape of a resident performing a work-up of a new patient (Noel). Immediately following the viewing, the faculty members rated the clinical skills of the resident. They also evaluated the overall clinical performance of the resident. There was significant disagreement between the raters. With one resident, for example, 5% of the faculty participants rated the overall clinical performance as unsatisfactory. However, this same resident's overall performance was rated as superior by 5% of the rater group. The performance was rated marginal by 26% while 64% rated it as satisfactory. A similar result was noted with a second resident. Based on these results, investigators concluded that evaluators base their ratings on different criteria and standards. Evaluators may also assign different weights to the criteria that they use for evaluation.

Mistake # 2

Underestimating the importance of specific faculty and resident comments

The Medical Student Performance Evaluation or MSPE, formerly known as the Dean's letter, is an important component of the residency application. It summarizes an applicant's performance and accomplishments during medical school. Typically created in the summer and fall of the student's fourth year by one of the Deans or his designee, the MSPE is used by residency programs to aid them in the resident selection process.

Although the MSPE contains information about preclinical performance and extracurricular activities, the focus tends to be on clerkship performance. In addition to providing residency programs with the overall clerkship grade, narrative information from clerkships is included. Where does this information come from? On evaluation forms, there is usually a section in which evaluators are asked to comment on a student's clinical performance. Comments about professionalism, knowledge, communication skills with other health care professionals, clinical reasoning, and clinical judgment are most common (Pulito).

While comments are generally positive, evaluators may also include negative comments. Since comments made by faculty and residents are often taken verbatim from these evaluations and placed in the MSPE, you must put forth your best effort in all rotations. Do not let your dislike of a specialty or a particular attending affect how hard you work or how well you work with others.

> *"Stacy rotated on our Obstetrics service, where she received a grade of Pass. She is interested in a future career in dermatology, and in evaluating her work ethic, we found that lifestyle issues did appear to be of importance to her."*

Such comments may sink your chances of matching into the residency program of your choice, or even your field of choice.

When reading the comments of an evaluator, you may at times notice a lack of correlation between the evaluator's comments and his rating of your performance. Comments may be quite positive but the numerical ratings may not reflect that. Why does this happen? First, an evaluator may not feel comfortable writing anything negative in the comments section. Second, an evaluator may place a higher value on factors that he did not discuss in the comments section. You may be described in the comments section as "hard-working," which is certainly a valued attribute. If the evaluator judged your problem-solving ability to be average, though, and gives that section more weight than work ethic, your ratings will be lower overall.

Mistake # 3
Glancing over your clerkship evaluation form

Clerkships will generally make available to you a copy of the evaluation form. Often the form is included as part of the clerkship orientation material. If not, you might find it on the clerkship's website. If you are unable to find it anywhere, it is imperative that you ask the clerkship director for a copy. You should look over this form early in the rotation.

When you are looking over the form, your goal is to be well informed of the criteria on which you will be evaluated. This requires much more than a cursory glance.

The typical clerkship evaluation form consists of a number of general categories. These categories may include the following or variations of the following:

- Patient care
- Fund and application of medical knowledge
- Clinical judgment and problem-solving
- Professionalism
- Interpersonal and communication skills

These general categories are commonly subdivided into subcategories. For example, under the "professionalism" category may be the following subcategories:

- Working relationships
- Relationships with patients
- Attendance

Next to each category is often a rating scale, which is usually numeric. The evaluator is instructed to mark a certain point on the scale which reflects the student's performance level. For example, an evaluator may be asked to rate the student's relationship with patients on a scale of one to five, with five being the highest score. To guide evaluators, clerkship directors often place written descriptors of what constitutes high, middle, and low scores. On the Baylor College of Medicine "Evaluation of Student Performance" form, for example, the highest mark for "relationship with patients" is given to the student that has the patient's "full confidence" and "works exceptionally well with difficult patients."

You must become familiar with the written descriptors on the evaluation form. This will help you determine the specific type of behavior that will earn you the top marks in each category.

For example, the Baylor evaluation form also asks evaluators to rate students in the category of patient-specific fund of knowledge. In this category, the form clearly states that the highest marks should be given to the student who "assimilates and applies relevant literature." There are a variety of ways in which students can demonstrate use of the literature. Examples include sharing a journal article with the team or listing references from the literature in a write-up. When students don't show me any signs that they are assimilating and applying relevant literature, I bring this to their attention at their mid-rotation feedback meeting. Quite often, these students are surprised to learn that they cannot receive the highest rating in this area unless they demonstrate that they are turning to the literature. In talking with these students, all of them had seen the evaluation form, but this important point was either missed or was not internalized. My advice is to read your evaluation form carefully at the start of your rotation and then revisit it several times during the rotation. You should also consider filling out the form yourself as a self-assessment tool, an exercise that may give you some insight into your progress towards meeting the clerkship's goals.

Tip # 1

As soon as you start a new clerkship, look over the evaluation form. Familiarize yourself with the criteria on which you will be evaluated. What descriptors are used to describe top performance in each category?

Mistake # 4

Remaining unfamiliar with the goals and objectives of the rotation

Clerkship directors will make students and evaluators aware of the goals and objectives for the rotation. For students, this information is generally communicated during the clerkship orientation and can often be found in the orientation syllabus. It is imperative that you read this information. Without this knowledge, it will be difficult to meet these expectations. If you don't meet the goals and objectives of the rotation, you won't receive the best possible ratings.

You also need to ascertain and meet your evaluators' expectations. Your residents and attendings have their own expectations, and you must learn precisely what those are in the first few days of the rotation. You might end up meeting the clerkship's objectives but fall short of meeting your evaluators' expectations.

Tip # 2

Each evaluator will compare your performance to a certain standard of performance that he has in mind. How can you determine the evaluator's standard of performance? In addition to learning about the evaluator's expectations, ask him to describe what he considers an ideal student.

Mistake # 5

Not knowing who will be evaluating you

At most schools, residents and attending physicians are asked to complete evaluations of your performance. Although less common, other members of the healthcare team, including interns and nurses, may also be asked to provide evaluation information. At the start of the clerkship, determine which team members will be formally evaluating you. As obvious as this may seem, many students overlook this important detail.

Tip # 3

Are evaluations of your clinical performance weighted differently at your school? In other words, do attending physician evaluations carry more weight than resident evaluations? This is important information.

While clerkship directors will have a record of whom you are working with, attending and resident assignments do commonly change. For example, a family emergency may require your attending physician to be away for much of your rotation, requiring you to work with another attending. Your clerkship director may not be notified of the change. He won't realize that the new attending needs to be contacted for information about your performance.

Tip # 4

Inform your clerkship director of the residents and attending physicians who have served as your supervisors, especially if there has been a change in supervisor assignments.

Mistake # 6

Failing to realize that team members will talk to one another about your performance

Even if you learn that a team member has no formal input into your evaluation, realize that those with input can, and often do, seek the opinions of other team members. This tends to be a problem for students who consciously perform at a high level for those with input but at a lower level for those whom they feel have no say in their evaluation. Since the attending physician will often approach your intern and resident in order to supplement his own assessment, don't give them any reason to speak less than glowingly.

Tip # 5

Your evaluator will often solicit opinions of your performance from other team members. The evaluator will be looking to see if team members' thoughts are consistent with his own. In the event of inconsistency, your evaluator may question his own assessment.

Did you know...

Faculty often receive information about students' performance from residents (Pulito). 66% received input about interpersonal/communication skills with other health care professionals. 56% received input about surgical/medical knowledge. 44% received input about clinical reasoning/clinical judgment, professionalism/dependability, and interpersonal skills with patients.

Mistake # 7

Underestimating the importance of the write-up and oral case presentation in your evaluation

Ideally, your evaluators will base their ratings on direct observation of your work. For example, the evaluation of your ability to take a history and perform a physical exam should be based on direct observation. The literature has shown, however, that faculty members often don't observe students during a history and physical. How then do faculty rate students in these areas? In my opinion, if a faculty member has insufficient data to rate a student in a particular area due to lack of observation, he should refrain from evaluating a student in that area. In fact, most evaluation forms give the evaluator the option to mark "not observed."

While some will mark "not observed," others will proceed to rate you based on inferences made from their interactions with you during rounds. In particular, the quality of your oral case presentations and write-ups will be used to draw conclusions about your skill in taking a history and performing a physical exam. If your evaluator feels that your oral case presentation and write-up on a particular patient was complete, he may conclude that your history and physical exam was complete as well. This conclusion may or may not be true.

Did you know...

In a study of 322 students at the University of Virginia School of Medicine at the end of their third year, 51% reported never having a faculty member observe them while taking a history (Howley); 81% had never been observed performing a complete physical examination.

Did you know...

In one study, five of the nine faculty participants rated a student's ability to take a history and physical exam from factors other than direct observation (Pulito). They wrote that "in the clinic setting, for example, if a student presents a patient to an attending and is verbally facile, succinctly describing a focused history and physical examination, the inference may be drawn that the student expeditiously obtained the relevant history and performed an appropriate physical examination."

9

Mistake # 8

Performing poorly during an observed history and physical examination

In recent years, the importance of direct observation has received considerable attention. Clerkships now strongly encourage evaluators to observe their students performing a history and physical examination. If your supervisor wishes to observe you, you should ascertain his expectations before the observed patient encounter. If you're unsure of his expectations, refer to the recommendations listed in the following boxes. You should follow these recommendations even when not observed.

During an observed history...

- Begin your patient encounter by greeting the patient and family member(s) if present. Make good eye contact while shaking hands.

- Introduce yourself properly as a medical student, explain your role in the patient's care, and obtain consent to proceed with the history and physical exam.

- Inquire about the patient's physical comfort, and respond to any emotions the patient expresses.

- Sit with your body position bent forward slightly.

- Start the interview with the question "Could you tell me why you came to the hospital?"

- Listen to the patient's story carefully. Avoid taking extensive notes while the patient is talking.

- Let the patient speak without interrupting. Encourage the patient to continue by nodding, saying "uh-huh," or "please go on."

- Initially, ask open questions to encourage the patient to elaborate. As the interview progresses, ask closed questions to further characterize the patient's symptom(s).

- Avoid the use of medical jargon. Instead use common language the patient can understand.

- If the patient shows emotion, acknowledge and encourage the patient to discuss how he is feeling.

- Periodically summarize the information that you receive to ensure that you have understood correctly.

- Toward the end of the interview, ask the patient what he thinks is causing the illness. Ask the patient about his concerns and expectations.

During an observed physical exam...

- Begin by asking the patient for permission to proceed with the physical examination.
- Before laying your hands on the patient, wash your hands with soap and water.
- Prepare the patient for the different parts of the exam by informing him what you plan to do.
- Respect the patient's privacy. Do not expose any more of the patient than is absolutely necessary.
- Provide the patient with feedback during the exam (e.g., "your heart sounds fine").
- Be attentive to the patient's comfort during all aspects of the exam.
- If the patient asks a question during the exam, either answer the question or inform the patient that you will address it when the exam is complete.
- At the end, summarize the key findings.
- Complete the physical exam with a statement that informs the patient of what will happen next.

Mistake # 9

Not seeking a mid-rotation feedback meeting

Of critical importance is the mid-rotation feedback meeting, a meeting that you should have with every team member that supervises you. At the mid-point of the rotation, you need to be informed of your progress in meeting expectations.

During this meeting, you and your supervisor can discuss your experience to date. You will want to know about your strengths as well as your weaknesses. Keep in mind that you may be surprised by what you learn. As disconcerting as it may be to learn that you are falling short of your supervisor's expectations, it is far better to learn about this now than at the end of the clerkship. With half of the rotation remaining, you can work with your supervisor to develop a plan for improvement. Students often don't have a clear idea of what they need to do to improve. If you find yourself in this situation, ask your supervisor for specific recommendations.

Mistake # 10

Remaining unaware of the factors that can cloud your evaluation

The clinical evaluation of students during rotations is far from perfect. Evaluators can be affected by a variety of factors, some of which can lead to ratings that are lower than the student deserves. These sources of bias are shown in the following table.

Rating error	Description
Central tendency	The evaluator rates everyone as average regardless of performance because of laziness or the desire not to appear too harsh or lenient. It can also occur when the evaluator has difficulty rating a student accurately because he has observed the student infrequently or briefly.
Severity bias	The evaluator is extremely harsh in his assessment regardless of performance ("hawk").
Horn effect	The student is rated lower across the board because of one factor that is particularly bothersome to the evaluator. A student may be above average in working with others, paying attention to detail, and fund of knowledge but, because of tardiness, the performance is rated lower.
Recency bias	The student is rated lower because his most recent clinical performance was suboptimal (over-emphasis on recent performance). With recency bias, an evaluator fails to take into account the entire period of evaluation.
Primacy bias	The student is rated lower because his early performance was suboptimal (over-emphasis on early performance). The evaluator is not able to get past the student's bad start.
Contrast effect	Rather than comparing the student's performance against the expectations, goals, and objectives of the clerkship, the student is compared with the occasional student who far exceeds the highest standards. This can lead to a lower rating than the student deserves.

To guard against these errors, evaluators ideally should be trained on how to complete evaluation forms properly. Unfortunately, schools don't often offer this training and, even when they do, evaluators may not take advantage of the opportunity. As a result, rating errors can and do occur. This is not because of any ill will. Evaluators are simply unaware that they are making these errors. What can you do to avoid being a victim of a rating error? Here are some recommendations:

- Work with your evaluators as closely as you can, letting them observe you as you complete your tasks and fulfill your responsibilities. If your evaluators have observed you frequently, they are less likely to rate you as average (provided that you have performed at a high level). Average ratings sometimes result when students are observed infrequently.

- Finish your rotation on a high note. As obvious as this may seem, for some students it can be difficult to put into practice. Why? Because as the rotation draws to a close, students naturally start spending more time preparing for the end-of-clerkship exam and less time reading about their patients. Do not lose sight of the fact that your evaluation will be completed either at the end of the rotation or soon after the rotation ends. Your performance at the end of the rotation will be fresh in the minds of your evaluators. Your work early in the rotation may not be remembered as well. Students who end their clerkship with a whimper rather than a bang may find that this is reflected in their evaluation.

- Don't underestimate the importance of making a good first impression. With every task you complete, strive to do your best work right from the start. This is especially true for your oral case presentations and write-ups. If you start off impressively, you may be seen as a student who is further along than most. Of course, after a good first impression, you must maintain a high level of performance.

- To avoid a lower rating due to severity bias, you need to have a number of evaluators submit evaluations. For example, you may happen to work with an attending physician who is more stringent. Even if you perform at a high level, it may not be reflected as such on his evaluation form. To lessen the effects of this single evaluation, you will need to have other evaluations that speak more favorably of you. In fact, the literature supports this, with studies showing that multiple ratings are necessary to provide a more reliable estimate of clinical competence.

Note that even if you heed the above recommendations, you can't guarantee that a rating error won't occur. Clerkship directors realize that rating errors can occur and make attempts to overcome the effect of these tendencies. In many rotations, clerkship directors will solicit multiple evaluations from those that supervise your work. When a number of evaluations are obtained, assessments can be averaged, leading to a more accurate assessment of your performance. This will mitigate the effect of any one person's rating error.

Did you know...

At a study performed at five medical schools, 107 surgery faculty members each evaluated four or more students (Littlefield). A total of 1482 ratings were obtained. From these ratings, the investigators were able to determine that 14% of the raters were significantly more stringent. Stringent raters were shown to rank students with true clinical ability at the 50th percentile at the 23rd percentile or lower.

Mistake # 11

Failing to realize that you may benefit from a rating error

While rating errors may lower your evaluation unfairly, you may also benefit from them, as shown in the following table:

Rating error	Description
Halo effect	The student's performance is rated higher across the board because the evaluator is particularly impressed with one aspect of the student's performance. A student's high level of enthusiasm may lead an evaluator to rate other aspects of his performance just as well, even if the student is mediocre in these areas.
Leniency bias	The evaluator is extremely lenient in his assessment regardless of performance ("Dove"). This tends to happen with students who are especially well liked by evaluators or when evaluators feel uncomfortable giving low ratings.
"Similar To Me" bias	The student is rated higher because the evaluator and student share something in common (e.g., *alma mater*, friend, personality, style, values).
Recency bias	The student is rated higher because his most recent clinical performance was significantly better than his previous performance (over-emphasis on recent performance). For example, a previously lazy, disinterested student picks up his work, energy level, and enthusiasm during the last week of the rotation, leading to higher ratings.

If you haven't performed as well as you would have liked during the first half of a rotation, don't assume that you can't receive a good evaluation. Since evaluation forms are completed either at the end of the rotation or soon after the rotation ends, evaluators can be influenced by what happens toward the end of a rotation. For this reason, it is important to finish the rotation on a high note. If you have performed well at the end, this is likely to be fresh in the mind of your evaluator.

Did you know...

At a study performed at five medical schools, 107 surgery faculty members each evaluated four or more students. A total of 1482 ratings were obtained. From these ratings, the investigators were able to determine that 13% of the raters were significantly more lenient. Lenient raters were shown to rank students with true clinical ability at the 50th percentile at the 76th percentile or higher (Littlefield).

Mistake # 12

Underestimating the likeability factor

Don't underestimate the power of being liked. Your interpersonal skills, your communication skills, your ability to interact well with team members, and your overall likeability can definitely influence your final evaluation.

Did you know ...

In a survey of LCME accredited schools, 48% of Internal Medicine clerkship directors felt that grade inflation did exist (Speer). Among the factors that directors felt contributed to grade inflation was "a tendency to reward one aspect of a student's skills, that is, interpersonal skills, over skills in such areas as problem solving and history and physical examination..."

Did you know...

How much can likeability influence your ratings? Consider the results of two studies. In one study, faculty were asked to view videotaped student case presentations in an effort to determine what effects personal characteristics of students have on the ratings of student performance (Wigton). This study demonstrated that personal characteristics could significantly influence the ratings with self-assurance of the presenter identified as an important factor. Wigton concluded that presentations are not "evaluated solely on content and organization." In another study, faculty observed students interviewing standardized patients on videotape. Two nationally recognized experts were also asked to do the same (Kalet). When compared with the experts, it was shown that likeability was a significant factor that influenced faculty ratings.

Interpersonal skills can and do influence the assessment of student performance. Don't ignore this aspect of your performance. We discuss in later sections recommendations for enhancing communication and rapport with patients and team members.

Mistake # 13

Moving to the next rotation without learning all you can from your previous experience

Too often, students leave clerkships without the benefit of a final face-to-face meeting with their evaluators. Although you would hope that your attending and resident would initiate this meeting, many don't. If not, you should ask if the two of you can meet to discuss your clerkship experience and evaluation. Clerkships expect that evaluators will have this final meeting with their students.

During this meeting, you should receive a verbal assessment of your performance. Your main goal is to process the information so that you can improve your future performance. If you're not sure what actions you can take, you should ask for specific recommendations. If your attending has been particularly impressed with your performance, you may wish to ask for a letter of recommendation. Although some students may hesitate to do so, there is absolutely no rule that says you have to wait until the start of the residency application process.

Tip # 6

When you are ready for the attending to write a letter of recommendation, make it as easy as possible for him to write a glowing letter. As months pass by, specific memories of your performance might fade, making it difficult for letter writers to create a letter with specific examples and details that back up their praise. For this reason, with every rotation, keep track of your accomplishments and the compliments you receive. File this information carefully, including write-ups, patient thank-you notes, list of specific patients and their conditions, and handouts from talks. At the appropriate time, provide this information in order to remind your attending of how you excelled.

These meetings can also have unintended consequences. There is some data to suggest that face-to-face discussion can lead to grade inflation. Two ward evaluation systems were compared at the University of Michigan Medical School (Coletti). In the old system, faculty filled out an evaluation form after the student had completed the rotation. It was rare for a faculty member to have a face-to-face discussion with the student to discuss the evaluation. In the new system, faculty were asked to fill out the same evaluation form but also had face-to-face final meetings with students. Significant grade inflation was found with the new system. The average grade increased from 5.11 ± 0.11 to 5.62 ± 0.07, with a 5 equaling high pass and 6 equaling honors.

Mistake # 14

Failing to encourage your evaluators to turn in their evaluations

Picture this scenario. You've performed at a very high level during your rotation, frequently receiving kudos from your attending physician, Dr. Bauer. You're pleased that you've made such a favorable impression and feel confident that he will give you a great clinical evaluation. Several weeks after the rotation, you are disappointed with your clerkship grade. Your clerkship director informs you that while you did meet the criteria for honors based on your exam score, your overall grade fell just short of honors. Your overall score was pulled down by the average on your clinical evaluations. As you dig deeper, you learn that out of all your evaluators, only Dr. Bauer didn't submit an evaluation. If he had submitted the evaluation, would your score have been pushed into the honors range?

17

As a student, this may seem far-fetched. Unfortunately, this scenario plays itself out frequently in medical schools across the country. Clerkship directors will tell you how difficult it is for them to get faculty and residents to not only complete and submit clinical evaluations, but also to do so on time. At many schools, systems are in place to frequently remind evaluators of their responsibility. Despite this, it can still be difficult to collect these evaluations. As one clerkship director told me, "It's the bane of my existence."

Did you know ...

In a survey of U.S. and Canadian deans for student affairs, survey participants described a variety of problems with the clinical evaluation system, including tardy submission of clerkship evaluation forms (Hunt). Over 30% of evaluation forms were turned in more than two months late.

If you are fortunate, you will work only with supervisors who understand the importance of submitting clinical evaluations and who comply with the rules of the rotation. Unfortunately, at some point you may find yourself working with an otherwise well-intentioned supervisor who delays completing the evaluation, only to have the deadline for submission pass. If you have performed at a high level and such a stellar evaluation is not submitted, your overall grade may be lowered.

Rather than taking a passive attitude, it's better to be proactive and prevent such a situation. In fact, some rotations encourage students to give evaluation forms directly to residents and faculty several days before the clerkship ends. The idea is that residents and faculty will find it harder to resist a request to complete an evaluation when it comes directly from the student. If your clerkship has such a policy in place, be sure to approach your evaluators at least a week before the rotation's end, hand them the evaluation form, and schedule a day and a time to discuss your overall performance.

The meeting should preferably take place before the rotation ends. Scheduling a meeting after the rotation ends introduces variables that may prevent this meeting. For example, your next rotation's schedule may not allow you to meet at a time that is convenient for your attending.

If your clerkship sends clinical evaluation forms directly to evaluators, you can still encourage them to complete and submit these forms. To begin with, set up a final meeting to discuss your overall clinical performance. Often this will spur evaluators to complete the evaluation as a way to organize their thoughts and prepare for the meeting. Hopefully at the meeting your evaluators will show or give you a copy of the completed evaluation form.

Before leaving the rotation, ask the clerkship director when clinical evaluations are due. Evaluators are generally asked to submit these forms by a certain date to ensure that students receive the grades they deserve. Once aware of the deadline, you can always call the clerkship office and speak with the coordinator to find out if the evaluation has been submitted. If there is no sign of the evaluation, and the deadline for submission is rapidly approaching, you may wish to contact the evaluator or the clerkship director. In this way you can be actively involved in ensuring that you are evaluated in a fair manner.

Tip # 7

If you have impressed an attending physician, you want him to submit an evaluation. You may even expect that this will happen. Unfortunately, when clerkship directors ask evaluators to complete and submit evaluation forms, some do and some don't. To ensure that an evaluator has submitted your evaluation form, check in periodically with your clerkship coordinator.

Mistake # 15

Feeling that all is lost after a poor clinical evaluation

As upsetting as an unfavorable evaluation can be, it is just one component used to determine your clerkship grade. Evaluations are typically gathered from a number of people who have supervised your work. The unfavorable evaluation may be just one of a handful. If the others are glowing, it may have little effect on your grade.

If you disagree with your clerkship grade, schools will usually allow you to appeal. Most schools have a policy in place that guides students through the process. Since guidelines for appealing a grade differ from school to school, it is important that you familiarize yourself with the process at your own school. Following are some important points about the appeals process.

Tips on appealing a clerkship grade

- Comply with the appeals policy at your school. Failure to follow the rules may nullify your request.
- Be aware that there is often a time limit. If you fail to appeal your grade within the specified time period, it's highly unlikely that your school will even consider it.
- The first step in the process is often meeting with the clerkship director.
- At this meeting, you will be given the opportunity to present your side. The clerkship director will want to know the basis for your appeal. Don't forget to bring any documents (write-up, etc.) that support your position.
- A meeting such as this one can invoke a variety of emotions. You must avoid displaying these emotions. An emotional response may weaken your chances of having the grade changed.
- After hearing your concerns, the clerkship director may then meet with your evaluator(s) to hear their thoughts. After reviewing the entire situation, the grade may remain the same or be changed.
- If you are unhappy with the clerkship director's decision, you can make a further appeal, usually to the department chair, one of the deans at your school, or a specific committee.

In discussions with clerkship directors, it seems that successful appeals are the exception rather than the rule. However, if you feel that an error has been made, you should certainly consider it. It is possible, for example, for the clerkship to make a mathematical error in the calculation of your final grade.

Commonly Made Mistakes

With Patients

As a third year medical student, you finally have the amazing opportunity to take care of patients on a daily basis. You will learn a tremendous amount from your patients, not just about their disease but also about yourself and your calling. Physicians often look back fondly on their third year of medical school, vividly recalling patients they took care of and the lasting impact these patients left on them.

Before you start your third year of medical school, you will have had some interactions with patients. You were probably introduced to the art of taking a history and performing a physical examination during your physical diagnosis course. Now, as a third year medical student, you will continue to develop your skills in this area while taking on additional responsibility in the care of patients. While your previous experience will have been helpful, most students still have some anxiety about their ability to interact with patients. These feelings, which are entirely natural, will diminish with time and experience. In this chapter, our focus is on the patient. In particular, we focus on the mistakes that students make when interacting with patients.

Mistake # 16

Harming the patient

"First, do no harm."—Hippocrates

A report by the Institute of Medicine, widely described in the mainstream media, found that as many as 98,000 deaths occur yearly because of medical errors (Institute of Medicine). Numbers like that are hard to fully comprehend, but other studies have found that medical errors are shockingly common. In response to the Institute of Medicine study, researchers surveyed practicing physicians and members of the public. They found that 35% of physicians and 42% of the members of the public reported errors in their own or a family member's care (Blendon).

Even as a medical student, you can do great harm to your patients. You can directly harm your patient in many ways. You may transmit a nosocomial infection. You may write an illegible order that is misunderstood by the nursing staff, and your patient may then suffer a potentially fatal overdose. You may make a prescribing error, inadvertently substituting one medication for another that sounds similar, such as Toprol for Topamax (an antihypertensive for a migraine medication). You may fail to document your patient's medication allergy, thus bypassing all of the pharmacy computerized safeguards.

You are the team's expert on your own patients, and therefore you have the ability to prevent and catch medical errors. Prevention begins with a thorough history and physical exam, a comprehensive problem list, a complete medication list, and an accurate list of drug allergies. These items alone can prevent many medical errors. Sound too obvious? Researchers at the University of Illinois looked at drug allergy documentation by physicians, nurses, and medical students, and found that 20% of individuals failed to document drug allergies in their admission notes (Pau).

Recognize that your interns are inexperienced, overworked, and fatigued, and may not be able to catch all of your mistakes. Although you don't have ultimate responsibility for patient care decisions, you are on the front lines of patient care and therefore play a critical role in the prevention of medical errors.

Mistake # 17
Transmitting a nosocomial infection

How are antibiotic-resistant pathogens most frequently spread from one patient to another in healthcare settings? *Via the contaminated hands of clinical staff.* That means you (How-to guide: improving hand hygiene).

Hand hygiene is described as "the simplest, most effective measure for preventing nosocomial infections" and yet a review of studies that looked at average compliance rates found that most studies estimated compliance rates to be less than 50% (Pittet). There are numerous studies that examine how best to encourage compliance among health care professionals, and can be summarized by saying that no one method is uniformly successful.

Hand hygiene is probably the one area in medicine in which I encourage you to teach yourself. Many medical students learn their practices by observing their interns, residents, and attendings. Unfortunately, as studies have demonstrated, these physicians may or may not be compliant with the best practices to avoid nosocomial infections. Lankford and colleagues found that "health-care workers in a room with a senior (e.g. higher ranking) medical staff person or peer who did not wash hands were significantly less likely to wash their own hands" (Lankford). Your mission is to protect your patients. Cleanse hands between every single patient encounter, even if you were wearing gloves, even if you only shook hands for a second, and even if no one else does so. Hand hygiene may include hand washing with soap and water, hand disinfection with disinfectants and water, or the use of alcohol-based hand rubs. If you wash your hands, use your paper towel to turn off the faucet and open the door. Recognize also that doctors and their accessories can serve as fomites. Nosocomial infections have been transmitted by way of artificial nails (Gupta). Contamination with potentially pathogenic bacteria has been demonstrated on white coats, neckties, and stethoscopes (Saloojee). In one study, *Staphylococcus aureus* was isolated from 38% of stethoscopes, which underscores the need for frequent cleansing between patients (Marinella).

Patients can and do die from nosocomial infections. Recognize that effective prevention of transmission begins with your own personal commitment.

Mistake # 18
Introducing yourself inappropriately

When meeting a patient for the first time, it is important that you introduce yourself properly. The patient should not only know who you are but also your specific role in his care. For example:

"Hello, I'm Shawn Patterson. I'm a third year medical student who is part of the team that will be taking care of you while you are here in the hospital. With your permission, I would like to ask you questions related to your medical history."

Since you haven't yet received your M.D. degree, you should never introduce yourself as "Doctor." Not long after you start clerkships, you'll notice that other healthcare professionals will, at times, introduce you as a "student doctor" or "student physician." While these individuals are well-intentioned, this tendency can be deceptive to patients. The danger with attaching the word "doctor" or "physician" to "student" is that the patient may assume that you have the qualifications and responsibilities of a doctor. To avoid any misunderstanding, it is always best to introduce yourself as a medical student.

If a team member introduces you as a "doctor," clarify your position and role to the patient at the appropriate time. Do so in a way that avoids any embarrassment to the team member. Even though that individual meant no harm to the patient, patients should have no misunderstandings about the healthcare professionals participating in their care. Once informed, patients are usually receptive to having a medical student involved in their care. For those who are not, we should certainly respect their wishes.

Did you know...

In a videotaped analysis of histories performed by senior medical students, 30% of all students did not introduce themselves by name (Rutter). 44% neglected to mention that they were medical students.

Mistake # 19
Referring to your patient as a disease

Never lose sight of the fact that your patient is a person—not a disease or illness. He is not simply the "patient in room 432" or the "patient with heart failure." Remember that your patient has family, friends, interests, an occupation—in other words, your patient has a life just like you.

Mistake # 20
Forgetting to care

Fresh out of basic sciences, students are usually focused on learning how to perform tasks related to patient care. While learning these skills is important, do not forget that which brought you to the medical profession in the first place—your desire to help people. If you are like most students, a significant factor in your decision to become a doctor was the great opportunity to make a difference in peoples' lives. Now, as a third year medical student, you have this opportunity. Show patients that you care.

Tip # 8

Imagine if your mother or father were being treated by a physician. Wouldn't you want that caregiver to not only be technically competent but also caring? Strive to do the same with your patients.

Did you know...

In telephone interviews with 192 patients cared for at the Mayo Clinic, researchers identified seven ideal physician behaviors (Benadapudi). Patients felt that the ideal physician is confident, humane, empathetic, personal, respectful, forthright, and thorough. Note that technical skills were not one of the seven ideal behaviors. The authors suggested that patients may be inclined to assume that a physician is competent.

Mistake # 21

Following a script

New clerks often want to conduct a medical interview using a scripted format. Students are concerned that they may miss some critical information if they don't ask every single question on their list. While this concern is only natural, following a scripted format impedes effective interviewing. If you are only focused on the next question on your list, you won't be able to respond empathetically to the patient who expresses emotion. "I'm so worried about what will happen to my kids if this chemotherapy doesn't take care of my breast cancer." As a patient, how would you feel if your physician didn't bother to acknowledge this statement?

Did you know...

In a videotaped analysis of histories performed by senior medical students, "patients were often forced to repeat key phrases such as "I was feeling very low' as many as 10 times in order to get students to acknowledge their mood disturbance" (Rutter).

Reading questions from a list and writing extensive notes during a patient encounter will also prevent you from making eye contact with the patient. This can hamper your efforts to foster a relationship with the patient. Your patient may wrongly assume that you lack interest in what he is saying. To establish the rapport needed for a positive outcome, don't forget about the importance of maintaining eye contact.

Tip # 9

In the inpatient setting, you will usually have the opportunity to go back to the patient if you miss something during the medical interview. If you keep this in mind, you may feel less of a need to rely on a scripted list of questions.

Mistake # 22

Taking it personally

Your patients will generally be good people. Good people, when faced with the stress of illness, can sometimes act in uncharacteristic ways. You may encounter a patient who lashes out at you through no fault of your own. Rather than taking this personally, consider the patient's situation. Being sick enough to be hospitalized is frightening for most people. Patients commonly feel afraid, confused, and powerless. They feel that they have no control over what's happening to them. These feelings may overwhelm them and cause them to respond to you with anger or frustration. It's important not to take their words, actions, or behavior personally. In dealing with the angry patient, keep the following points in mind:

- Understand why the patient is angry. Generally, patients become angry when we fail to meet their expectations.
- Listen carefully to the patient. Too often, in our hurry to fix the problem, we fail to listen properly.
- Rather than standing over the patient or by the door, ask the patient if you can sit down. Do not sit on the patient's bed.
- Begin by saying, "Mr. Woods, the nurse informed me that you have some concerns regarding your care. Could you fill me in...?"
- Let the patient speak without interrupting. Avoid the tendency to interrupt the patient to ask a question or offer an explanation. Instead, let the patient speak until he has finished.
- After the patient is finished, summarize what you have heard to make sure you have understood him properly. "So, Mr. Woods, as I understand it, you expected..."
- After the patient has expressed his concern, ask him how he feels about the situation. Then acknowledge that feeling. "I can understand how that would make you feel..."
- Determine what will make the patient feel better. "What can I do to make you feel better about this now?"

- Finish your conversation by asking the patient if he is satisfied with your understanding of the situation and your plan to address his concerns.

Tip # 10

Hospitalized patients often feel as if they have no control. This is a distressing feeling, one that you can diminish by keeping your patients well informed of what will happen next.

Did you know ...

In a survey of second-year medical students at the Kansas University School of Medicine, researchers asked students to report personal characteristics of patients that might evoke a negative personal reaction, interfering with their ability to provide quality clinical care (Walling). Comments included:

"Patients who are violent or mean to staff"

"People who treat me with animosity"

"Vulgar, disrespectful, antagonistic patients"

"Drug/alcohol/substance abusers who have horrible, rude, or unpleasant attitudes"

"Chronic complainers who never seem to appreciate care"

"People who don't take responsibility for their actions (everything is everyone else's fault)"

This study raised concerns that students may lose objectivity when caring for patients with certain personal characteristics.

Mistake # 23

Using medical jargon

Some healthcare professionals have a tendency to talk to patients as if they were colleagues. If you haven't witnessed this yet, you definitely will during your third year. I still remember as a medical student hearing a liver specialist tell a patient why she had abnormal liver function tests. He was convinced that the patient had hepatic steatosis (fatty liver) and was throwing this word around without defining it. The patient had a perplexed look on her face as he explained to her what the work-up would entail.

In your interactions with patients, remember to avoid medical jargon. Don't use medical terms such as CHF or COPD when explaining to a patient the possible reasons for his difficult breathing unless the patient clearly understands these terms. Instead, replace these medical terms with language that is easily understood.

Mistake # 24

Answering the patient's questions without exercising caution

You will usually spend much more time with your patients than other team members. Because of this, patients will often direct questions about their condition to you. This may place you in an uncomfortable and awkward position. On the one hand, you would like to address these concerns, but on the other hand, you may not have the knowledge or experience to answer these questions. How should you handle this situation?

Don't be afraid to simply say that you do not know the answer to the question. Tell the patient that you will discuss his concerns with the team. Inform the patient that you or another team member will be back to address the issue.

Tip # 11

Take care in answering a patient's questions. If you give the wrong answer, intentionally or unintentionally, you could create a very difficult situation. If you are even slightly less than 100% confident, then it's best to inform the patient that you will return with the answer.

Mistake # 25

Putting the team at risk for a lawsuit

Why do patients sue their physicians? With so much money at stake, there are numerous studies devoted to answering this question. Why do some patients sue their doctors when there hasn't been a negative outcome? Why would some sue over a tiny scar? Why do some patients, on the other hand, truly experience medical negligence, and then decide not to sue? While physicians may expect that medical errors would be most likely to trigger a lawsuit, several findings point to communication, or rather miscommunication, as the major factor.

A number of authors, based on anecdotal evidence, have suggested that communication issues play an important role in a patient's decision to sue. Beckman *et al* went further and studied depositions made by patients and families who were bringing a malpractice suit (Beckman). They found that physician relationship issues played a role in 71% of the depositions. They found four themes within the relationship issues. These included perceived desertion of the patient, delivering information poorly, and either failing to understand the patient perspective or devaluing the patient or family views.

These findings underscore the need for students and physicians to always maintain respectful interactions with patients and families. Even if medical science tells you the patient is completely wrong about the cause of his cancer, listen carefully to his point of view and acknowledge his beliefs with respect. Ensure that the patient knows that you are always available to answer questions or respond to concerns. Learn from your attendings and residents how best to deliver bad news. Lastly, even if your team believes that another physician or hospital was medically negligent, it is not your place to discuss this with the patient. Suggestions by another healthcare professional of prior malpractice may also lead to a decision to sue (Beckman).

Mistake # 26

Spending insufficient time on patient education

You will have fewer patients to follow than any other team member. As a result, you will have extra time to spend with your patients. Use this time to educate your patients on their illness. Let them know where things stand, what's in store for them on a particular day, and what they can expect in the long-term. Most patients appreciate patient information brochures. These can be found in your hospital library or online. If provided online, obtain information only from reputable sources. Some patients are actually told to seek out their own information, but a simple Google search may lead to commercial, biased, or even fraudulent sites. Patients may also be interested to hear of local support groups, such as the Scleroderma Foundation or the Arthritis Foundation. Some patients wish to become more involved in their own care, and are not sure how to proceed. The Agency for Healthcare Research and Quality (AHRQ), part of the U.S. Department of Health and Human Services, publishes brochures that patients may find helpful. The website www.ahrq.gov/path/beactive.htm

includes information on topics such as taking a medication safely, planning for surgery, and helping to prevent medical errors.

Accompany your resident or attending when they visit your patient to discuss discharge instructions. Return to the patient's room later to make sure the patient understood all instructions. You and your team have worked hard to provide the patient with effective treatment. Now, as the patient is being prepared for discharge, you need to ensure that he is ready to assume responsibility for his own care. Make it a point to:

- Speak to the patient in language he can understand
- Spend whatever time it takes to educate and counsel the patient. Be sure that the patient is familiar with the illness, the names and dosing schedule of all medications, and side effects of therapy
- Determine if the patient actually understands the discharge instructions (verbal and written)
- Allow the patient to ask questions about the diagnosis and treatment plan

This is a critical time for communication. Your efforts will help the patient remain compliant with therapy and remain healthy.

Did you know...

In a study involving 47 patients at the time of hospital discharge, researchers sought to determine the level of understanding patients had of their discharge diagnoses and names, purpose, and common side effects of prescribed medications (Makaryus). They found that only 41.9% knew of their diagnosis or diagnoses. Even less were able to list the names (27.9%), purpose (37.2%), and common side effects (14.0%) of their medications.

Mistake # 27

Underestimating the importance of including family members

Physicians often underestimate the influence of family members on patient care, thus overlooking a great resource. Case Western Reserve University School of Medicine researchers noted that in 32% of all family practice office visits, family members were present (Medalie). The management of chronic disease in the outpatient setting often requires the involvement of family members to ensure compliance and successful therapy. Discharge planning and education following hospitalization also requires the input of family members. Clinical trials have shown that significant improvement can be realized in certain patient behaviors when a family member is involved in the treatment. This includes how faithfully patients keep appointments, take their medications as prescribed, and stick to the treatment plan (Levine).

Tips for communicating with family members

- Include family members whenever possible when communicating with patients. There are numerous reasons to do so, not the least of which is that it demonstrates respect for the patient and those important to him. Many physicians will walk into a room, look at the patient, and never acknowledge the person who has just spent the night at the bedside. You need to introduce yourself properly and ask about them and their relationship with the patient.

- Before including any family member or loved one in a discussion, ask the patient if he would prefer that you speak to him alone.

- News of certain health conditions, such as diabetes or cancer, can be overwhelming to patients. A family member or close friend may be able to listen better and actually process what you say. They may be the ones to take notes and ask relevant questions.

- If a patient does not speak English, a family member may not be the best translator. Some family members are overwhelmed by bad news and are unable to function well. Children may not have sufficient comprehension of medical issues in order to translate well. Even adult children, particularly those raised in America, may be able to speak their native language at home, but may lack the knowledge to fully translate medical terms. In issues involving personal questions, patients may not be honest if a family member is translating. A patient may not give an accurate sexual history if their child is the translator. Hospitals do have translators available, and many subscribe to telephone translation services for those languages infrequently encountered.

- When planning lifestyle modifications, a spouse or caregiver must be involved. If you recommend a change in diet, recognize that in order to be successful the entire family must be involved. Particularly when a spouse does all the grocery shopping and cooking, such information may actually need to be directed primarily at them.

- Interventions such as smoking cessation efforts work best with the support of the family. You can involve them in the discussion and make clear to them how important they are to the patient's success.
- With some types of chronic disease, family members become caregivers. The care of a patient with dementia is exhausting, emotionally and physically, and has been shown to affect the health of the caregiver. Some caregivers make Herculean efforts day after day and have no one that recognizes that fact. Do what you can by acknowledging and praising their efforts.

Commonly Made Mistakes

At the Start of a Rotation

Making the transition from clerkship to clerkship is challenging, and how well you handle being "new" again will play a major role in your chances for rotation success. The start of a new rotation is always difficult and it's common to feel ill at ease during the first few days. After all, you won't be familiar with how things work.

In the first few days, lay the groundwork for a successful experience. The key is to quickly ascertain the rules, responsibilities, and expectations of the rotation. Only after you become comfortable will you be able to do your best work. In this chapter, we discuss common mistakes students make during the first few days of a new rotation.

Mistake # 28

Waiting too long to request time off

Important events in our lives sometimes take place during busy periods at school or work. Clerkships are no exception. To increase the likelihood that you will be able to attend the wedding of a loved one or present your research at a medical conference, you must notify the clerkship coordinator well before the start of the rotation. You can then be placed on a team whose schedule allows you to leave without causing too much difficulty for the team. Clerkships generally, although not invariably, accommodate students who place requests for time off well in advance. The key is to contact the clerkship early. As some students have found out the hard way, once the schedule is set, your request may be denied.

If you are given approval for time off, make sure that you inform all team members. I recall one student who was given permission to attend a four-day conference to present his research. He informed his resident and intern but failed to inform me, his attending physician. Needless to say, I was not impressed with his lack of professionalism.

Remember that you are part of a team. The team functions best when all of its members are present. So if you need to be away, recognize that someone else will have to pick up the slack. Don't forget to thank those who fill in for you. Before you leave, volunteer to make up any time you will miss.

Mistake # 29

Letting the luck of the draw dictate who you will work with

Students often leave their team assignments to chance. What's wrong with this approach? This assumes that it makes little difference who's doing the teaching. In actuality it makes a big difference. Imagine yourself, unsure of your specialty choice, at the start of a new clerkship. You hope at the end of it you'll be able to make an informed career decision. Unfortunately, you're assigned to an uninspiring attending, and end the clerkship disappointed with your experience. You discard the specialty as a possible career choice. Were you able to make an informed decision or was your decision colored by your experience?

This is a common scenario. Even if you are certain that your future lies in a different field of medicine, there are many compelling reasons to seek out great teachers. You'll be working long, tiring hours with your team. An inspiring attending can motivate you to do your best work. Dedicated attendings work hard to help students excel with their oral case presentations and write-ups, skills that are transferable to all rotations. In short, it behooves you to do everything possible to seek out attendings known to be great teachers.

Did you know...

At the University of Michigan Medical School, researchers determined that "attending faculty's clinical teaching ability has a positive and significant effect on medical students' learning" (Stern). They found that ratings of teaching ability were strong predictors of students' performance on the end-of-clerkship NBME subject examination.

Did you know...

Researchers at the Medical University of South Carolina found that "students with attendings who received poor teaching evaluations performed more poorly on OSCE data-gathering stations than did students with attendings rated as average or good" (Blue). Students who worked with attending physicians with higher teaching evaluation scores were found to score higher on the NBME surgery subject examination.

One to two months before your clerkship begins, call the clerkship office for a list of attendings on service during your rotation. Share this list with students in the class above you or with classmates who have already completed the rotation. At many schools, attendings are evaluated by their students. In some cases, schools make these evaluations available to students for review. If your school allows this, take advantage of the opportunity, making note of teachers who are highly regarded by your predecessors. After you have identified attendings known as excellent teachers, contact the clerkship office to see if you can be placed on one of these teams. The key is to make sure you call early enough. You clearly want to call before team assignments are made. Keep in mind that your fellow students may have the same idea. Don't be surprised if the clerkship is not receptive to your request. Some rotations make it a policy not to accept student requests for team assignments.

Mistake # 30
Lacking the equipment to do the job

As with any job, in order to do it well, you need to have the proper equipment. The tools that you need are listed in the following table, according to rotation.

Clerkship	Equipment needed
Internal Medicine	Stethoscope Penlight Reflex hammer Tuning fork Visual acuity card Ophthalmoscope
Surgery	Stethoscope Penlight Scissors Paper tape Kerlix Cover sponges
Pediatrics	Stethoscope Penlight Ophthalmoscope Otoscope with pneumatic attachment Calculator Reflex hammer Measuring tape Tongue blades Toy (for distracting apprehensive children)
Obstetrics/ Gynecology	Stethoscope Penlight Reflex hammer Pregnancy wheel Bandage scissors Tape Gauze
Psychiatry	Stethoscope Penlight Reflex hammer Tuning fork

You will, of course, need something to carry all this equipment in. Many students place their equipment in their coat pockets while others prefer to carry it in some type of bag. Make sure you label your more expensive tools so that they may be returned to you if lost.

Mistake # 31

Lacking the necessary books

It is better to have the books you need in your hands before the rotation starts. Your fellow students will be able to inform you of books the clerkship requires or recommends. This information can also be found in the clerkship orientation material, which some rotations send to students before the start of the rotation. Many rotations also post orientation information on their website.

Your classmates may tell you about other helpful books, as will your intern, resident, and attending physician. After speaking with them, you may feel tempted to go on a shopping spree. Before you make the bookstore owner's day, I encourage you to take a look at the books that have been recommended. If the information in the book fits well with the way you process information, then you should consider buying it.

Keep in mind that many of these books are also available at the medical school library. You can also try the hospital library or you can borrow the book from a classmate. If you don't obtain books before your rotation starts, make sure you do so in the first day or two of the clerkship. The idea is to arm yourself as soon as possible with the resources you need to excel.

Mistake # 32

Starting the rotation without talking to students who have recently completed it

Classmates who have recently completed the rotation are a valuable source of information. They can give you a better idea of what to expect. Your goal is to learn how you can maximize the learning opportunities presented by the rotation. Most students would also like to receive outstanding evaluations, and classmates can help in this area as well. Rather than relying heavily on the advice of one or two individuals, I recommend that you talk to as many people as you can. You definitely need the answers to the following questions:

- Describe what you did during a typical day.
- What is the exam format?
- What are the must-have books?
- What things did you find most difficult during the rotation?
- What would you have done differently?

37

- Who will be evaluating me?
- How will I be evaluated?

It is also useful to contact upper levels at your school for their insight, especially if your clerkship is the first one of the academic year. Keep in mind, though, that the information you receive may not be current as changes are often made at the end of an academic year.

Tip # 12

Find out in advance the name of the attending physician with whom you will be working. Then check with fellow students to learn more about this attending. What is his style? How does he like to do things? What are his pet peeves? This is valuable information that can help you get off to a good start.

Mistake # 33

Reading clerkship orientation information after the rotation starts

It is common for clerkships to send students a welcoming letter several weeks before the start of the rotation. Along with this letter may be forms for parking, computer access, and name badges. You may be asked to complete and return these forms prior to the start of the rotation. Failure to follow these instructions will require you to deal with these issues on the first day of the rotation, while your colleagues will be off and running.

If you are sent clerkship orientation information, be sure to read it prior to the first day of the rotation. If you haven't received any information, turn to your clerkship's website where detailed information may be available. At the very least, you need to know when and where to report, and if driving, where to park. Students who take the time to carefully read over clerkship information are better prepared for the first few days of the rotation.

Tip # 13

A new clerkship is like a new job. There is a job description which discusses the requirements of the clerkship and your responsibilities as a student. Take the time to read this information. Because most students don't do this before that all-important first day, they often have little to no idea of what's in store for them.

Mistake # 34

Forgetting that the clinical evaluation counts much more than the exam

New students often don't realize that the grading system used during clinical rotations is very different from that used during the basic science years. During the basic science years, your course grade was based on objective findings. In other words, it depended solely on your exam performance. In your clinical rotations, the bulk of your grade will be based on clinical evaluations submitted to the clerkship director by your superiors, generally residents and attending physicians. While most clerkships will have exams at the end of the rotation, the weight the exam carries in the overall determination of the grade is considerably less than the clinical evaluation.

Tip # 14

Although you will still have an exam at the end of the clerkship, it generally counts much less than your clinical evaluation. Don't focus so much on the exam that you let your clinical evaluation suffer.

Mistake # 35

Missing important information during the clerkship orientation

Clerkships often begin with an orientation. During the orientation, the clerkship director will provide you with an overview of the clerkship. The director will use the orientation to set the tone for the rotation, discuss his educational philosophy, inform you of the clerkship's expectations regarding student performance and attitudes, and convey other key aspects of the rotation. They will often discuss the following aspects of the clerkship:

- Course goals and objectives
- Overall course management and leadership
- Course policies and procedures, including hours of duty, overnight call policy, number of patients admitted on call nights, number of patients to follow at any given time, and guidelines for the written and oral presentation of newly admitted patients

- Student responsibilities, including required assignments and deadlines
- Attendance requirements
- Lecture/conference schedule
- Professionalism policy
- Recommended/required reading
- Learning resources
- Test/examinations
- Grading/evaluation process
- Whom to notify in the event of an emergency

A considerable amount of information will be presented. It is imperative that you pay close attention. If need be, take notes. Many students have run into trouble because they missed something important. I still remember one student who performed at an honors level but received a final clerkship grade of pass. She didn't realize that her write-up had to be submitted to the clerkship director for review by a certain date.

If you have questions, be sure to ask. Try not to leave orientation without knowing who your evaluators will be, when this evaluation will take place, and what qualities will be evaluated. When asking questions about the evaluation process, take care in how you obtain this information. If you seem preoccupied with concerns related to your grade, it will reflect poorly on you.

Mistake # 36

Making a poor first impression

After orientation, you will usually be asked to join your team. When meeting the team, your initial focus should be on making a good first impression. Your objective is to connect immediately with team members in such a way that you establish comfort, trust, and rapport. A good first impression can set the tone for a successful experience, while a bad first impression can be disastrous. Since bad first impressions are powerful and tend to last, you will need to expend considerable time and effort to overcome such an impression.

Your appearance is a major factor in first impressions. Consider that team members are meeting you for the first time and have no idea of the type of person you are or the quality of work you perform. Your team members will make assumptions about your ability, character, and potential based largely on your appearance and the way in which you initially interact with them. This perception, whether right or wrong, will govern the way you are regarded and treated by the team.

Before meeting the team, make a quick trip to a mirror. Perform a final self-check. How does your hair look? Is there anything caught in your teeth? Do you have any open buttons? The idea here is to not be remembered for your appearance. Many students have made memorable entrances. If you are remembered for your entrance, it's generally not for a good reason. I still remember the student who had bits of Kleenex stuck to his nose.

What others will first notice is your entrance—the way you walk into the team room, your dress, and your manners. Enter the room confidently, energetically, and with a nice relaxed smile on your face. Avoid walking in with sagging shoulders or a slumped posture, body language that suggests you are tired or exhausted.

You should wait momentarily for other team members to offer their hand to you, but if a hand is not extended, don't be afraid to initiate the handshake. In today's world, gender is no longer an issue and it is perfectly appropriate for both men and women to offer their hand. Shake hands using a firm grip. Make sure that your handshake is not weak or limp but avoid a crushing grip. Since many students can't evaluate the quality of their own handshakes, solicit input from friends or colleagues. While shaking hands, maintain eye contact. With direct eye contact and a great handshake, you will project confidence.

As you shake hands with team members, smile cordially, speak clearly, and address each person by name. Don't forget to repeat your own name. An example:

"Dr. Khan, I'm Josh Stein, a third year medical student assigned to your team. It's a pleasure to meet you."

Addressing each person by name is important. People like to hear their names being said. Do not address a team member by first name unless you are clearly invited to do so.

Students who make a polished entrance project confidence, energy, and poise, the very qualities that team members value in their students.

Mistake # 37

Dressing inappropriately on the first day of the rotation

Students tend to dress conservatively on the first day of the rotation. However, some students, perhaps basing their dress on recommendations from colleagues or for other reasons, dress down on their first day. They may even show up for duty dressed in scrubs. Others may forgo the tie.

Do not lose sight of the fact that a large part of the first impression you make has to do with your dress style. Even if others have told you that it is acceptable to dress casually, resist the temptation to do so. While a more casual dress style might have sufficed for them, it may not meet the standards of your team. For this reason, dress conservatively for the first day of your rotation and don't make any changes until your attending informs you of what is and is not considered appropriate attire. If the attending does not initiate a discussion about appropriate attire, you may do so.

Tip # 15

Team members will draw conclusions about your abilities based on your dress and appearance. Don't underestimate the importance of looking your best.

Even your lab coat may send the wrong message. I've seen too many medical students show up with dirty, unwashed white coats. Although that stain may only be iodine, to a patient it looks like blood. At some point, your coat may be beyond salvage. Invest in a new coat. In the following box, we list some other professional appearance mistakes. Some may seem quite obvious. I feel obligated to list them, however, since I have seen many students make these mistakes.

Professional appearance mistakes

- Too much make-up
- Heavy perfume/cologne/shaving lotion
- Flashy or excessive jewelry
- Dirty or unkempt hair
- Dirty fingernails
- Chipped nail polish
- Clothing that is too tight, stained, or wrinkled
- Provocative clothing (e.g., low neckline, see-through, short skirts)
- Clothing that is too casual (e.g., jeans, sweatpants or shirts, tee shirts, loud ties, halters)
- Visible body piercing or tattoos
- Improper footwear, including dirty or scuffed shoes, tennis shoes, open-toed shoes, high heels
- Buttons or pins expressing political or social opinions or affiliations

---

Mistake # 38

Taking the first few days too lightly

Most students dislike the first few days of a new clerkship. First days can be confusing, difficult, and overwhelming. The length of time it takes for students to adjust varies from one student to another. Some students take weeks to adjust while others are seemingly ready after just one or two days. Your goal is to shorten the duration of your adjustment period. Only after you reach a certain comfort level will you be able to do your best work. In the real world, the adjustment period for new employees generally takes months. This luxury is lacking in clerkships that may just last a total of four to eight weeks.

One reason why students take considerable time reaching their comfort zone is that they take the first few days of the rotation too lightly. Few students take full advantage of the grace period that team members give them early in the rotation. Generally, during this period, little is expected of students beyond familiarizing themselves with the rules, responsibilities, and expectations of the new clerkship. Yet many students don't put forth the effort to

43

learn the rules of the new rotation. It is no wonder then that many students start off their new rotation on the wrong foot.

The early impressions you make on your team will play a large role in your clerkship success. Savvy students realize the importance of these first few days, seize this time as an opportunity to distinguish themselves from other new students, and establish a professional presence. In contrast, other students get caught up thinking about how much they don't like the "new student" feeling. These are thoughts that only add to their insecurity and hamper their efforts to get acclimated to their new rotation. The best way to put an end to the discomfort and insecurity of being new is to know how to handle these challenges with poise.

Mistake # 39

Failing to let go of the previous rotation's culture

The start of a rotation is difficult for those students beginning their very first rotation as well as experienced students. Students who have completed other rotations often assume that their experience can only help them in their new rotation. They fail to understand that previous experience can also be a hindrance in the transition phase. Much of this difficulty has to do with the culture of rotations. In short, every rotation has its own culture which governs behavior, dress, interactions, and how things get done. Behaviors and actions that served you well in meeting the needs of a previous rotation will often not fit the culture of your new clerkship.

As a new student, you may need to let go of some of the behaviors that led to success in your previous rotation. You may argue that some of this know-how should transfer to your new rotation. You're right—some of it does. Some of it, however, clearly doesn't. In your old rotation it may have been acceptable to speak directly with your resident about issues pertaining to your patient. You would assume that the same approach would work just as well in your new rotation. However, the new clerkship may operate differently, with students expected to speak first with the intern. You will have erred if you internalized the rules of the previous rotation.

Savvy students consciously let go of behaviors that won't serve them well in a new clerkship.

Mistake # 40

Not understanding the culture of the new rotation

Every rotation has its own unique culture. The rotation's culture will govern everything you do, from how you dress to how you interact with other team members. Your team members want you to fit into this new culture as soon as possible. Why? Because only after you fit into this new culture will you be able to reach your full potential as a productive team member.

You can learn about a rotation's culture by paying close attention to the way things are done. Keep your eyes and ears open to learn as much as you can about the rotation and the people you are working with. Watch your intern, resident, and attending physician. How do they communicate with one another? How do they work together? How do they behave? Is there someone on the team who seems to be working at a high level? If so, why is that person more effective and efficient than others?

Students who take the time to understand the culture of their new rotation, including its nuances and subtleties, will reach a comfort level sooner than their colleagues.

Mistake # 41

Focusing on the wrong elements of the job

If you are like most new students, you're probably most concerned with learning how to perform patient care tasks. These include admitting patients, writing daily progress notes, presenting patients, and performing procedures. Are your team members also worried about your ability to perform these tasks? Of course they are. However, your superiors, having worked with students in the past, recognize that you have the ability to perform these tasks. With time (hopefully not too much time), they know you will learn how to accomplish this work.

What are they most concerned about? Their most pressing concerns have to do with issues unrelated to task performance. These concerns include how well you will fit into the team, your willingness to embrace new ideas, and your ability to work effectively with other team members. When team members are asked about what impresses them most about new students, the ability to perform tasks is much lower on the list. Ranked much higher

45

are the abilities to learn the rules of the rotation quickly, to get along with the team, to display the proper attitude and work ethic, and essentially fit in. Note that these are not skills related to task performance but rather so-called "soft" skills concerned with how you communicate and interact with others. Since you will be working closely within the team structure, it is not surprising that the team members place such importance on these soft skills.

Tip # 16

Your success depends not only on the quality of your work but also in the way in which you deal with people. Don't lose sight of this important point. "In fact, several decades of research in emotional intelligence demonstrated that 80-90 percent of the difference between outstanding and average performers is linked to emotional intelligence" (Arond-Thomas).

The challenge that faces you in the first few days involves establishing your reputation. You should quickly become known as a student with a strong work ethic, a positive attitude, a willingness to learn, and the desire to be a productive team member.

Mistake # 42

Not meeting with the resident and intern

You will typically meet your intern and resident after your orientation. At some point during the first day, you will want to sit down with the resident and intern, separately, to discuss the rules of the rotation, your responsibilities, and their expectations of you. Since interns and residents are busy, do not assume that upon meeting you, they will drop everything to have this discussion. You may have met them at a particularly busy time.

In a perfect world, the intern and resident would initiate this meeting. As this may not happen, though, you may need to be proactive. When there is a lull in the action, ask the intern or resident if you can meet to discuss your upcoming month together. While you can meet with them together, it is recommended that you have separate meetings because their expectations will differ. Your goal is to meet and hopefully exceed the expectations of each and every team member.

Some residents and interns are savvy. They understand the importance of this meeting and will take the time to fill you in on the specifics of the rotation. Others don't recognize the value of this meeting and have only brief discussions. These discussions are often lacking in structure and short on the specifics students really need. Too often, students leave these meetings unclear about their work responsibilities. To increase the odds that you will leave this meeting with the information you need, be sure to have a list of questions ready.

Questions to ask your resident and intern at your initial meeting

- What are your expectations for me?
- What are my work responsibilities?
- Can you go over a typical day with me?
  - What time should I arrive in the morning?
  - What time do work rounds begin?
  - Where do we meet for work rounds?
  - What time are attending rounds? Where do they take place?
  - Do we have afternoon rounds? When and where do we meet?
  - How does this schedule differ on a weekend day?
- What is our call schedule?
- What are my responsibilities on call?
- What procedures do you expect me to perform?
- How would you like me to present patients during work rounds?
- Can you go over your preferences regarding the writing of the daily progress note?
- Is there a particular time of the day the progress note needs to be written by?
- Can you show me the paperwork I need to be familiar with (progress notes, lab request forms, x-ray request forms, consult requisitions, etc.)?
- Can you provide me with a list of important phone numbers (lab, x-ray, pharmacy, etc.)?
- Where can I safely keep my bag and other personal items?
- Where do you recommend that I work?

You may be overwhelmed by the amount of information you receive about ward logistics, the daily and weekly schedule, rules, and responsibilities. For this reason, take notes. Learn as much as you can about how things operate so that you can get off to a good start.

Tip # 17

Although you will want to know when your work day ends, take care in how you ask. You don't want to come across as someone who won't be working hard. Rather than asking directly, try a more roundabout approach. Ask the resident or intern to describe a typical day's schedule. Then take note of the last activity of the day. That will give you some idea of when the day will end.

Mistake # 43

Not meeting with your attending physician

Meeting with the attending physician sometime during the first few days of a new rotation is an absolute must. You will want to learn about his expectations of you as a student. Remember that these expectations will differ from that of the intern and resident.

Ideally, this meeting should take place on the first day of the rotation. As with residents, not all attendings make it a point to have this meeting. If the attending does not initiate the meeting, simply approach him and ask, "Dr. Nguyen, do you have some time today to meet with me to discuss our upcoming month together?" Don't be afraid to initiate this meeting. I have yet to meet an attending who wouldn't be receptive to this approach.

What are the consequences of not meeting? Failure to do so will leave you feeling confused about the rotation and the attending's expectations of you as a student. For example, when asked to present a new patient to the attending, you are prepared to deliver your thorough 15-minute oral case presentation. Just before you begin, the attending says, "Be sure to keep this to less than 5 minutes." Imagine your anxiety as you think quickly of how to cut your 15-minute presentation to five minutes or less. An initial meeting with the attending to discuss such preferences would have averted such a scenario.

If you are fortunate, you will have an attending physician who spells everything out for you. More often than not, however, the attending will be short on specifics. To guard against this common scenario, you should have a plan in place to obtain the necessary information. Basically, you should ascertain what the attending considers an ideal student. You will want to listen for answers to the following questions:

- What are the attending physician's expectations for me as a student?
- What does the attending view as my clinical responsibilities?
- How will the attending evaluate my performance?
- How would the attending like me to present patients?
- Does the attending want me to turn in patient write-ups? If so, does he have any preferences regarding the write-up?

If some key information is lacking, ask. Too often, students don't ask questions because they don't want to seem ignorant. However, your goal is to know as much as possible up front rather than being informed as problems arise.

While your resident and intern may be able to provide you with some insight regarding the attending physician's preferences, you need more information than they are able to provide. That's why you should always have a meeting with the attending.

Tip # 18

Ask your attending how often you will be meeting to discuss your progress. Let your attending know that you wish to improve and are open to suggestions.

Mistake # 44

Meeting only your immediate team members

You do not just work with your intern, resident, and attending physician. You also work with nurses, ward clerks, medical assistants, pharmacists, social workers, radiology technicians, physical therapists, and others. You will be working with and relying on a variety of healthcare professionals during your clerkship.

On your first day, meet as many of these individuals as you can. It can be as simple as:

"Hello, my name is Susan Ward. I'm the medical student working on Team A this month, and Dr. Reddy is my resident. It's nice to meet you, and I'm looking forward to working with you."

This simple effort on your part can help set the proper tone for your working relationship with these individuals.

In particular, you will want to meet:

49

- **Nurses**

  It's important to cultivate a good relationship with nurses because it can make your rotation and care of patients easier. There are many physicians, including residents, who never understand this, always choosing to erect a barrier between themselves and the nursing staff. Sometimes physicians take on an air of superiority with nurses, coming across as arrogant and condescending.

Did you know ...

In a survey examining the impact of physicians' disruptive behavior on nurses, 86% and 49% of nurses and physicians, respectively, stated that they had witnessed disruptive behavior from a physician (Rosenstein). Of the nurses, 22% stated that disruptive behavior occurred weekly. Over 50% of all respondents felt that there was a strong link between disruptive behavior and negative clinical outcomes, including patient safety, quality of care, and patient satisfaction.

  Strive to be the student and future physician who treats nurses with respect. If you do, you may be rewarded in a number of ways. Because nurses spend more time with the patient than any other healthcare professional, they may share with you important information regarding your patient's condition. You may benefit from their teaching, even though their training and knowledge is different than yours. They may help you with blood draws, arterial blood gases, and placement of intravenous lines. These are procedures that students should be comfortable performing. Nurses can also be of great help early in the rotation when students are not comfortable with their new environment. They can help you be more efficient during these trying times.

  How do you develop a solid working relationship with nurses? During the first few days of the rotation, introduce yourself to the nurses. Treat them with respect and encourage them to share their thoughts regarding your patients. When your team has decided on the diagnostic and treatment plan for the day, personally convey this to the nurse. It's through these types of interactions that a professional atmosphere is created, one which is essential to providing the best possible patient care.

- **Social workers**

  Social workers perform a variety of functions in the hospital setting.

  They may be responsible for the following:
  - Providing counseling for patient and family to help them cope with the many issues that surround illness and hospitalization (i.e., social, financial, psychological)
  - Identifying community resources
  - Treatment planning
  - Discharge planning/coordination of post-hospital services (e.g., home visits)

  You will quickly realize how valuable social workers are in the care of your patients.

- **Radiology file clerks**

  These clerks can make your life easier by pulling x-rays and scans for you when needed for rounds and conferences.

- **Radiology technicians**

  If you establish good rapport with technicians, you are more likely to have your x-rays and scans done sooner rather than later.

- **Lab personnel**

  The time will come when you need assistance. For example, you may need some help reviewing a peripheral blood smear or performing a gram stain.

- **Pharmacists**

  Clinical pharmacists are a rich source of information, providing detailed information about the safe use of medications, including interactions and side effects. In a review examining the role of clinical pharmacists, Kaboli described the findings of two recent Institute of Medicine reports. These reports "recognized that pharmacists are an essential resource in safe medication use, that participation of pharmacists on rounds improves medication safety, and that pharmacist-physician-patient collaboration is important" (Kaboli). In some hospitals, clinical pharmacists round with the team. In other hospitals, a quick call to the pharmacist can provide the information needed to select the most appropriate medication, along with the correct dose and duration of therapy. Many students, not to mention residents and attendings, don't take advantage of this expertise.

- **Ward secretary**

   The ward secretary provides clerical support for the patients and staff on the ward. Responsibilities may include notifying residents when newly admitted patients have arrived on the floor, entering physicians' orders into the computer system, calling transport to take patients for tests, and facilitating the discharge of patients.

By being aware of the responsibilities of these healthcare professionals, you will be able to call upon them when you require their assistance. When working with them don't forget to use the words, "Please," and "Thank you." Being polite, respectful, and nice will go a long way in establishing a positive working relationship.

Mistake # 45
Forgoing the hospital tour

To reach a comfort level which will allow you to do your best work, you must become familiar with the layout of the hospital and ward in which you will be working. If you don't know where to go or where to find things, you can't possibly do your best work.

If a tour of the hospital is offered as part of the orientation, then you should take advantage of it. If no such tour is offered, ask your resident or intern to give you one. If they are too busy, take yourself on a tour. Start with your ward. Locate:

- Supply rooms
- Dirty/clean utility rooms
- Staff bathroom
- Nursing conference room
- Patient rooms. Determine how patient rooms are numbered.

Then take a tour of the rest of the hospital. Locate:

- Lecture halls/rooms
- Call room
- Medical records
- Lab
- Radiology department, including the radiology file room where patient films/studies are kept

- Emergency room
- Library
- Vending machines
- Cafeteria
- Gift shop
- Resident/student lounge

Mistake # 46
Following instructions poorly

Following the instructions given by your team members will be of obvious importance throughout the clerkship. It is especially important, however, during the first few days of a new rotation. Rest assured that team members will be observing you closely to see how well you follow directions. Here are some tips in this regard:

- Pay attention. Do not let internal or external distractions affect your ability to concentrate.
- Ask for clarification if the instructions don't make sense. It is always better to ask a question than to make an error that could have been avoided.
- Observe your team members performing the tasks that you will be expected to do.
- Write down important points so that you'll remember them when it's time for you to perform the task.
- Perform the task as soon as you can. The sooner you perform the task, the sooner you will be comfortable doing it

---

Before doing a task, you must know...

1) what you are supposed to do
2) how to do it
3) why you should do it
4) when to begin
5) when to finish
6) what the finished product should look like
7) how to do it the right way (the right way is their way)
8) the importance of the task, relative to your other responsibilities (i.e., priority)

After the task, you must receive specific feedback about your performance.

Mistake # 47

Asking few, if any, questions

As a newcomer, you are not expected to know how things work in your new setting. While some of your questions will be answered during orientation, others will remain unanswered. These are the questions that should be asked of your team members. Having worked with students in the past, your team members fully realize that you will have many questions during the first few days of a new rotation. Don't be afraid or embarrassed to approach any team member for assistance. Sometimes students feel that this is a sign of weakness. In reality, asking questions is a sign of strength.

Your goal is to complete any task the right way the first time. You want to avoid spending too much time on the task, and you want to avoid having to repeat the task. From drawing blood to ordering a bone density scan to preparing the patient for their bone marrow biopsy, you need to get it right. Ask questions, listen carefully, and take notes.

Mistake # 48

Having unrealistic expectations

Every student begins a new rotation with certain expectations. Conversations with fellow students and upperclassmen may have given you an idea of what the rotation is like. You'll have your own idea of rotations based on previous clerkships. You may be frustrated to find that some of these expectations are not met. "It was done so much better in the other rotation." "Things are nothing like Jill said they would be."

Despite these initial feelings, many students end up with a very positive experience. Once they adjust, they often find the satisfaction that was missing during the first few days. Be patient with your new team and yourself. Factor in the time needed to adjust to a new rotation and a new team. Above all, avoid unrealistic expectations.

Tip # 19

Don't begin your rotation with preconceived notions. Although you may have heard that your resident or attending is hard to work with, reserve judgment. Start the rotation with an open mind and base your opinion on your own experiences.

Mistake # 49
Displaying a negative attitude

During the first few days of the rotation (as well as throughout), you should be upbeat and positive. That's easy to say and harder to do. The start of a clerkship can be challenging, not to mention frustrating, as you try to become comfortable in a new environment. Students often feel that things are not going as well as they expected or as well as they would like them to. Remember that this is only natural. Remain positive, remember your previous accomplishments, and visualize yourself succeeding during this clerkship.

You may be asked about previous rotations. Even if your experiences were negative, you must remain positive when discussing these. Be especially careful not to say anything negative about a colleague. Although you may feel you are being truthful, your new team may come away with a different impression.

Mistake # 50
Sticking your foot in your mouth

Right before the start of the noon lecture, the speaker was patiently waiting for students to grab their food and take a seat before starting the talk on EKG interpretation. Two students nearby began talking about their rotation experience.

"So who's your attending this month?" asked Taylor.

"I got Dr. Morelli. I haven't met him yet because he starts in a few days," replied Leticia.

"Oh, you got screwed over. I've heard that he expects you to live, eat, and breathe medicine," responded Taylor.

"That figures. I always get stuck with these anal types. There goes my life for the next month," said Leticia in exasperation.

Unbeknownst to either student, the speaker, who could hear every word, was the aforementioned Dr. Morelli.

The hospital is a very public place and you never know who might be within earshot of your conversations. Early in a rotation, there is a tendency for students to talk about their initial experiences when they meet at lectures or conferences. Students often freely discuss their feelings about their intern, resident, or attending physician, sharing complaints about team members with one another. There is a real danger that these conversations may be overheard by the very team member under discussion or may be passed along to that team member by someone else.

Mistake # 51
Trying to make a big splash

Resist the temptation to start your new rotation with some sort of bang. The opportunity to make significant contributions as a team member will be coming your way. In the first few days, focus on understanding your new clerkship rather than trying to bring too much attention to yourself. In the early days, this may lead to an embarrassing moment or major mistake.

Tip # 20

Really use your powers of observation during the first few days of a rotation. Observe how the team members perform tasks, interact with one another, and handle themselves in different situations.

Mistake # 52
Making the wrong mistakes

As a new student, your work, behavior, and actions will be closely watched. Under such scrutiny, you may wonder how it's possible to avoid mistakes. It's not. Realize that you will make mistakes. Your goal is to make the right mistakes.

What are the "right" mistakes? These are mistakes that are made naturally in the process of learning. For example, if you have never written a daily progress note before, you will probably make mistakes the first time you do so. Contrast this type of mistake with more serious mistakes, such as those that call into question the strength of your character. You never want your honesty, integrity, sense of responsibility, or reliability called into question.

If you find yourself making one of the "right" mistakes, learn from your mistake, own up to it, and take corrective action so that it doesn't happen again. Operate with the philosophy that mistakes will occur, but the same mistake won't occur twice.

Did you know ...

Errors made by students have been divided into two types (Bosk). The first type is technical or judgmental errors. These errors are to be expected as part of the learning process and are the result of inexperience or lack of knowledge. The second type of mistake has to do with professionalism or lack thereof. Examples include arguing with other healthcare professionals, failing to establish rapport with patients, and dishonesty. These are the "wrong" mistakes to make.

Mistake # 53

Failing to build effective relationships

Your team is a group working towards a common goal—the delivery of outstanding patient care. The success of the team and yourself depends on how well your group works together. As simple as this seems, it's easy to lose track of the team concept, especially in the first few days.

Unless you build good relationships with team members, rotation success will be elusive. In the early days of a new rotation, many students are overwhelmed, and feel that their time is best spent in the library or secluded in the conference room. However, it's difficult to become a top performer if you don't place an emphasis on establishing rapport with your team members. That's why it's important to take the time to develop these relationships, especially in the early days of a new rotation. If opportunities to spend time with the team present themselves, take advantage of them.

Go to lunch with the team. Take a coffee break with them. These are ideal times to learn about your team members.

Mistake # 54
Failing to master the tasks of the job

The focus of this chapter has largely been on creating a profes-sional presence that sets the stage for clerkship success. How-ever, outstanding task performance remains critical to success. In the first few days of the rotation, you will be informed of your responsibilities, including tasks that you are expected to com-plete. Team members expect that these tasks will be done and done well.

Typically, your intern, resident, or attending physician will provide you with some training to help you get started. If you've com-pleted other rotations, you may think that some of this training is unnecessary. If you take this instruction too lightly, you risk run-ning into problems that could have been easily avoided. For example, if you have written daily progress notes in previous rota-tions, you may feel confident about your abilities. Keep in mind, though, that while there is a consistent format and structure of a progress note, differences exist in how notes are written from clerkship to clerkship. Some of this has to do with the preferences of your team members as well. Listen carefully to the specifics of how your team members want the notes written.

Mistake # 55
Being overwhelmed with your work responsibilities, and letting these feelings paralyze you

In the first few days, you may feel overwhelmed with your work responsibilities. This is an entirely natural feeling. Some students let these feelings paralyze them, however, and find it difficult to move forward. With so much information being passed to stu-dents in the first day or two, team members realize how difficult it is to fully grasp everything. Few team members would expect their students to learn everything at once. Nor do they expect you to do everything right the first time, although that should be your goal. Don't be afraid or embarrassed to ask for additional assis-tance.

Tip # 21

At times you will feel overwhelmed. Don't let it get you down. Do the best that you can and don't be afraid to ask for help when you need it. With every day that passes, you will become more comfortable in your new surroundings.

Mistake # 56

Slacking off

You wouldn't have reached this point in your career if you weren't a hard worker. But your new team doesn't know that. There's no better time to demonstrate your strong work ethic than the first day of a new rotation. Work hard throughout the day, stay late, volunteer to help your residents, and try to do more than required.

You'll be busy during the first few days of a rotation learning the ropes. Even if you aren't busy, you should be. This holds true for the entire rotation. On some days, you'll finish your work early, well before the rest of the team. I've seen students kick up their legs on a table or surf the internet. It's far better to stay engaged in patient care activities such as checking on your patients or reading about their issues.

Tip # 22

It's not enough to just work hard. You must also make sure that team members see you working hard.

Mistake # 57

Believing there's only one way to skin a cat

You may have performed tasks in a specific way on a previous rotation. Never assume that's the way it should or will be done in a new rotation. "When I was at St. Joseph's hospital last month, we wrote our admission orders this way." Team members never want to hear this type of comment. Remember that many tasks are done differently from one rotation to another. Even within a rotation, such as when an attending changes, things may be done differently.

Mistake # 58

Maintaining a stone face

When you first start, your team will know nothing about your character and your abilities. Your goal is to appear confident and friendly, and to quickly build rapport with your team members. A smile is one of the most basic techniques for doing so.

Tip # 23

It's natural to be nervous when starting a new rotation, but you don't need to show it. Rather, you should exude confidence. You can do that by smiling and conducting yourself in such a way that says, "I'm looking forward to working with this team."

Did you know ...

Researchers observed the nonverbal behavior of 36 Harvard medical students while they interviewed a patient or parent during their pediatrics clerkship (Rosenblum). This analysis was compared with the final clerkship grade to determine if nonverbal behavior was predictive of grade. They found that the "profile of the highly evaluated student-physician, irrespective of gender, was that of an individual who showed greater smiling..."

Mistake # 59

Waffling on whether to reveal your career interests

Team members commonly ask students about their career interests, often early in the rotation. Some students are honest while others lie. Many answer the question vaguely. Why would students give a vague or deceptive response? They are concerned that their clerkship experience will suffer if they let the team know they are going into a different field of medicine. The fear is that residents and attendings may teach less, opportunities during the clerkship may become limited, and clerkship grades may ultimately suffer.

It is my feeling that a student's clerkship experience should not change based upon his career interests. Having said this, however, I recognize that there are evaluators out there in all clerkships who might provide a different experience for students interested in their own specialty. Although this does occur, I sincerely believe that it is not as prevalent as many students think. The question is often asked casually in conversation just to learn more about you. If you're not sure of your career interests, you can say, "I haven't finalized my career plans. I've found several rotations to be very interesting, so I'm keeping an open mind." If you are certain of your career plans, always emphasize your interest in the current rotation. If it pertains to your field of choice, mention that as well. "I'm going into internal medicine, and one of the reasons I took this rotation was to become more comfortable with ENT issues, since I'm likely to encounter those in a primary care setting. I've really been looking forward to this rotation."

Mistake # 60
Staying in observation mode

During the first few days, little is expected of students beyond familiarizing themselves with the rules, responsibilities, and expectations of the new clerkship. Team members sometimes assume that the best way for students to gain this familiarity is to simply observe.

While observing does have its merits, you can't truly reach a comfort level until you start doing what you are expected to be doing. In other words, you must begin the work of patient care. For this reason, you should ask your intern, resident, or attending to assign you a patient starting from day # 1 of the rotation. Once you are assigned a patient, you can proceed to perform the daily tasks involved in patient care (i.e. writing progress notes, writing orders, obtaining lab test results, etc.).

You will see that many team members, in an effort to ease you into the rotation, will not assign you a patient. These well-intentioned team members may not realize that observing rather than performing delays students from reaching a comfort level that allows them to do their best work. If you find yourself in this situation, you should inform your team that you want to get your feet wet right away. There is no better way to do so than by picking up a patient on the first day of your rotation.

Tip # 24

Ask the resident to assign you a patient. Begin the rotation with no more than one or two patients at a time. Assume primary responsibility for your patients and strive to perform all patient care-related tasks. As you become familiar with your tasks and develop your skills, accept more patients.

Mistake # 61

Remaining unfamiliar with the chart

The medical chart is the vehicle by which all healthcare professionals involved in the care of the patient communicate. Irrespective of whether the chart is written or electronic, components of the chart can be divided into the following areas:

- Orders
- Admission notes
- Progress notes
- Consultant notes
- Nursing notes
- Lab tests
- Radiology reports

On the first day of the rotation, spend the time necessary to familiarize yourself with the components of the chart. Every morning, you will rely on the chart to bring you up to speed on your patient's hospital course. It will help you answer the question, "What has happened to my patient while I was away from the hospital?" During the workday, you will often turn to the chart to see what others (nurses, therapists, consultants) have written or recommended. The sooner you become familiar with its contents, the sooner you will become an efficient, competent student.

On Call

The phrase "on call" refers to a period of time when a team is responsible for admitting new patients. Call structure varies from one institution to another but in general, call can either be during the day or night. New students often approach their first call with some trepidation, but being on call is an excellent time to work up new, interesting patients, and to spend time with your team. This chapter reviews common mistakes made by medical students during call.

Mistake # 62

Starting Day #1 of the clerkship without knowing if you are on call

If you haven't received any information about the call schedule prior to the start of the rotation, call the clerkship office to see if the schedule has been created. Some students will be on call the first day of the rotation. If you happen to be one of them, you need to know this before the start of the rotation. You can then prepare for the experience properly.

In some rotations, student call assignments are not set in advance but are created on the first day of the rotation. If the clerkship operates in this manner, it is best to assume that you will be on call on the first day.

Mistake # 63

Remaining unfamiliar with your responsibilities

New third year medical students often approach call with apprehension, anxiety, or even a sense of dread. Much of this has to do with being unfamiliar with your on call responsibilities. Even students who have taken call on other rotations have feelings of uncertainty. That's because the experience varies from clerkship to clerkship.

During the clerkship orientation, the clerkship director will probably provide you with information regarding on call expectations. Prior to your first call, be sure to review this information. Keep in mind that the information may be general. For example, the director may inform you that students are required to pick up and evaluate two new patients per call. What may be lacking is advice on how you should evaluate these patients. For specifics, you will need to meet with your intern and resident, who will be on call with you.

Note that every resident and intern operates a bit differently. For this reason, at the beginning of the rotation, check with them to learn about their expectations. Experienced students may bypass this step, assuming that what worked well for them in previous rotations will suffice. These students are sometimes surprised when team members voice displeasure over their on call performance. To avoid starting off on the wrong foot, always meet with your superiors, regardless of your level of experience.

During the meeting, your goal is to learn how you should spend your time on call. Generally, you will be asked to focus on the evaluation of newly admitted patients who are assigned to you. Your intern and resident can also inform you of your other responsibilities.

Mistake # 64
Being inadequately prepared for your call

You won't have a successful experience unless you have everything you need. Of key importance are the following items, all of which should be placed in your on call bag:

- Change of clothes
- Personal hygiene items
- Snacks (food/beverages)
- Medical equipment
- Books/resources

In order to perform at a high level while on call, you must take care of yourself. This includes eating properly. Know the cafeteria's hours of operation but keep in mind that work on the wards may prevent you from getting food before it closes. Be sure to bring snacks.

In order to perform a complete history and physical examination, as students are expected to do, you need to have the proper medical equipment. Don't assume that equipment will be easily available on the wards. Prior to your first call, talk with your intern and resident to determine what is and is not available. When a student forgets to bring in an item, some aspect of the physical exam will not be performed. During the next day's rounds, the attending physician will inevitably ask why that portion of the exam was omitted. Rest assured that the attending will not be impressed with the reply, "I didn't do the funduscopic exam because I didn't have an ophthalmoscope."

Mistake # 65
Not being visible or easily accessible

Students on call are presented with a variety of opportunities to learn, but only if they are visible or easily accessible. Students commonly express an interest in helping the team during call, asking the resident and intern to page them when needed. These students may then retreat to the call room or library to study while waiting for a page.

What's the problem with this approach? It doesn't take into account how call works for residents. Typically, call is very busy, with multiple competing demands placed on their time. Since every minute is precious, they may find it easier to take care of the matter themselves rather than page you, wait for your response, and then instruct you on what to do and how to do it. In the time that it takes to reach and instruct you, they may be able to accomplish not only that task but several others.

For this reason, a far better approach is to be physically present. If your intern allows it, consider shadowing him. If shadowing is discouraged, plant yourself where the intern and resident can't help but notice you as they scurry around completing their work. The idea is to be around but not in the way. Students who adopt this approach will be presented with many more opportunities to learn.

Mistake # 66
Picking up a patient later
rather than sooner

It is best to pick up a patient as early as possible during the call. The sooner you are assigned a patient the sooner you can begin the evaluation. The evaluation of a newly admitted patient takes considerable time, especially for students. Remember that you not only have to take a history and perform the physical examination, but you also have to read about the case, prepare the oral case presentation, and complete the patient's write-up. If you are expected to pick up more than one patient during call, then picking up your first patient early is even more important.

Typically, it will be the resident who will assign you a patient. In assigning patients to students, residents sometimes have the tendency to wait for the "exciting case." This case may never come and you will then be assigned a patient whose evaluation you could have started hours ago. In some cases, students are never assigned a patient because "the case" never arrived. In this case, students lose out on a valuable learning opportunity. You should also realize that both your attending physician and clerkship director are expecting you to pick up one or more new patients while on call. If this doesn't happen, it reflects poorly on you. For these reasons, don't let your resident deny you a patient because he doesn't think it is of good teaching value. In many cases, what residents consider "boring" may have great teaching value for students.

Mistake # 67

Working up an insufficient number of patients

Clerkships often require students to work up a certain number of patients while on call. This is generally communicated to students during the clerkship orientation. It is your responsibility to inform your resident of this requirement before your first call. Often, residents are not aware of the requirement and then proceed to assign their students an insufficient number of patients. When your present the following day to the attending, he may wonder why you didn't pick up enough patients.

Mistake # 68

Evaluating the patient superficially

As a junior medical student, the expectation is that you will be thorough, performing a complete history and physical examination. Every part of the physical examination must be done, even if you don't think that it is relevant to the issue that brought the patient into the hospital. Thorough patient evaluations performed by students have often revealed important information not obtained by other team members.

Since you will rarely be observed taking the history and performing the exam, you may wonder how others will know how thorough you have been. The thoroughness of your evaluation will be assessed by the attending during rounds the next day when you deliver your oral case presentations. Review of your patient write-up will provide further information.

Mistake # 69

Obtaining an incorrect medication history

Obtaining and documenting the patient's medication regimen would seem to be straightforward. Even within this area, though, the potential exists for errors. Some patients rely on memory, while others bring in a typed list of their medications. Others may bring in their brown bag or plastic grocery bag full of medication bottles and hand them over to you. Don't just copy information about drug names and dosages from the list or bottles. Ask the following questions each time:

- Which medications is the patient actually taking?
- Are they following the schedule as prescribed?
- If not, why not? Are they taking the medication less often due to side effects? Are they rationing their pills due to cost?
- Are they taking the medication more often than prescribed? Why? Do they feel it may be more effective that way?
- Are they taking any over-the-counter medications?
- Are they taking any nutritional supplements?
- Are they taking any herbal or natural medications, such as St. John's wort, gingko biloba, or colloidal silver?

It may be understandable that patients would leave out certain drugs. In the case of over-the-counter medications, nutritional supplements, herbal products, or "natural" medications, many patients just don't see these as medications. However, they have the potential to cause serious side effects, such as increased bleeding time or drug rashes. Some may lead to potentially dangerous drug interactions.

In the case of prescription medications, all physicians would agree that accuracy is paramount. However, researchers who looked at medication regimens among elderly patients found that family medicine faculty and residents didn't always document accurate information. In evaluating congruence, defined as agreement between the physician and patient regarding all prescription medications, dosages, and frequency, they found a rate of only 58% for residents (Bikowski). As a medical student performing a thorough evaluation, strive for a congruence rate of 100%.

Mistake # 70

Not evaluating the patient on your own

When you are assigned a patient, you may be given the choice of seeing the patient alone or with the rest of the team. Although both options have merit, I encourage you to opt for the former for a variety of reasons:

- You must perform a thorough history and physical examination, while your intern and resident are more interested in a focused history and physical. If you see the patient together, you will usually have to come back to the patient's room to fill in the gaps.

- If you do see the patient with the residents, they will often allow you to start the interview but at some point will take over. Remember that while you only have a few patients to work up, they must evaluate many new patients. Because they are pressed for time, they may be forced to make you an observer. While there is much that you can learn from watching experienced team members interact with a patient, observation alone can only take you so far. To gain comfort evaluating a newly admitted patient, you must be an active participant.

- At this early point in your career you are developing your own style and becoming comfortable with the process of performing the history and physical exam. Having your resident and intern next to you may be anxiety-provoking.

For the reasons cited above, I recommend that you see newly admitted patients on your own. If possible, see the patient before the residents, but recognize that this may not be possible. If your patient is severely ill, your residents will need to evaluate the patient as soon as possible. They may ask you to either accompany them or evaluate the patient after they are through.

Mistake # 71

Spending too much time reading and not enough time with the patient

After being assigned a patient, students will often read about the patient's symptoms or condition before performing the history and physical. Reading about the patient's medical problems is beneficial, but save the bulk of your reading for later. When patients are admitted, there is much that needs to be done. As a student, you should assume "ownership" of all newly assigned patients. You want to be an active participant, involving yourself in all aspects of the patient's initial care. That's hard to do if you spend considerable time in the call room or library reading. A better approach is to quickly review key aspects in the work up of the patient's symptoms and then proceed to evaluate the patient.

Mistake # 72

Functioning as the patient's medical student

You should always strive to function as the patient's intern, not just as a student. To do so, you must be familiar with the intern's role in the evaluation and management of a newly admitted patient. The intern is responsible for the following:

- Obtaining the history
- Performing the physical examination
- Gathering the results of laboratory test data
- Gathering the results of other diagnostic studies (x-rays, electrocardiograms, etc.)
- Using the above information to determine the cause of the patient's symptom(s) or, if this is not possible, a list of possible causes (differential diagnosis)
- Deciding on which further diagnostic testing is needed to confirm the diagnosis and exclude other considerations
- Developing and instituting a treatment plan
- Writing the patient's admission orders
- Following through to make sure the orders are implemented
- Recording the history and physical examination in the patient's medical record (i.e., admission note or write-up)
- Preparing an oral case presentation which will be delivered to the attending physician on the following day (post-call day)
- Periodically checking in on the patient to assess the patient's condition and response to therapy
- Answering patient's questions as well as family's questions

The student who takes it upon himself to care for the patient as if he were the patient's intern is not only presented with tremendous learning opportunities but is also held in high regard for his contributions to patient care. This is precisely the type of student you want to be.

Following is a step-by-step approach to the evaluation of a newly admitted patient.

Step-by-step approach to evaluating a new patient

Step 1: Have a patient information template available to collect all patient data. After you have been assigned a patient, enter the patient's name, room number, and medical record number on your template. You will need this information to locate the patient and to access important patient information. Having the data on the template will help you organize the information for write-ups and oral case presentations

Step 2: Check to see if there are previous medical records ("old charts") on your patient. Because it can take time for hospital personnel to pull medical records for review, it's a good idea to call the medical records department and request the records as soon as the patient is assigned to you. You will need this information to complete your work-up. If the records are already on the floor, look them over and see if they contain any information that is relevant to the patient's current reason for hospitalization. Record this information on your template. If the records are not yet available, you can always look them over after you have performed the history and physical.

Step 3: Before seeing the patient, review the emergency room or clinic notes which prompted the admission. Patients will generally be admitted either through the emergency room or from their personal physician's office. Usually the chart will have a note reflecting this encounter.

Step 4: If you are not familiar with the work-up of the patient's chief complaint, read about it quickly.

Step 5: See the patient and perform a complete history and physical examination.

Step 6: Gather all test results (i.e., laboratory, EKG, imaging, etc.). Record this information in your patient template.

Step 7: Review and organize the information you have collected. Consult books and other resources to help you formulate an assessment and plan. Ask yourself the following questions:

- What is the differential diagnosis?
- What is the most likely diagnosis (i.e., working diagnosis) and why?
- What further evaluation is needed to support my working diagnosis?
- What treatment should I recommend?

The answers to these questions will help you create your own assessment and plan.

Step 8: Present the information and offer your assessment and plan to the resident. Present the case as you would to the attending physician. This will be good practice for the next day's attending rounds. Do not forget to ask the resident for feedback, especially about your assessment and plan.

Step 9: Write the admission orders. Remember to have all orders reviewed and co-signed by your intern or resident.

Step 10: After the patient is "tucked in," read about the patient's issues using a variety of resources, including handbooks, textbooks, and the literature. This will allow you to prepare a high quality write-up and oral case presentation. You will also be better prepared for the attending physician's questions.

Reviewing an old chart efficiently

Old charts (see step # 2 above) are sometimes enormous. You may wonder how you can possibly review a chart of this size with so much to do and so little time. Fortunately, you can usually obtain the necessary information with the following approach:

1) Look for the most recent hospitalization

2) Locate the discharge summary. In the discharge summary, you should be able to find the following:
   - Reason for hospital admission
   - Hospital course, including the results of important tests and response to treatment
   - Medication list at the time of discharge
   - Discharge diagnoses

3) If the discharge summary is not available or is lacking information, your job becomes harder. First, locate the admission note, which is usually the first note or two in the progress notes section. From there, read each progress note in chronological order to obtain the necessary information.

Mistake # 73

Letting others write the admission orders

Admission orders are written after a newly admitted patient is evaluated by the intern and resident. Admission orders are essentially instructions for nurses and other healthcare professionals in patient care. Orders are normally written by interns, but when students are involved in the care of the patient they are often allowed to write them.

If you aren't offered the opportunity to write orders, don't hesitate to ask. Keep in mind that interns may not be able to let you write orders, especially if there is a hospital policy against it. Also, if the patient's condition is such that orders need to be written promptly, then the intern won't have the luxury of waiting for you to complete your evaluation before writing orders. Even when you don't have the opportunity to write the admission orders, you can always take an order sheet, write your own orders, and then compare yours with the intern's actual orders.

Mistake # 74

Writing incorrect medication orders

Writing orders is a major responsibility, and each and every time you do so you need to ensure complete accuracy. One aspect of writing orders is prescribing medications. In this one aspect alone, the potential exists for multiple errors. In a study that looked at the incidence of adverse drug events and potential adverse drug events, researchers found that prescribing errors were common and contributed to over half of all significant adverse but preventable drug events (Bates).

Prescribing errors are common. The issue for physicians and physicians-in-training is how to prevent them. Garbutt and colleagues studied the behavior of house staff and medical students in regards to safe prescribing practices (Garbutt). They describe in their article a number of safe prescribing behaviors that focus on different aspects of prescribing. These include confirming information about the medication itself (e.g. spelling), checking patient information (e.g. renal function), double-checking orders once completed, how to write the orders correctly, and special considerations with verbal orders.

They asked respondents to report if they always followed specific safe prescribing practices. The results indicated that routine use of these behaviors was poor. Among students, they found that—

- 85% reported always checking prescribing information before prescribing new drugs.
- 75% reported always checking for drug allergies before prescribing.
- 54% reported always double-checking dosage calculations.

- 52% reported always avoiding the use of dangerous abbreviations.
- 25% reported always checking for renal impairment before prescribing a medication that is renally excreted.
- 23% reported always checking for potential drug-drug interactions.

With every medication order you write, ask yourself the following:

1) Have I consulted a prescribing reference before writing a new medication order?
2) Is the patient allergic to this medication?
3) Is the medication contraindicated in this patient (e.g. beta-blockers in severe asthma)?
4) Is the medication teratogenic? If so, is the patient pregnant, trying to become pregnant, or breastfeeding?
5) Will this medication interact with any of the patient's other medications?
6) Does the dose need to be adjusted for renal dysfunction (including dialysis), liver dysfunction, weight, or age?
7) Have I spelled the medication correctly?
8) Have I avoided the use of abbreviations?
9) Is the dosage, route of administration (i.e., oral, intravenous, subcutaneous, intramuscular), and dosing schedule correct?
10) Did I date and time the medication order?
11) Have I signed and printed my name along with my beeper number?
12) Is my handwriting legible?
13) Does it need to be administered as soon as possible? If so, have I conveyed this to the nurse?

Always have your intern, resident, or attending review the order for accuracy prior to cosigning.

Adapted from Garbutt JM, Highstein G, Jeffe DB, Dunagan WC, Fraser VJ. Safe medication prescribing: training and experience of medical students and housestaff at a large teaching hospital. Acad Med 2005; 80(6): 594-599.

As a final note, I would like to emphasize that students must avoid the use of dangerous abbreviations. Examples of such are listed here.

Examples of dangerous abbreviations		
Dangerous abbreviation	**Why?**	**Instead, write out ...**
Q.D.	The period after the "Q" may be misread as an "I." This may lead to four-times-daily dosing rather than the intended once daily dosing.	"every day"
MSO4	This abbreviation is often used for morphine sulfate but it may be misinterpreted as magnesium sulfate.	"morphine sulfate"
AZT	AZT has been used as an abbreviation for azidothymidine, an antiretroviral medication. This may lead to confusion with azathioprine, an immunosuppressant medication.	"azidothymidine"
U	"U" is often used as abbreviation for units. However, when the "U" follows a number as in "Insulin 5U", it may be mistakenly read as a zero. This could lead to a tenfold increase in the drug dose.	"units"
HCT	HCT, a commonly used abbreviation for hydrocortisone, may be misinterpreted as hydrochlorothiazide.	"hydrocortisone"
µg	This is an abbreviation commonly used for micrograms. When handwritten, it may be mistaken for "mg."	"mcg"

Mistake # 75

Going into attending rounds without having first met with the intern or resident

After you complete your history and physical examination, gather your thoughts. Working up a patient is like solving a puzzle: you have all these pieces of information and you have to see how they fit together. Once you do this, you will be able to establish a diagnosis and then formulate an appropriate treatment plan. During the problem-solving process, questions that you cannot answer will inevitably arise. For this reason, make it a point to sit down with the intern or resident to go over the case. If they do not initiate this meeting, you should. Don't forget how busy they are. While you may be ready to have your meeting, they may need to deal with other issues that take precedence. Be patient.

Failure to have this meeting can have disastrous consequences for the next day's attending rounds. Your attending will want to know how well you understand your patient and his problems. If you have questions that remain unanswered from the on call day, there's a good chance that the attending will ask you those very questions. To avoid this, you need to meet with the intern or resident on the day that you admit the patient. Don't delay until the next day. Issues may arise that prevent you from having your questions answered.

During your meeting, present the case, including your assessment and plan, to see if it is in agreement with theirs. This will be good practice for attending rounds. Keep in mind that your residents can often predict the questions the attending physician will ask.

Mistake # 76

Leaving for the day without offering to help the team

Medical students are often the first team members to finish since they have fewer patients and less responsibility for patient care. When you complete your work, don't just leave. I've heard of medical students who make it a point to tell the team that their responsibility, per the clerkship director, is for a maximum of two patients while on call. Forget the "requirement." As a team player, you should be going above and beyond the minimum requirements. You should offer to help other team members. The on call

75

day is busy and stressful for the entire team. Any assistance that you can provide will be appreciated.

Tip # 25

Although you may have completed your work, don't leave without offering to help other team members.

Mistake # 77

Arriving for rounds with the post-call look

To avoid oversleeping after an overnight call in the hospital, set your alarm. If you didn't bring an alarm, you can ask a colleague to page you or you can arrange a wake-up call through the hospital operator. As I have witnessed, arriving late for rounds is not the best way for a student to start the post-call day.

After an overnight call, students don't always look their best. Call is definitely busy, but it is still important to take time before rounds to clean yourself up. Avoid that post-call, disheveled look. Always dress your best and be well groomed. Your appearance remains important in projecting the right degree of professionalism for your team and your patients.

For more information about being on call, see also ...	Chapter	Mistakes
Psychiatry Clerkship: 150 Biggest Mistakes And How To Avoid Them	4	46 – 60
Internal Medicine Clerkship: 150 Biggest Mistakes And How To Avoid Them	3	22 – 36
Surgery Clerkship: 150 Biggest Mistakes And How To Avoid Them	9	111 – 125
Pediatrics Clerkship: 101 Biggest Mistakes And How To Avoid Them	3, 14	21 – 35 87 – 90

When Presenting Newly Admitted Patients

After you are assigned a new patient, it is your responsibility to evaluate the patient. You will be expected to present the findings of your evaluation during attending rounds, typically on the day following the patient's admission. The term "present" means to tell someone about a case, usually in a formal manner. The purpose of these oral case presentations is to inform the attending physician of the patient and his illness.

As a physician, you will not take care of patients alone. Since you will be relying on other healthcare professionals, it is important that you develop good communication skills. You must be able to present patient information clearly and concisely. This is essential for good medical practice and proper patient care. During rotations, you will see that considerable emphasis is placed on helping students acquire and develop effective oral case presentation skills. This chapter focuses on the mistakes commonly made during oral case presentations.

Mistake # 78

Underestimating the importance of the oral case presentation

During an oral case presentation of a newly admitted patient, your goal is to convey the story of the patient's illness along with the findings of your evaluation. The presentation will generally conclude with your assessment of the patient's clinical status and the treatment plan. In order to make informed decisions about the appropriate diagnostic work-up and therapeutic plan, the attending physician must be given an oral case presentation that is accurate, complete, and concise.

Although your attending may not have been with you during your patient evaluation, he will draw conclusions about your ability to evaluate and treat patients from your presentation. It also serves as a means by which he can assess your fund of knowledge. From your presentations, the attending will learn how competent, reliable, and thorough you are. Therefore, the quality of your oral case presentations will significantly influence your grade. One of the keys to impressing your attending is to deliver outstanding oral case presentations on newly admitted patients.

Tip # 26

No matter how well you understand your patient's illness, if you can't clearly and confidently convey your thoughts during the oral case presentation, you will not be seen as competent or effective.

Did you know ...

In their article titled "Identification of Communication Apprehension in Medical Students Starting a Surgery Rotation," Lang and colleagues wrote that "much of a student or resident's evaluation is based on oral presentations: case presentations..." (Lang).

Did you know ...

In their article titled "Assessing student performance on a pediatric clerkship," Greenberg and Getson found "a highly significant relationship between students receiving a final grade of honors and an 'A' on their case grade" (Greenberg).

Mistake # 79

Being unaware of the qualities of an outstanding oral case presentation

If you talk to enough attending physicians, some common adjectives and descriptors associated with outstanding oral case presentations will emerge. These are listed here for you on the following page.

Characteristics of an outstanding oral case presentation

- Well organized
- Clear
- Concise
- Complete
- Follows the expected order or format
- Includes relevant aspects of the history, physical exam, laboratory testing, and other data, including pertinent negatives
- Free of irrelevant information
- Thorough but not overly laden with detail
- Allows the listener to develop a coherent and accurate picture of the patient's problems
- Accurate
- Shows knowledge of major and minor issues
- Minimal use of notes
- Good eye contact
- Excellent assessment and plan

Features that are universally regarded as signs of a poor oral case presentation are listed here.

Characteristics of a poor oral case presentation

- Includes irrelevant facts
- Rambling
- Disorganized
- Ill-prepared
- Major omissions
- Unclear
- Skipping around (e.g. lab data is included in the HPI)
- Inattention to detail

Your goal is to consistently deliver outstanding oral case presentations and in this chapter we provide you with sound advice to help you reach this goal.

Mistake # 80

Presenting the case without realizing what the attending is seeking

The type of presentation expected depends on whether the patient is newly admitted or not. On post-call days, you will formally present your newly admitted patient to the attending. He expects a complete presentation because he is not familiar with the case. If he is familiar with the case, you should instead provide a quick update on the patient's progress.

Mistake # 81

Presenting the case without knowing how much time you have

The duration of the oral case presentation varies depending upon the preferences of the attending physician, but typically ranges between 5 and 15 minutes. At the beginning of the rotation, you should ask the attending how much time you have to deliver your presentation. Remember that your attending has a preconceived notion as to how much time your oral patient presentation should take. He may not volunteer this information so you must ask. Do so early in the rotation, preferably before you ever present.

Mistake # 82

Presenting for longer than the allotted time

Once you know how much time you have, your goal is to prepare and practice your presentation, making sure that it does not exceed the allotted time. It is very easy to do so. If you were to include every piece of information that you obtained during your patient encounter, the presentation would easily exceed the time that you have been given.

Many students don't adhere to the time limit imposed by the attending. This is a sure-fire way to annoy team members. When presentations last longer than expected, they take time away from other activities that need to be done during attending rounds. Time on the floor is precious. With so many tasks to accomplish in a relatively short period of time, it is imperative that the team stays on schedule during rounds. Your team will thank you if you are sensitive to this need.

Tip # 27

While rehearsing the oral case presentation, you need to time yourself.

Mistake # 83

Presenting a case with too little or too much detail

Before listening to your presentation, the attending physician has a preconceived notion as to the amount of information he wants to hear. Your goal is to avoid delivering case presentations that are too detailed or that are not detailed enough. For students, the former tends to be more of a problem than the latter.

Successful students must communicate an organized, succinct history, physical exam, assessment, and plan without losing the attending's attention. This can be a challenge, considering that there is so much material to convey on any given patient. Students often fear that they will leave out key details if they don't present all of the data learned. They also worry that they are too new to medicine to be the judge of what should and should not be included. It is no surprise, then, that students commonly make the mistake of presenting too much information. Students who are able to convey only the relevant details sound impressive because they are presenting at an above average level for their training.

How do you know how detailed your oral case presentation should be? You can learn about the attending's expectations by meeting early in the rotation. You can then tailor the presentation to meet his needs. Don't worry if your first few presentations contain too much or even too little information. With time and practice, you will become more proficient.

Mistake # 84

Presenting a verbatim reading of the patient's write-up

The oral case presentation should not be a verbatim reading of the patient's write-up. Instead, it should be a carefully edited version of the write-up. Oral and written case presentations have different purposes. The latter is much more comprehensive. Oral presentations, however, are meant to rapidly convey key informa-

81

tion. By reading your write-up aloud for the oral presentation, you will present information that is overly detailed.

It is also difficult, if not impossible, to keep the attention of your audience if you present a verbatim reading of your write-up. When presenting, you need to keep the audience engaged and interested. That's difficult to do if you are reading the write-up out loud. Lesser reliance on notes allows you to maintain eye contact with your listeners, which helps keep your audience interested. It also conveys to the attending that you have a firm grasp on your patient's medical problems. Keep in mind that it is acceptable to glance at your notes occasionally. For example, when reporting medication dosages and laboratory data, it may be necessary to refer to your notes. If you are able to deliver polished oral case presentations without relying too heavily on notes, you will be seen as an accomplished, effective student.

Mistake # 85
Not practicing your oral case presentation

Practice. Practice. Practice. By practicing your presentation over and over, you will become much more familiar with the patient information. Knowing the material that you are conveying is one of the best ways to prevent nervousness. Since you will be giving your presentation by speaking it, you must practice by speaking it as well. Practicing it silently in your mind robs you of the opportunity to hear yourself say the words. By hearing yourself say the words, you become more confident in your delivery.

To deliver a polished oral case presentation, you must practice not only on your own but, if possible, with others. Practice it before family, friends, or fellow students. It is particularly important to practice with your resident or intern before presenting to the attending. If your resident doesn't ask you to present the case to him beforehand, ask if you may do so. After your practice run, the resident may offer suggestions on how to polish the presentation, or may identify problems that require correction. Since residents have considerable experience delivering oral case presentations, their advice should be taken seriously. They can help improve your presentations significantly, allowing you to shine when you present the case to your attending.

Tip # 28
Videotaping is an underutilized but very effective way of improving the quality of your oral case presentations.

Mistake # 86

Speaking softly

In our normal conversations, we generally speak in a softer voice. During an oral presentation, however, you need to adjust the volume of your voice, depending on the setting and circumstances. For example, if you are presenting in a larger room with team members spread throughout, your goal is to be heard clearly by the person sitting farthest away.

At other times, you may be asked to present in the hallway between patient rooms. In this more intimate setting, your focus will again be on making sure that all team members can hear you. However, you don't want to speak so loudly that you compromise patient privacy.

In my experience, speaking too softly is more of a problem for students than speaking too loudly. For some, this is the natural way they speak. For others, this stems from fear or nervousness. Since we often have difficulty evaluating the volume of our own voice, solicit feedback from others and make changes if necessary.

Mistake # 87

Speaking too quickly or too slowly

In delivering your presentation, your goal is to speak slowly enough to be easily understood by the audience. If you speak too slowly, however, your listeners may cease to pay close attention to what you are saying. If you speak too rapidly, then it will be difficult for you to enunciate each word clearly, correctly, and distinctly.

In my experience, speaking too quickly is the more common problem for students. With so much information to convey in a fixed amount of time, students will sometimes increase the pace of their speech so they can finish within the allotted time. If you find yourself in this situation, determine if there is information that you can leave out. Usually there will be, and by doing so, you won't feel pressured to speak too rapidly. Rushing through a presentation may also be due to nervousness. The best way to combat nervousness is to prepare thoroughly.

The most interesting presentations are given by students who vary their rate of delivery. By speeding up and slowing down when necessary, they are able to emphasize certain points, making their presentations more interesting. You can learn about your rate of delivery by recording your presentation, reviewing it, and making adjustments where you see fit.

Tip # 29

To avoid delivering a boring presentation, vary your rate of speech. Slow down if you want to emphasize certain points. A short pause is particularly effective in this regard.

Mistake # 88

Speaking in a monotone

If you ever listen closely to a dynamic speaker, you will notice that the speaker varies the pitch and tone of his voice during the speech. By doing the same, your audience will find your presentation much more interesting.

Utilizing a monotone voice can make even the most interesting content come across as boring. To avoid this common pitfall, you must practice your presentation, paying careful attention to the pitch and tone of your voice. Recording and listening to your presentation is a useful way to evaluate your own pitch and tone. Also, as with other aspects of your oral case presentation, rely on the feedback of others.

Tip # 30

The tone of your voice reveals your feelings and attitudes. Be aware of how you sound by recording your presentation and listening to it. Students who have delivered monotonous presentations often don't realize it until they hear themselves speak.

Mistake # 89

Mispronouncing words

While practicing your oral case presentation, be sure you are comfortable pronouncing all words. Students commonly make pronunciation errors during case presentations, and these mistakes can affect your credibility. A student who is knowledgeable about his patient may not be perceived as such when words are mispronounced.

At times, you may realize that you are unfamiliar with a word and how it is pronounced. If so, consult a medical dictionary or team member who can educate you on the proper pronunciation. In other cases, you may be unaware that you are saying a word incorrectly. This is yet another reason to present your case to the resident before presenting to the attending. After hearing your presentation, they can inform you of any mispronunciations.

Pronunciation errors are particularly common during the medication section of the oral case presentation. I can't tell you how many times my students have mispronounced medications such as tamsulosin, carvedilol, irbesartan, and rosiglitazone.

Tip # 31

Students want to be seen as intelligent and competent. To be perceived as such, you must speak well. Students who deliver polished oral case presentations understand the importance of voice quality (volume, rate, pitch, and tone), pronouncing words properly, and speaking clearly.

Mistake # 90

Speaking with annoying speech habits

Oral case presentations should be polished and free from extraneous words or phrases such as "uhh," "um," "like," or "you know." The use of these phrases, also known as fillers, is distracting. Listeners may conclude that you lack knowledge about your patient or his medical conditions. Often, these annoying habits are manifestations of nervousness. The best way to prevent the use of these fillers is to become comfortable with your presentation.

We are often unaware of our own use of these fillers. For this reason, while practicing in front of others, be sure to ask if they note any use of fillers. If so, continue practicing your presentation in order to eliminate them. If you don't have the opportunity to receive feedback from others, record your presentation so you can evaluate yourself. You might be surprised to learn how often you use these fillers. Strive to replace them with a short, silent pause.

Did you know ...

In one study, eleven faculty members from the Department of Internal Medicine independently viewed the same 17 videotaped student case presentations. Most raters placed high value on three communication skills: economy, fluency, and precision of language. In the article, these skills were defined as shown below:

Economy—"the information's relevance and avoidance of unnecessary content"

Fluency—"the student's ability to articulate without verbal tangles, with a minimum of qualifiers and hesitations"

Precision in language—"unambiguity in phrasing, appropriate use of terms, and avoidance of lay jargon"

This study demonstrated that the faculty's assessment of oral case presentation quality was regularly influenced by the way in which the information was conveyed by the student (Elliott).

Mistake # 91

Minimizing the importance of body language

Do not forget that you will be communicating in two ways during your oral case presentation—verbally and nonverbally. Your audience will pay close attention to not only what you say but also how you say it. To make a strong favorable impression on your listeners, be sure to:

- Maintain eye contact with team members. Rotate your eye contact to keep all listeners engaged. Students who are able to make eye contact are seen as more credible, competent, and confident.

- Display good posture, whether you are standing or seated. Students who slouch give the impression that they are indifferent, even if they feel otherwise. With good posture, you are also more likely to speak more clearly.

- Never invade a colleague's space. If you are presenting in a large room, this is unlikely to be a problem. In a hallway, a team is often huddled close together. If you notice signs of another team member's discomfort, adjust your body position so that you are at a comfortable distance for interaction.

- Avoid distracting behaviors such as playing with your hair, jewelry, or tie. Understand that students are usually unaware that they are engaging in these behaviors. During your dress rehearsal, ask your resident or friend if you are displaying any such behavior.

Mistake # 92

Letting the awkwardness and discomfort of the first few oral case presentations get to you

Even with considerable preparation, students often feel awkward and uncomfortable with their first few oral case presentations. Don't worry if your presentations seem a bit rough at first. These are natural feelings, which will abate with practice, time, familiarity, and an understanding of the attending physician's preferences. With time, your oral case presentations will become more polished.

Mistake # 93

Paying poor attention to other student presentations

In many of your rotations, your team will include other students. These students will also be expected to present newly admitted patients. It is important to listen closely to your fellow students when they present. Pay careful attention to the attending physician, as they often make suggestions for improvement. Learn from other students' mistakes, making sure not to repeat them.

Mistake # 94

Letting your anxiety take over

Students often feel anxious before delivering an oral case presentation. This is only natural. In fact, a certain degree of nerves can spur you into delivering a fine performance. However, uncontrolled anxiety can prevent you from giving the best possible presentation.

To reduce your anxiety, consider some of the following suggestions:

- Don't view your nervousness as a negative. You need that burst of adrenaline to perform well.

- Practice over and over. The best way to avoid anxiety is to feel confident about your presentation. You gain this confidence from practicing until you know your presentation like the back of your hand.
- While practicing, visualize the room, the audience, and yourself during the presentation. Picture yourself impressing the team. Studies have actually demonstrated that positive thinking in "speech-anxious subjects" can reduce subjective anxiety and cardiovascular responses (Hu).
- Realize that your anxiety is not as apparent to your audience as it is to you. From speaking to many students, I know this to be the case.
- Get off to a good start by knowing your introduction (typically the history of present illness) very well. If you are able to convey the first part of your presentation with poise, you will gain confidence, allowing you to relax and shine during the rest of the presentation.
- Remind yourself that you know more about your patient than any other team member.

Mistake # 95
Following an improper format or order

There is a proper order to the presentation of patient information. Oral case presentations that do not adhere to the expected order are considered disorganized and are difficult to follow. The order and content, to some extent, varies from clerkship to clerkship. During your pediatrics clerkship, you will be expected to present the patient's birth, neonatal, and feeding history. These elements are not required during the internal medicine rotation.

Even within a clerkship, you will at times encounter differences when working with different attendings. Do not assume that an order that served you well with one attending will fit the needs of another. Learn your attending physician's style and follow a format that suits his preferences. The traditional format of the oral case presentation is described in the following table.

Component of the oral case presentation	Some important points
Patient identification	Start your presentation with the name of the patient, location of the patient, and any other identification information that is required to access medical records (i.e., medical record number)
Chief complaint	Keep it one sentence long Include duration of the complaint
History of present illness (HPI)	Make sure it is chronological Discuss chief complaint in more detail (onset, intensity, severity, precipitating factors, relieving factors, progression of illness, etc.) Include associated symptoms Include pertinent positives and negatives (let your differential diagnosis guide what you include) Include elements of past medical/surgical history, medications, social history, and family history that are relevant to the present illness Include degree of impairment caused by the patient's illness Include any therapy instituted by patient and/or physician along with response to treatment
Past medical/ surgical history	Relevant or pertinent past medical or surgical history should be included in the HPI Include only important PMH/PSH Leave out minor diagnoses Do not repeat previously stated information
Medications	Group together any medications given for the same condition Don't forget to include over-the-counter or herbal medications
Allergies	For drug allergies, include the type of reaction
Social history	Relevant or pertinent social history should be included in the HPI and need not be repeated here
Family history	If the information obtained is not relevant to the patient's current illness, then consider saying, "the family history was noncontributory."

Review of systems	If the information obtained is not relevant to the patient's current illness, then consider saying, "the review of systems was noncontributory." Do not repeat previously stated information
Physical examination	Begin with brief description of patient's general appearance followed by vital signs Follow expected order* Include both pertinent positives and negatives If an aspect of the physical examination is normal, it may be acceptable to say that it is "normal" or "unremarkable" (ask attending physician for his preferences)
Lab/imaging/other studies	Ask attending if he wants all results or only abnormal lab test results Start with basic lab tests first Bring electrocardiogram, x-rays, CT scan with you for the attending physician to review
Summary	Generally a three to four sentence summary of the patient's clinical presentation
Assessment/plan	This is your opportunity to demonstrate your reasoning skills and fund of knowledge Use information obtained (history, physical exam, labs, etc.) to argue for a particular diagnosis Discuss other possibilities (differential diagnosis) and why they are less likely Offer diagnostic and therapeutic plan

*A commonly used order is as follows: general appearance → vital signs → HEENT (head, eyes, ears, nose, throat) → neck → thorax → heart → lungs → abdomen → rectal → pelvic/genital → extremity → neurological/musculoskeletal

As you progress through each aspect of the presentation, take care not to "jump around." For example, physical examination findings should not find their way into the history of present illness. Students who do so confuse their listeners.

Tip # 32

Don't stop your oral case presentation when you reach the assessment and plan, as some students do, because you fear that your assessment and plan may be incorrect. Present your conclusions with confidence. Even if you are wrong, the fact that you committed to a diagnosis and provided support for it will be looked upon favorably by your attending.

Did you know ...

55 verbal case presentations of house officers and medical students were observed during an inpatient ward month at a teaching hospital affiliate of the Wright State University School of Medicine (Marinella). Students reported the chief complaint in only 61% of their presentations.

Mistake # 96

Transitioning without the use of headings

As you progress through your presentation, you should keep your listeners oriented by using standard headings. When you are ready to present the patient's past medical history, you might start by saying, "The past medical history was remarkable for ..." Before delving into the physical exam, you might say, "On physical exam ..."

Mistake # 97

Presenting irrelevant information

Students are often unsure about what information should be left out of the presentation. It can be difficult to determine whether a detail is relevant or not. With time and experience, of course, you will become more comfortable making these decisions. Here are some tips:

- Include the detail if it helps build your case. With every oral case presentation, your goal is to convey patient information that provides support for the diagnosis.
- Include the detail if it helps your listener take care of the patient.
- If you are not sure whether the detail is relevant, omit the information. Be prepared to provide the information if your listener asks for it.
- If your attending keeps asking for the same type of information during or after your presentation, then you should include it in your next presentation.

Mistake # 98

Letting interruptions fluster you

In the perfect student world, an attending would never interrupt during an oral case presentation. The reality is that many attendings will interrupt with varying frequency. Many students are annoyed when their attendings interrupt with questions or comments. These often throw off a students' train of thought. While some students are able to handle this with poise, others become flustered and disoriented. Some students are unable to recover.

As you prepare and practice your presentation, you must realize that most of the time you will be interrupted. Students tend to assume that an attending will only interrupt them if there is something lacking in their presentation. However, an attending may interrupt to ask questions because it is simply his style. He may interrupt to ask for a clarification or because he missed something you said. Questions or comments may also indicate that your attending is interested in what you have to say.

How do you handle these interruptions? First, realize that you probably will be interrupted. Second, understand that an interruption does not mean you are presenting poorly. In fact, it usually indicates that your attending is paying close attention. If the attending asks a clarifying question, answer it and move on. If the attending asks a question to gauge your knowledge base, then answer it to the best of your ability. In many cases, your reading will allow you to answer the question. If you don't know the answer, don't become flustered. You are not expected to have answers to every question.

Mistake # 99

Not obtaining feedback

Ideally, your attending would initiate a feedback discussion with you shortly after each and every oral case presentation. During this discussion, he would inform you of any mistakes and recommend areas for improvement. If you find yourself working with such an attending, consider yourself fortunate. More often than not, however, you will not receive timely feedback. In fact, some students receive no feedback whatsoever. While attendings realize the importance of providing feedback, they are sometimes unable to do so. Rounds may be particularly busy or there may be other constraints on their time. Others simply dread giving feedback. They feel uncomfortable giving any feedback that is less than perfect.

To prevent this from happening, you must take an active role by asking for feedback from your attending and resident. Do not feel that you are imposing. Attendings realize that giving feedback is one of their many responsibilities.

Obtain feedback soon after you present. If days pass, you are more likely to receive nonspecific information. Do not settle for vague statements. What does "you're doing a good job with your oral case presentations" mean? Instead, ask the attending to provide you with specifics. Armed with specific feedback, you will be in a position to correct mistakes and build upon each presentation, leading to improved performance.

If you are having difficulty obtaining feedback, consider handing out an oral case presentation evaluation form to the attending physician with each presentation. A few clerkships have adopted this strategy, providing their students with a form to use. If your clerkship has not, it shouldn't stop you from creating your own form. Or you may choose to use ours, on the next page

Mistake # 100

Letting one mistake throw off your presentation

Mistakes can and will happen during presentations. Do not let one mistake affect the remainder of your presentation. If an error is made, correct it and move on. If you lose your train of thought or your mind just draws a blank, refer to your notes and keep going. The point here is to remain calm and composed, which will allow you to recover more easily and move on.

Mistake # 101

Not projecting confidence

The most polished presenters are able to project confidence throughout their presentation. To exude confidence, you must feel confident, and to feel confident, you must prepare well. Barbara Linney in her article, "Presentations that hold you spellbound", said "presentation content is important but even more so body language and voice quality because the best of messages will fall on deaf ears if you don't look and sound confident" (Linney).

Oral case presentation feedback form

	Strongly disagree	Marginal	Agree	Strongly agree
The patient was clearly identified (name, age, sex, race, pertinent past medical history)				
The chief complaint was clearly stated				
The HPI was chronologically organized				
Pertinent positive information was included				
Pertinent negative information was included				
Physical exam included general appearance				
Physical exam included vital signs				
Physical exam was presented in logical order				
All pertinent physical exam findings were presented accurately				
No extraneous information was presented				
Pertinent/significant labs/studies were included				
A problem list was conveyed				
Problem list was presented in descending order of importance				
Plan was presented—not just an assessment				
Presents with minimal use of notes				
Voice volume and quality appropriate				
Accurately pronounces words				
Presents in a lively manner or in a way that holds attention				
Good time management				
Adequately responds to questions and requests for clarification or additional information				
Is knowledgeable about illness or topic, including up-to-date literature				

Mistake # 102

Lying

When presenting a patient to your attending, honesty is always best. There are many times when you may be tempted to stretch the truth or lie in an attempt to make your history and physical exam more complete than it actually was. If your attending asks you about the patient's dorsalis pedis pulses and you did not check them, do not say they were normal. Simply tell the attending that you did not examine the pulses and learn from your mistake. It is not possible to deliver the best possible care to patients unless team members are honest.

Mistake # 103

Ignoring audience response

As you deliver your presentation, pay close attention to how it is received. This requires you to make eye contact with your listeners. Watch for body language cues that indicate approval, confusion, frustration, or other emotions. It's up to you to read these nonverbal cues and then respond appropriately. If you sense that your listeners are growing impatient with the length of your presentation, you can shorten the remainder by cutting out the less important details.

For more information about the oral case presentation, see also ...	Chapter	Mistakes
Psychiatry Clerkship: 150 Biggest Mistakes and How To Avoid Them	6	88 – 103
Internal Medicine Clerkship: 150 Biggest Mistakes and How To Avoid Them	3 Appendix A	76 – 116
Pediatrics Clerkship: 101 Biggest Mistakes and How To Avoid Them	5, 10, 16	40 – 46 74 – 76 95 – 96

Commonly Made Mistakes

On Write-Ups

The write-up or written case presentation is a detailed account of the patient's clinical presentation. You were probably introduced to the process of writing a case presentation during your physical diagnosis course. During most, if not all, rotations, you will be asked to do write-ups on patients you admit. One of the major purposes of the write-up is to help you develop the written communication skills needed to take care of patients. These are skills that will serve you and your patients well throughout your medical career. In this chapter, we discuss mistakes students commonly make on write-ups.

Mistake # 104

Underestimating the importance of the write-up

During your rotations, you will be expected to complete write-ups on any patient that you admit into the hospital. These write-ups will often be placed in the patient's medical chart, along with those of other team members. Student write-ups are generally the most detailed document in the chart. They are likely to be referenced by other healthcare professionals, not only during the patient's present admission but for many years to come. For this reason, it is important that you are accurate.

Students are often asked to turn in write-ups for review. In most cases, it is the attending who will review them. At some schools, the clerkship director may also review write-ups. The reviewers will draw conclusions about your ability to perform a comprehensive patient evaluation and appropriately record the result of this evaluation. In addition to your ability to collect information, reviewers will assess your ability to identify and evaluate problems, generate an accurate differential diagnosis, demonstrate clinical reasoning, and formulate a management plan. Write-ups should not be taken lightly since the quality of the write-ups plays a large role in the determination of your overall grade.

> **Did you know...**
>
> Kogan and Shea wrote that "Assessment of the write-up is believed to be important because it evaluates a student's ability to collect information; identify, prioritize, and evaluate problems; demonstrate clinical reasoning; develop management plans; and communicate through a written record. These are important clinical skills that students are expected to be proficient in prior to graduation" (Kogan).

Mistake # 105

Not ascertaining the expectations of the attending physician

"If you don't know where you're going, you won't know how to get there." This expression definitely applies to the written case presentation. In order to meet the expectations of the attending, you need to know these expectations before you submit your first write-up. This is particularly true when you change clerkships as the content of the write-up, to some extent, differs from one specialty to another. Even within a clerkship, expectations will vary among different attendings. Do not assume that what served you well with one attending will fit the needs of another.

> **Tip # 33**
>
> The quality of your write-ups will significantly contribute to the attending's impression of your clinical performance. Keep this in mind as you prepare them.

Mistake # 106

Late submission of the write-up

Clerkships generally require students to turn in write-ups within a specified period of time. Your evaluation will suffer if they are submitted late. Timely submission of the write-up offers another advantage. The attending may be able to return it to you before the next one is due. The feedback you receive will help improve subsequent write-ups.

Doubtful that you would commit this mistake? Just about every student I have worked with has made this mistake.

Students miss submission deadlines for a variety of reasons. Among the most common is perfectionism. Students always feel as though a write-up could be better. At some point, though, you have to let it go. When missing the deadline, students too often say nothing, thinking the attending won't notice. Even if he doesn't say anything, chances are he's noticed. Therefore, a better approach is to keep your attending informed of your progress. If your write-up will not be completed on time, ask for extra time. Most attendings would be receptive to such a request. The key is in how you word this request. Consider the following two requests:

"It's been so hectic on the wards that I haven't yet completed my write-up. Is it okay if I turn it in tomorrow?"

"I would like to put some polishing touches on my write-up. Would it be okay if I turned it into you tomorrow instead of today?"

With the former request, the student offers an excuse. With the latter request, the student does not offer any excuses. He instead presents his request in such a way that suggests that the write-up is essentially done save a few tweaks here and there.

Tip # 34

Aim to turn in write-ups on time. There's always going to be something you want to change, word differently, or explain better. At some point, you simply have to let it go. You don't want the evaluation of your write-up to suffer because you submitted it late.

Mistake # 107

Submitting an incomplete write-up

It's not just the student who completes a write-up on a newly admitted patient. The residents and attending will do the same. Their documents will also be placed in the medical chart, typically as an admission history and physical. These experienced clinicians will generally produce a more concise and abbreviated document. In contrast, your write-up will be expected to be very detailed, reflecting what should be a thorough patient evaluation on your part. Many clerkship evaluation forms ask evaluators to grade students on their ability to perform a comprehensive history and physical exam. Since attendings are generally not present while you perform the patient's evaluation, they will often rely on your write-ups to give them an idea of your proficiency. The chief means by which you can demonstrate the thoroughness of your patient work-up is by turning in a comprehensive, complete, and detailed write-up.

> **Did you know...**
>
> In a study in which three student write-ups were evaluated by seventeen faculty members, incompleteness was the most common error students made (McLeod).

> **Did you know...**
>
> After videotaping clinical interviews performed by medical residents, contents of each videotape were compared with the medical record to determine the adequacy of medical history documentation. Researchers found that "residents recorded a little over half of all medical history information observed on the videotapes" (Moran).

Mistake # 108
Submitting an illegible write-up

Doctors and their poor handwriting skills are the subject of many jokes. However, 7000 deaths a year in the United States are attributed to medication errors, some of which are the result of poor penmanship. Bad handwriting can also be found in other sections of the medical chart, including your write-up. When it does, it prevents other healthcare professionals from understanding or accessing key information. Their inability to read your work wastes time. If information is misconstrued or simply missed because handwriting is indecipherable, then the patient may be harmed. Even as a third year medical student, you will undoubtedly feel the pressures of time. This can lead to hastily written notes, write-ups, and orders. To avoid compromising patient safety, recognize that poor penmanship can have serious consequences. You must guard against this tendency now and in the future by making a conscious effort to practice good penmanship.

Mistake # 109
Submitting your write-up without comparing it to previous ones

When a write-up is returned to you, review it closely for any critical comments. Make a list of these comments and then refer to this list each time you prepare a write-up. As an increasing number are returned, your list of comments will grow. Compare your next write-up to the list to ensure that you have not made the same mistakes.

Mistake # 110

Not doing a tremendous job on the first write-up

You know the importance of making a good impression the first time you meet someone. The same holds true for your first write-up. By producing an outstanding first write-up, you will set the proper tone. Your goal is to show the attending that you are more advanced than most students at your level. Turning in a high quality first write-up can go a long way towards creating this impression. In the remainder of this chapter, we will provide you with the information you need to produce an outstanding write-up.

Tip # 35

Appearance makes a difference. If you hold your write-up out in front of you, does it look good? Is it pleasing to the eye? Before the attending physician begins reading the write-up, his first impression will be based on how professional it looks. Coffee stains, crossed-out lines, endless paragraphs, and poor spacing won't make your attending want to read any further.

Mistake # 111

Submitting a write-up with poor grammar and incorrect spelling

Poor grammar and incorrect spelling often find their way into student write-ups. These are hallmarks of carelessness, an image that no student wants to cultivate. An otherwise high quality write-up will not be seen as such when the write-up is peppered with misspelled words and poor grammar. Avoidance of such carelessness is imperative for your future career as well. Should you ever be named in a lawsuit, you will want your documentation to be free of these errors. Even if the care provided has been sound, poor documentation with spelling errors, poor grammar, and sloppy penmanship will create an impression of carelessness.

Tip # 36

Your write-up should be neat, with perfect grammar and flawless spelling. What do misspelled words and poor grammar say about you? They suggest that you don't pay attention to detail. Even if the content of your write-up is stellar, it may not be perceived as such if you are sloppy with spelling and careless with grammar.

Did you know...

In a study in which three student write-ups were evaluated by seventeen faculty members, poor readability/misuse of language was the second most frequent problem type (McLeod).

Mistake # 112

Submitting a write-up with improper abbreviations

Physicians frequently use abbreviations in their write-ups. While abbreviations are generally acceptable, it is common for students to use unapproved abbreviations. When an unapproved abbreviation is used, the potential for misinterpretation exists, leading to a medical error that could jeopardize the patient's care. For example, if your patient is taking hydrochlorothiazide and you list this medication as "HCT" in the medication list of your write-up, another team member may interpret "HCT" as an abbreviation for hydrocortisone. Make sure that the abbreviations you use are approved, preferably by your own institution.

Mistake # 113

Submitting an inaccurate write-up

Since write-ups often become a part of the patient's permanent medical record, make sure that your work is accurate. Once you have written and placed the write-up in the patient's medical record, it cannot be changed. It has the potential to be used as evidence in legal proceedings such as a malpractice case.

Did you know ...

To determine the accuracy of medication histories, researchers evaluated 115 hospital medical records (Beers). The written record was compared to a structured history taken by a member of the study's research staff. An error was defined as "either the failure to record the use of a medication the patient claimed to use or the recording of a medication that the patient denied using." At least one such error was found in 83% of all patients.

Did you know ...

In a study performed to assess adequacy of medical record documentation, researchers learned that key information was not documented regularly (Cox). Previous history of heart failure was not documented in 58% of patients hospitalized for myocardial infarction.

Mistake # 114

Submitting a disorganized write-up

There is a proper order to the presentation of patient information. Write-ups that do not adhere to the expected order are considered disorganized and are difficult to follow. The order in which information is presented generally does not differ from the oral case presentation. Write-ups begin with subjective data followed by objective data (physical examination), assessment, and plan. Components of the subjective portion of the write-up include the identifying data, chief complaint, history of present illness, past medical history, medications, allergies, social history, family history, and review of systems.

Keep in mind that the content of the write-up will differ, to some extent, from specialty to specialty. For example, while the prenatal, birth, and neonatal histories are important in the pediatric patient, this information generally has no bearing on the adult patient. If you are unsure of the proper order, you should ask.

Mistake # 115

History of present illness errors

The history of present illness or HPI is a description of why the patient is here now. It is considered to be the most important element of the history. As such, it should flow like a story, giving the reader a clear idea of the events that transpired before the patient sought medical attention from you. A well-constructed HPI...

- Begins with an introductory statement that includes the patient's age, race, sex, and relevant past medical history.
- Is chronological. The story should begin when the patient was last in his usual state of health (i.e., baseline), and trace the development of symptoms from onset to the current time.
- Identifies time of symptom onset.
- Identifies duration of symptom.
- Addresses why the patient has sought medical attention now.
- Explores the patient's chief complaint thoroughly, including onset, precipitating/palliative factors, quality, region/radiation, severity, and timing/temporal aspects.
- Includes pertinent positives and negatives.
- Includes any therapy initiated by the patient, as well as therapy prescribed by other caregivers. Also includes response to therapy.
- Includes relevant features of the past medical history, social history, medications, family history, and review of systems.
- Includes patient's concerns, fears, and thoughts about what may be accounting for his symptoms.
- Includes the degree to which the illness is affecting the patient's quality of life.

Did you know ...

In a study in which three student write-ups were evaluated by seventeen faculty members, poor characterization of symptoms and signs was the third most frequent problem type (McLeod).

Mistake # 116
Problem list errors

Clerkships often prefer that the write-up includes a problem list, which is a compilation of the patient's active medical problems. To identify problems that should be included on the list, a useful technique is to start at the beginning of the write-up and circle all symptoms, known illnesses, abnormal physical exam findings, and abnormal test results (laboratory, EKG, imaging, etc.). Everything that is circled should be listed as a problem with the exception of inactive problems. An inactive problem is one that has no bearing on the present illness or the patient's future health. An example would be tonsillectomy performed as a child in an adult patient.

Mistake # 117
Submitting a write-up that lacks an appropriate assessment and plan

No other area of the write-up causes students as much distress as the assessment and plan. New clerks tend to write a brief assessment and plan section. An example of a brief assessment and plan:

A – Unstable angina

*P – Rule out myocardial infarction with enzymes and
treat with aspirin, beta-blocker, and heparin*

What's wrong with this assessment and plan? The student does not describe what led him to believe that unstable angina was the most likely diagnosis. He does not include any information from the patient's history, physical exam, or testing that supports his assessment. There is also no discussion about other conditions (i.e., differential diagnosis) that could cause similar symptoms. The plan is also very brief with no rationale given.

Do not lose sight of the fact that the attending physician will assess your understanding of the patient's disease, including your knowledge of appropriate management and therapy, based on the quality of your assessment and plan. In this section, it is not only important that you commit to a diagnosis, even if you are less than 100% certain, but also that you provide support for it. You must also offer a differential diagnosis and explain why other conditions in the differential diagnosis are less likely. End this section with the diagnostic and therapeutic plan.

To assist you in the development of this important section, below is a step-by-step approach to writing the assessment and plan.

Step-by-step approach to developing the assessment and plan

Step 1—From the patient's problem list, determine the patient's most important problem. List it as problem # 1 under the assessment and plan section.

Before listing the problem, ask yourself if you have made it as specific as possible. If the patient is admitted for chest pain and the etiology of the chest pain is not clear, then you would list it as:

1. Chest pain

If, on the other hand, your initial evaluation of the patient's chest pain reveals that he is having a myocardial infarction, then you would list it as:

1. Acute myocardial infarction

Step 2—Provide a differential diagnosis

The differential diagnosis is a list of conditions that could account for a patient's illness. Start your assessment with a statement that provides your reader with the differential diagnosis that you have considered.

1. Chest pain

While the differential diagnosis for chest pain is extensive, in this hospitalized patient, we will first consider the potentially life-threatening and common etiologies. Life-threatening causes of chest pain include unstable angina, myocardial infarction, pulmonary embolism, aortic dissection, pneumonia, pneumothorax, esophageal rupture, and pericardial tamponade.

Note that, thus far, the assessment and plan only includes a differential diagnosis. It's always a good idea to comment on the life-threatening causes of a patient's symptom, since that is what concerns physicians the most in a newly admitted patient.

Did you know ...

Faculty at the University of Minnesota Medical School were asked which aspects of student performance discriminated better between average and superior medicine clerks (Parenti). Formulation of a reasoned differential diagnosis and plan was found to be more discriminating than any other aspect of student performance.

Step 3—State the most likely diagnosis (working diagnosis)

A definitive diagnosis may be established in some patients immediately after your work-up. More often than not, though, you will have a working diagnosis. In other words, you and your team will make a likely diagnosis based on the patient's clinical presentation and the results of testing. As the patient's hospital course is observed, the results of further testing become available, and the response to therapy is assessed, a definitive diagnosis will be established. Before that happens, however, you will have to complete your write-up. Therefore, you will have to commit to a working diagnosis.

With that in mind, you will have to determine which of the entities in the differential diagnosis is the most likely (or working) diagnosis. You will do this by reading about each of the considerations in the differential diagnosis. As you read, determine which of these conditions best accounts for your patient's presentation. That is your working diagnosis (see example below).

> *1. Chest pain*
>
> *While the differential diagnosis for chest pain is extensive, in this hospitalized patient, we will first consider the potentially life-threatening and common etiologies. Life-threatening causes of chest pain include unstable angina, myocardial infarction, pulmonary embolism, aortic dissection, pneumonia, pneumothorax, esophageal rupture, and pericardial tamponade.* ***Of these possibilities, unstable angina or myocardial infarction is the most likely diagnosis.***

Tip # 38

You may be hesitant to commit to a particular diagnosis because you fear you may be way off track. It is always better, however, to commit. Those who do commit show the attending that they have thought about the case. The same can't always be said for those who don't commit.

Step 4—Provide support for your working diagnosis

After you have stated what you believe to be the most likely diagnosis, you should proceed to inform your reader how you came to that conclusion.

In support of this is his history of coronary artery disease. Up until one week prior to admission, the patient described only exertional chest pain. He then began experiencing more frequent episodes of chest pain, lasting longer in duration and even occurring at rest. These episodes of pain are otherwise similar in nature to his previous episodes of stable angina. Although his physical exam did not reveal any findings consistent with ischemia or infarction, the patient was examined when he was free of pain. EKG findings revealed ST-segment depression in the inferior leads, which were not present on an old tracing. When chest pain becomes more frequent, lasts longer, or occurs at rest, it raises concern for unstable angina and myocardial infarction. Lending further support to our working diagnosis is the EKG changes.

Note that in providing the reader with support for the diagnosis, data from the patient's history, physical exam, and testing are weaved in to make a strong argument.

Step 5—Inform the reader why other considerations in the differential diagnosis are either not the cause or are a less likely cause of the patient's illness

After stating the working diagnosis and providing support, discuss other considerations in the differential diagnosis and why they are less likely to account for the patient's illness.

Aortic dissection is quite unlikely given the description of the pain (pressure sensation in the center of his chest rather than a sharp, tearing pain), lack of radiation (pain of aortic dissection often radiates to the back), lack of physical exam findings (pulses symmetric and normal in all extremities), and normal mediastinal size noted on chest x-ray. Pneumothorax was also considered but, again, the description of the pain was not typical (pressure sensation rather than a sharp, pleuritic pain), shortness of breath was absent (shortness of breath is common in patients with pneumothorax), classic physical exam findings were not present (decreased breath sounds, hyperresonance to percussion), and the patient had a normal chest x-ray. Pulmonary embolism always needs to be considered in the differential diagnosis of chest pain, especially given the fact that most diagnoses of this condition are made at autopsy. Therefore, we must always think of it as a possibility. This patient has no risk factors for pulmonary embolism, lacks symptoms and signs of deep venous thrombosis in the lower extremities, and does not have any other findings supportive of this diagnosis. Pericardial tamponade... Pneumonia... Esophageal rupture...

In discussing other considerations in the differential diagnosis, provide reasons why you think they are less likely. Incorporate data from the history, physical exam, and testing to support your argument.

Step 6—Provide your diagnostic and therapeutic plan

Many attendings prefer that students write the plan as a list or outline. Include both the diagnostic and therapeutic plan.

The diagnostic and therapeutic plan for this patient with chest pain due to an acute coronary syndrome includes—

1) Bed rest with continuous EKG monitoring

2) Oxygen

3) Serial cardiac enzymes (CK, CK-MB, troponin) to rule out myocardial infarction

4) Aspirin

> *Aspirin therapy has been shown to reduce the risk of death or MI in patients with unstable coronary artery disease not just in the acute setting but also long-term.*
>
> *- Chewable 325 mg aspirin given in the ER*
>
> *- Will continue aspirin therapy daily at a dose of 81 mg po*

5) Clopidogrel

> *In combination with aspirin, clopidogrel has been shown to reduce the rate of cardiovascular death and reinfarction to a greater effect than when aspirin is used alone*
>
> *- Loading dose of 300 mg po given*
>
> *- Will continue clopidogrel therapy daily at a dose of 75 mg po*

6) Metoprolol

> *Beta-blocker therapy has been shown to reduce mortality in patients with myocardial infarction*

> *- Metoprolol 5 mg IV given and then repeated twice for a total of 15 mg. This was followed by 25 mg of metoprolol given orally with this dosing to continue every six hours.*

7) Heparin

> *Studies have shown that the addition of heparin to aspirin will lead to a further reduction in the risk of death and myocardial infarction in patients with unstable coronary artery disease.*

> *- Will use low-molecular-weight heparin in this patient*

8) Ramipril

> *In the HOPE trial, ramipril was shown to reduce mortality and myocardial infarction in all patients with coronary artery disease.*

> *- Will begin ramipril*

9) Atorvastatin

> *Several studies have shown that the early use of statins in patients with LDL-cholesterol levels above 100 mg/dL has beneficial effects in reducing ischemic events*

> *- Begin atorvastatin 20 mg po qd*

Tip # 39

Clerkship evaluation forms often ask evaluators to comment on a student's use of the literature. Because many students don't realize this, they fail to show their team that they are reviewing the literature. One place to demonstrate your use of the literature is in the write-up, particularly in the assessment and plan. Note that in step 6 above, I have made mention of the HOPE trial under "ramipril" to show how you can incorporate recent literature findings into an assessment and plan.

Step 7—Determine which one of the patient's problems is second in importance and list it as Problem # 2.

After listing Problem # 2, ask yourself if it is a known (established) or unknown diagnosis. For example, if the patient has had gout for 10 years, then that is an established diagnosis. For established diagnoses, you need not discuss a differential diagnosis. However, you should provide the reader with reasons as to why this diagnosis can be accepted in this patient, the current status of the problem, and the treatment plan.

> *2. Gout*
>
> *Patient was diagnosed with gout ten years ago when he developed acute right knee pain and analysis of the synovial fluid revealed the presence of needle-shaped, negatively birefringent monosodium urate crystals. Since then he has had several more attacks but none over the past five years. Because the gout is currently stable, we will continue his current therapy of allopurinol.*

If, on the other hand, Problem # 2 is thrombocytopenia of unclear etiology, then that is not an established diagnosis but rather an "unknown." With an "unknown," the assessment and plan should include a differential diagnosis, the most likely diagnosis, the diagnostic plan, and the therapeutic plan.

Step 8—Complete the assessment and plan section, making sure that you deal with each problem on the problem list in the manner described in Step 7.

Mistake # 118

Passing off the work of others as your own

Attendings realize that the assessment and plan section of the write-up is difficult for almost every student. Sometimes students feel tempted to take shortcuts. One involves copying the intern's or resident's assessment and plan verbatim. Attendings may want the student to review the assessment and plan with their residents, but no attending expects to read one that is identical to the house officer's. While the basic diagnostic and therapeutic plan is unlikely to differ, the student's version should be more detailed. It should be written in such a way that the attending is able to understand the student's thought process. And, of course, it should always be written in the student's own words.

Do not copy information directly from a text or journal article. While students are expected to turn to a variety of resources, the information learned should be stated in your own words. You also come across better if you are able to apply the information to your own patient. Being able to do so demonstrates that you have a firm understanding of the patient's illness. If you must copy information directly from a text, place quotes around the copied text and include the reference. In general, it's a good idea to include references regardless.

The prevalence of plagiarism has not been well studied in American medical schools. However, over the past five years in conversations with faculty at different medical schools, a handful have raised concerns about this issue, citing examples in which student plagiarism occurred and how it came to light. Recently, a colleague related a story about one of his third year medical students. As he read through the student's write-ups, he suspected that the words and ideas expressed in the discussion did not belong to the student. He punched in portions of the discussion into an internet search engine. Before long he came across a website that contained sections of the discussion word for word. The website was never referenced by the student. This was immediately brought to the attention of the clerkship director and others in the administration. The student now faces disciplinary action.

Did you know ...

In a survey of students at the Dundee University Medical School, 82% felt copying text directly without acknowledging the source was wrong yet 14% had either done or would considering doing it (Rennie).

Tip # 40

Medical schools have policies in place to deal with the student who passes off another's work as his own. The punishment is often severe. Attendings expect that you will turn to a variety of resources to analyze and understand your patient's problems. With that being the case, you should always cite your sources in the write-up.

Mistake # 119

Submitting the first write-up without having it first reviewed by the resident

After completing your write-up, ask your resident to review it. Some students are hesitant to do so, but you can inform the resident that you want to make sure that you get off to a good start. Take the resident's comments seriously and make changes where necessary. Keep in mind that the attending may have preferences of which the resident is not aware. While it can't guarantee a glowing review from the attending, it should elevate the quality of your write-up.

Mistake # 120

Not seeking feedback on the quality of your write-ups

Write-ups are very useful for learning. They are even more valuable when faculty provide regular feedback regarding their quality. As with your other clerkship assignments, it is imperative that you receive feedback. If you are fortunate, you will have an attending who provides feedback quickly, well before the next write-up is due. Unfortunately, feedback is often delayed or short on specifics that students can really utilize. To optimize their learning value, consider providing your attending with a write-up evaluation form, as shown on the following two pages. The use of this form can give you valuable information regarding your strengths and weaknesses.

Write-up feedback form				
	Strongly disagree	Marginal	Agree	Strongly agree
The write-up was turned in on time				
The write-up is legible and free of spelling errors/ poor grammar				
The patient is clearly identified*				
The chief complaint is concise and stated in the patient's own words				

The HPI begins with an introductory statement that includes the patient's age, race, sex, and relevant past medical history				
The HPI is chronologically organized				
Each symptom is explored (onset, precipitating/ palliative factors, quality, radiation, location, severity, temporal aspects)				
Pertinent positive information is included in the HPI				
Pertinent negative information is included in the HPI				
Past medical/surgical history, medications, allergies, social history, family history, and review of systems are included and complete				
Physical exam includes general appearance				
Physical exam includes vital signs				
Physical exam is presented in logical order				
All pertinent physical exam findings (positives and negatives) are included				
Breast exam in women is included				
GU/pelvic exam is included. If not performed, the reason is specified				
Rectal exam is performed				
Results of all test results are reported				
Problem list is complete				
Problem list is presented in descending order of importance				
An assessment and plan is given for all problems				
An adequate differential diagnosis is provided for each problem				
An adequate diagnostic and therapeutic plan is given for each problem				
Student is knowledgeable about illness or topic, including up-to-date literature				

*Your clerkship may ask you not to include the name, medical record number, or other identifying information on the write-up for purposes of patient confidentiality.

For more information about the write-up, see also …	Chapter	Mistakes
Psychiatry Clerkship: 150 Biggest Mistakes And How To Avoid Them	5	61 – 87
Internal Medicine Clerkship: 150 Biggest Mistakes And How To Avoid Them	4	37 – 75
Pediatrics Clerkship: 101 Biggest Mistakes And How To Avoid Them	4, 15	36 – 39 91 – 94

Commonly Made Mistakes

When Giving Talks

Medical students are often asked to give a talk to the team, usually pertaining to an issue that arises during rounds. Many students are overcome with a sense of dread when assigned a talk. Students don't realize, though, that a talk offers them the opportunity to really impress their team. While you can't control what an attending might ask you during rounds, you do have complete control over your talk. With sufficient preparation and practice, you should be able to deliver a terrific talk. Relish this opportunity to perform in front of the team, and recognize that an outstanding talk can go a long way towards impressing your team. In this chapter, we look at the mistakes students make when giving a talk.

Mistake # 121
Not volunteering for a talk

During attending rounds, an issue may arise that requires further research. Sometimes an attending will turn to the team and ask "Who would like to give us a talk about ...?" As team members pointedly try to avoid the attending's gaze, the request is often met with silence. This is not surprising. Most residents, interns, and students would rather not prepare and give a talk, if they had the choice. This reflects poorly on the entire team.

If the attending asks for a volunteer, you should be the first person to raise your hand. This is yet another opportunity to demonstrate your enthusiasm and initiative. You may not like the thought of giving a talk. However, as you will see in the remainder of this chapter, with adequate preparation and practice there is absolutely no reason why you cannot deliver an outstanding talk.

Tip # 41

Volunteer for talks with enthusiasm, even if it's the last thing you want to do.

Mistake # 122

Choosing the wrong topic

In most cases, the attending physician will assign the topic. If you are given the freedom to choose any subject you wish, consider the following carefully before you select a topic:

- It is always better to choose a topic that you know something about. If you recently cared for a patient with asthma, consider speaking about some aspect of asthma. If in your last rotation you spoke about pulmonary embolism, consider speaking about it again if it pertains to your current rotation. Speaking on a topic you know something about can shorten your preparation time.
- It should be a topic that you have an interest in.
- Be sure your topic will be of interest to your audience.
- Be sure that you can discuss the topic in the time you have been given. Realize that you may have chosen or been assigned a broad topic. For example, your topic may be lung cancer. It's hard to do justice to such a topic unless you have been given considerable time to speak. If you have only a short amount of time, ask the attending if there is a specific aspect of the topic he would like you to focus on. If he leaves it up to you, pick an aspect of the topic that would be relevant to your audience, such as the therapy of metastatic lung cancer.

Did you know ...

In a study of medical student talks, Yale medical students were asked to present a 30-minute talk on a topic of their choice during the Ambulatory Component of the Internal Medicine Clerkship (Kernan). At the orientation, students were told to avoid overviews or large topics. As an example, rather than talking about pneumonia, students were asked to focus on a particular aspect of pneumonia. Despite this recommendation, at the end of the rotation faculty evaluated student presentations and found that 35% were too broadly focused.

Mistake # 123

Preparing for a talk without knowing when you are expected to deliver it

Dr. Jones assigned the topics of thrombocytosis and asthma to his medical students, Paul and Sophia, respectively. He didn't tell them when they would give the talks and neither student asked.

Two days later, during rounds, he said, "Since we have a lull in the action, why don't we use this time for student talks?" Paul had assumed that he would have longer than a few days to prepare the talk. "Can I give my talk tomorrow? I just need a little more time to work on it." The attending then looked at Sophia. "Since we have some time, I can go ahead and give my asthma presentation," she said.

Even though it wasn't Sophia's intention to show up Paul, she clearly came across as the more prepared and responsible student. Never assume that you know what your attending is thinking. When assigned a talk, ask when you are expected to give it.

Realize also that talks are not always given on the date specified. A patient issue may consume more time than expected during rounds, preventing you from giving your talk. Having prepared extensively for your talk, you, of course, would like to just give it and get it out of the way. Unfortunately, you have little choice in the matter. There's not much you can do except be ready to give the talk on another day.

Tip # 42

Some attending physicians will give students a vague deadline. They may say, "There's no rush with the talk." Knowing when you are to give the talk is crucial information, so don't accept a vague deadline. Above all, do not view a vague deadline as a license to procrastinate. Get started right away.

If just a few days remain before the end of the rotation and no mention has been made of a talk you were assigned some time ago, you need to bring it up. You should never leave a clerkship without finishing any project, including an assigned talk. If you don't bring it up, the attending may assume that you "blew it off."

Mistake # 124

Being unaware of your allotted time

You cannot prepare properly for a talk unless you know how much time you will be given to speak. The duration of a talk will vary depending upon the preferences of the attending. Remember that your attending has a preconceived notion as to how much time your talk should take. A talk that lasts much longer than this takes time away from the completion of other tasks during rounds. One that is too short will prompt the attending to wonder how much effort you expended researching your topic.

Tip # 43

If the attending physician doesn't tell you how much time you have to speak, you should ask.

Never take up more than the allotted time. As Hoffman and Mittelman wrote in their 2004 article on presentations, "many speakers who have not adequately prepared their talk go beyond their time limit. The result is often an annoyed chairman, an irritated audience..." (Hoffman).

Mistake # 125

Procrastinating

After being assigned a talk, students do one of two things. They either begin working or they procrastinate. The latter option is chosen more often.

Students procrastinate mainly because of fear. Many fear they will do or say something that will make them look foolish. Others are scared to be the center of attention. These concerns weigh especially heavily on the minds of new clerks, who have not yet had the opportunity to give a talk in the clinical setting. You can alleviate these fears by preparing for your talk as soon as it is assigned. With adequate preparation, you can polish your talk and gain confidence in your ability to deliver it well.

Tip # 44

Start preparing right away. The more you prepare, the more confident you will be.

Mistake # 126

Preparing a talk without knowing your audience

Since you will generally give talks to your team, you will know your audience beforehand. Keep in mind that this audience is mixed. The team consists of members at different educational levels. You must always take into account the knowledge level of your audience. This will help you develop a talk that suits the needs of all listeners.

If you are assigned to speak before an unfamiliar audience, ask for information beforehand. During my psychiatry clerkship, the attending asked me to give a talk on obesity during psychiatry grand rounds. Having never attended psychiatry grand rounds, I was completely unfamiliar with the group. Only after finding out about the audience was I able to prepare a talk tailored to their needs and at a level that was appropriate for their educational background and expectations. Since many of the attendees were psychiatry faculty, I prepared a talk that took into account their knowledge and experience. Had the group consisted only of my fellow students, I would have prepared a very different talk.

Your audience analysis should yield answers to the following questions:

- How many people will be in the audience?
- How familiar is the audience with the subject?
- What is the educational background of the audience?
- What does the audience expect from me?
- How can I provide information relevant to their specialty?
- What would I like the audience to do with the information I present?
- What materials do I want to leave with the audience?
- What questions might audience members ask?

Students who carefully consider the composition and background of their audience are more likely to deliver a talk that meets the needs of their listeners.

Mistake # 127

Preparing a talk without knowing the purpose of the talk

For most talks, your general purpose will be to inform. You also need to determine the specific purpose of your talk. You can do so by considering the needs of your audience and establishing goals and objectives. Without a specific purpose in mind, you run the danger of preparing a vague and disorganized talk.

When developing a purpose statement, be specific. Consider the following two purpose statements:

I want my listeners to know how to manage an acute gout attack.

I want my listeners to be able to specify at least three types of medication that can be used to manage an acute gout attack.

The latter statement is clearly more specific. It's much easier to develop a focused talk when you have a specific purpose statement.

Mistake # 128

Failing to captivate the audience from the get-go

Start your talk with an introduction that leaves your audience eager to hear what else you have to say. You only have one chance to make a strong first impression. When you fail to grab their attention, it can be difficult to capture it later. For this reason, plan your introduction carefully. Too often, students begin their talk with one of the following types of statements:

I'm talking today about …

The subject of my talk is …

You should include the topic and purpose of your talk in the introduction. However, rather than using a bland statement to open the talk, begin with something that will stir interest. Examples include the following:

- **Asking a rhetorical question**

We all realize that pulmonary embolism is a major cause of death. Did you know that the diagnosis of pulmonary embolism is missed in approximately 400,000 patients per year? And that's just in the United States...

- **Making a bold statement or sharing a startling statistic**

  In the United States, 650,000 people are diagnosed with pulmonary embolism every year, with over 200,000 deaths.

- **Making a historical reference**

  More than 160 years have passed since Virchow's classic paper on thrombosis and homeostasis was published and we, of course, continue to use the principles of Virchow's triad in the diagnosis and management of patients with pulmonary embolism. From historical reports, Virchow was small in stature but possessed a quick wit. He was known to be sarcastic, particularly when he dealt with incompetence or inattention. Yet he could also be generous and friendly, recognizing those who had made significant contributions. If he were alive today, he would perhaps be impressed with the progress that has been made in the diagnosis and management of pulmonary embolism but he might also berate us for not making more progress. After all, pulmonary embolism remains a major cause of death in the United States...

- **Providing a thought-provoking quote**

  "Substantial and unacceptable." Those were the words of Dr. Kenneth Moser, referring to the morbidity and mortality rate of venous thromboembolism... (Moser KM: Venous thromboembolism. Am Rev Respir Dis *1990 Jan; 141(1): 235-49).*

- **Telling a brief story**

  If you've ever seen a patient die suddenly of a massive pulmonary embolism, it's not something that you will ever forget...

Using the above techniques, you can easily create an introduction that will capture the audience's interest.

Tip # 45

Since the audience's attention is best at the start of a talk, create an attention-grabbing opening that will keep them interested in the remainder of your talk.

Mistake # 129
Utilizing inappropriate resources

Do not use handbooks as your primary source of information. You should instead turn to larger, more authoritative texts and the recent literature. While the information in your handbooks may suffice for your fellow students, remember that your audience will also consist of an intern, resident, and attending physician.

If you are having difficulty finding data, seek the assistance of the research librarian. The research librarian is a wonderful yet underutilized resource. They don't have all the answers, but they generally have a good idea of how to help you find the information you seek.

Mistake # 130
Overloading your audience with information

Before you even organize your talk, you must first select material for your presentation. The real trick is determining what *not* to use. Your research will usually yield more material than you have time to talk about. You need to avoid information overload as there is a limit to what your audience can handle in a finite period of time. How do you know what to include and what to discard? When you are not sure, ask yourself if the information supports your purpose. Discard that which is irrelevant. As Starver and Shellenbarger stated in their 2004 article on presentations, "It is tempting to include lots of information about the topic, but be sure that it clearly fits the purpose of the presentation" (Starver).

Tip # 46

One of the most common mistakes students make is presenting too much information. Every point you make should support your talk's specific purpose. If it doesn't, cut it out.

Mistake # 131
Presenting inaccurate data

During your talk, you will present data that support your ideas. Your data must be accurate and relevant. Review all data several times to ensure that the information is accurate. Presenting accurate data is the key to coming across as a credible presenter.

Nothing will damage your credibility more than passing along inaccurate information. Even one inaccurate fact can call into question the accuracy of your entire talk. With statistics, ask yourself if the information is up-to-date. Presenting statistics that are many years old when more recent information is available is a surefire way to damage your credibility.

Mistake # 132

Practicing incorrectly

When practicing, strive to simulate the actual experience as closely as you can. Whenever possible, practice in the room in which you'll actually speak. If this is not possible, pick a room that closely resembles the real location of your talk. Doing so allows you the opportunity to become comfortable with the environment.

As you practice, do not just go over your talk in your head. There is a difference between going over a talk in your head and actually delivering it. For this reason, stand in the proper spot, imagine an audience in front of you, and rehearse your talk. Use your notes exactly as you plan to during the actual talk. If you will be using audiovisual equipment, practice with the equipment.

Tip # 47

As you rehearse your talk, time yourself to ensure that your presentation fits within the allotted time. If you run over, delete material rather than increasing the pace at which you speak.

You can learn a lot about how you will appear by videotaping yourself. This is a valuable yet underutilized way of improving performance. Play it back so that you can see and hear yourself as others will. Students are often surprised by what they learn from a videotape of their performance. Annoying habits are usually not self-evident but will often come to light during this type of review. It is better to learn about these habits during a practice session when you still have the opportunity to correct them.

Tip # 48

If you will be using audiovisual equipment, realize that problems often occur. A bulb in the projector may burn out. A slide may jam. Too often, when the unexpected happens, students stop their talk, hoping that the problem will be fixed. Unfortunately, problems are not always correctable. You must be able to continue your talk if an equipment failure cannot be corrected.

Mistake # 133

Reading your talk word for word

Many students write out their talk and then proceed to read it word for word. This is among the most common errors students make when giving a talk. It almost always leads to a monotonous delivery, a surefire way of boring your audience. It is also impossible to maintain eye contact with your audience save for an occasional upward glance. This will diminish your credibility.

Tip # 49

Talks that are read are boring. They lack spontaneity and rhythm. Think about the best speakers at your medical school. How many of them read their talks word for word? Keep in mind the words of Edwards who wrote that "... natural rhythm of telling a story with its pauses and eye-to-eye contact with the audience is lost when the talk is read" (Edwards).

Rather than reading your talk word for word, I recommend that you use note cards with no more than ten words on each card. You can use these words as a reminder of the points you wish to make and then proceed to formulate sentences to express these points. You may argue that this method is risky, but keep in mind that you will be practicing with these note cards. With sufficient practice, you will become comfortable developing sentences using the cues you have on the card. As you grow less dependent on your notes, consider memorizing your introduction, which will allow you to make an outstanding first impression.

If you are able to speak without detailed notes, it will enhance your image. Since so many students read their talks, attendings are impressed with students who can give a talk using a paucity of notes. It is this type of student who comes across brighter, more confident, and more articulate.

Tip # 50

When quoting an article or conveying detailed statistics, it is better to refer to your notes. You don't ever want to misquote or pass along inaccurate data.

Tip # 51

Should you memorize your talk? It's a risky option. What if you draw a blank? Even if you don't, chances are that you will come across robotic and stiff rather than natural and enthusiastic.

Mistake # 134

Speaking in a monotone

A particularly effective way to maintain your audience's interest is to vary your inflection. Too often, students speak with the same force, pitch, and pace, leading to a monotonous delivery. Speaking in a droning monotone bores listeners. It also suggests a lack of interest in the topic.

Is this the impression you wish to convey? Of course not. However, this is precisely the impression that many students make on their audience. You may be very interested in the subject matter. However, that does you no good if the force, pitch, and pace of your speech suggests otherwise.

Mistake # 135

Speaking without gestures

Students commonly remain seated during talks given to a small group, such as their team. In the seated position, students generally place their hands underneath the table. This robs them of the ability to gesture. It has been found that voice patterns often follow hand movements. When hands are kept under the table, it can hamper your ability to vary inflection. Gesturing, if done appropriately, can help you speak with inflection, leading to a more lively talk.

For this reason, I recommend that you give your talk while standing. Do not keep your hands in your pockets or clinging to a lectern. Instead, have them in front of your body with your palms open. In this position, you are able to effectively gesture.

Avoid gestures that indicate nervousness or lack of confidence. These include the following:
- Keeping your hands in your pockets
- Gripping the lectern or audiovisual equipment
- Biting your fingernails

- Playing with keys or coins in your pocket
- Rocking back and forth or from side to side
- Rubbing the back of your neck
- Playing with your hair
- Clenching your fists constantly
- Pacing back and forth
- Fidgeting with clothes or jewelry

If you still choose to give your talk while seated, don't forget to lean forward in your chair, a gesture that conveys enthusiasm and confidence.

Since we are usually unaware of how we gesture, it is useful to take note of your movements while standing in front of a mirror and practicing. You can also review your gestures on videotape and solicit feedback from others after they watch you rehearse. Take note of any inappropriate gestures and make a conscious effort to eliminate them during practice.

Tip # 52

Only 7% of a speaker's message is obtained through actual spoken words (Mehrabian); 55% is conveyed through nonverbal communication while 38% is transmitted through vocal tone.

Mistake # 136

Using fillers

Fillers are sounds like "um" and "er" that find their way into talks when speakers are thinking about what to say next. If you use fillers, listeners may conclude that you lack knowledge or are unsure of your information. "The speaker's voice, tone, and inflection are powerful tools for attracting an audience... Speakers are advised to refrain from speaking in a low, monotonous style and from taking long breaks with fillers such as 'uh...uh...'" (Hoffman).

Most students don't even realize that they use fillers. I recommend that you record your presentation and then listen to it. With this approach, you can determine if fillers are a problem for you. Once you are aware of the problem, you can proceed to replace these fillers with short pauses.

Mistake # 137

Speaking too quickly

You must take care to speak at a speed that allows your audience to understand what you are saying. Talks lead to a great deal of anxiety for most students. In students who normally speak at a reasonable pace, this anxiety can cause them to speak at a faster speed with few, if any, pauses. The effect can be poor enunciation with garbled words and sentences. "Too many ideas presented too quickly will not be understood, even to the most well-informed and intelligent audience" (Edwards).

You must make a conscious effort to slow down so that your listeners can follow you. Accomplished speakers will also pause periodically to allow their listeners to fully process what they have said. You should aim to do the same. In their article on lecturing, Brown and Manogue wrote that lecturers, to improve clarity, should "speak clearly, use pauses, and don't go too fast... Whilst these suggestions may seem common sense, observation of lectures suggest that they are not common practice" (Brown).

Mistake # 138

Letting your anxiety take control

Are you nervous about speaking? If so, you are far from alone. Some surveys have shown that public speaking is the number one fear, ranked ahead of even the fear of death. Anxiety affects everyone, even the best speakers. The best speakers, though, are able to make their jitters work for them. They have learned how to use that nervous energy to their advantage.

A little bit of nervousness can spur you into delivering a better performance. Too much anxiety, however, can be problematic, especially if it is discernible to the audience. They won't be able to relax and won't effectively process your information. While it is only natural to feel nervous, you need not express these feelings to your audience. Speakers often believe that audience members can easily tell when they are nervous. In reality, studies have shown that listeners are often unable to pick up on signs of anxiety.

Mistake # 139

Concluding your talk with a whimper

Some students conclude their talk by mumbling "I guess that's about all I have," or "I think I've gone over everything." These statements completely lack impact. Others even close with an apology. "I'm sorry I wasn't able to find more," "I'm sorry I couldn't get the projector to work," or "I'm sorry the talk went so long". In ending your talk, do not mumble and do not ever apologize. The conclusion is also no place for bringing up new points or rambling on and on. Students who don't take the time to think about their conclusion end up closing with a whimper rather than a bang.

To conclude in a way that leaves the audience with a lasting, powerful impression, begin with a phrase that tells your audience that you are wrapping up your talk. Examples:

In concluding, I want to …

Let me leave you with …

As a final thought …

To wrap up my talk …

Since most of your talks will be informative presentations, it is reasonable to close by briefly summarizing your main points. After doing so, end your speech in an interesting way, perhaps with a quote or rhetorical question. Since a talk is often assigned when a team member raises an issue pertaining to a patient, one particularly effective way of closing is to apply your information to that specific issue. "As the recent literature has shown, the diagnosis of pulmonary embolism may clearly be challenging. As in the case of Mr. Smith, however, a combination of diagnostic methods leads to improved sensitivity." To leave your audience with a strong, final impression, avoid reading your conclusion. Instead, know it well enough that you can deliver the conclusion with few, if any, notes.

Tip # 53

Avoid the all-too-common abrupt or awkward conclusion. Instead, use a strong conclusion to leave your audience with a favorable impression.

Mistake # 140

Avoiding eye contact

Without maintaining eye contact with your listeners, it will be difficult to keep them interested in what you are saying. Too often, students make no eye contact whatsoever, reading their talk word for word from their detailed notes. Even when students try to present without reading, they will often be looking elsewhere—at the floor, ceiling, table, or audiovisual material.

As you give your talk, make eye contact with your listeners. Not only will this keep them interested but it will also help you come across as more credible and confident. As Spinler wrote in her article on presentations, "eye contact is the most critical component of effective delivery" (Spinler). Looking into people's eyes while delivering a talk can be difficult for some students. If you find this unnerving, you need not look into people's eyes. Instead, focus on another part of the face such as the forehead, nose, or mouth. Your listeners will not realize the difference. As you make eye contact, do not be surprised if a team member is not paying attention to you. You may notice someone falling asleep. Don't let that bother you. Remember your audience is often a tired group. Don't be thrown off track if a pager goes off or if team members are engaging in conversation. As distracting as this may be, you should not let it affect your presentation.

If you are able to make eye contact, you can also learn about how your talk is being received. People communicate their attitudes and feelings by way of body language. Observe your listeners carefully to pick up on any negative nonverbal feedback and utilize this information to make an adjustment. You may need to adjust what you are saying, how you are saying it, or both. For example, if you sense your attending losing interest, you can vary the volume, pitch, or pace of your voice to keep him involved.

Mistake # 141

Showing little, if any, enthusiasm

In a perfect world, you would only be asked to speak about topics you love. Unfortunately, as a student, there will be times when you are asked to speak about a subject that does not interest you. However, it is important that you project enthusiasm about your assigned topic. A lack of interest is easily picked up on by audience members. When students are not interested in their topic, listeners won't find the talk interesting. If they don't find it interesting, they're not likely to view your talk favorably.

Tip # 54

As one attending physician once remarked to me, "There are no dull subjects, only dull presentations." If you don't have natural enthusiasm for a topic, find a way. Fake it if you must.

Mistake # 142
Giving a talk without using visual aids

Some people describe themselves as visual learners while others describe themselves as aural learners. While it is true that some learn better by seeing and others by hearing, a talk that meets the needs of both learning styles will have the most impact. As such, it behooves you to use visual aids during most talks. I say "most talks" because there may be factors that prevent you from using visual aids. If the attending has asked you to give a quick 2-minute "blurb" about something while standing in the hallway between patient rooms, the short duration and location of the talk clearly preclude the use of visual aids. For longer talks that will take place in an environment more conducive to the use of visual aids, there are compelling reasons to do so. Visual aids, if done well, can enhance your talk, making your presentation more interesting and enjoyable. Effective use of audiovisual aids can—

- Reinforce your statements.
- Help you direct the audience's attention.
- Help your audience comprehend your ideas and points.
- Make you appear more credible and professional.
- Lead you to deliver a more memorable talk.

Tip # 55

You may wish to forgo visual aids when your talk is brief or the setting in which you are giving the talk is not conducive to their use. Without visual aids, it is especially important that your content is interesting and your delivery is captivating.

Although a variety of visual aids are available, students most often use slides, PowerPoint projection, or overhead transparencies. All are useful presentation tools, but only when well done. While good visual aids can certainly complement your talk, bad ones can damage your talk. Below are some tips for PowerPoint presentations:

PowerPoint do's and don'ts

- Don't read the text.
- Use a font color that contrasts with the background color.
- Use the same background color throughout the presentation (medium blue is popular).
- Maintain consistency by using the same symbols and typefaces.
- Don't use full sentences. A good rule is to keep each line no more than 6-7 words.
- Don't place too many points on each slide (less is more).
- Use at least 18-font size (be sure that people in the back row can read the information).
- Avoid fancy fonts. Instead, choose a standard font like Arial or Times New Roman.
- Don't capitalize entire words unless it is necessary.
- Proofread your text for spelling, repeated words, and grammatical errors.
- Avoid overly complex tables, charts, graphs, or diagrams.

Should you provide your audience with a handout? A strong argument can be made for providing listeners with a handout. They can help the audience follow your train of thought. Most listeners will appreciate written material that they can refer to later. The fact that you produced a handout will also give your audience some idea of the effort you put into the talk.

As you prepare the handout, pay careful attention to its presentation. The handout should appear professional. Remember that its appearance is a reflection of you. If it appears unprofessional, your listeners may form a negative impression of you and what you have to say, even before you open your mouth. As always, proofread your work to avoid misspelled words and grammatical errors.

You can either provide the audience with the handout before or after your talk. The disadvantage of handing it out at the start is that your listeners may pay more attention to the handout than to

131

you. With complex subjects, however, you may find it preferable to have the audience follow your thought process.

Did you know...

Cleveland Clinic researchers sought to determine which features of a lecture were most important to attendees (Copeland). Features found to be important include:

Clarity and readability of slides

Relevance of lecture material to the participants

Presenter's ability to identify key issues

Presenter's ability to engage the participants

Ability to present material clearly and with animation

Mistake # 143

Allowing audience interruptions if you can't handle them well

Some students get flustered when a team member interrupts their presentation to ask a question. If you wish to have the audience hold questions until the end, be sure to state this at the beginning of your talk. If you don't mind interruptions, then you can certainly encourage listeners to ask questions during your talk.

Mistake # 144

Being afraid to say "I don't know"

At the conclusion of your talk, you should invite questions from your listeners. Few students end their talk with such a statement, but it is important that you do so. Many students would rather not take questions because they fear they won't know the answer. This is an entirely natural feeling, a concern that also weighs on the minds of experienced speakers. Experienced speakers will prepare for the question and answer period by anticipating questions. They then proceed to develop responses to these questions, providing for more polished replies. You can do the same.

You can begin the question and answer period of your talk by simply asking the audience, "Do you have any questions?" When asked a question in front of a large group, it's preferable to rephrase the question before answering it. This ensures that everyone has heard the question and also provides you with additional time to formulate an answer.

While you are expected to be well read about the subject of your talk, you are not expected to have all the answers. In the event that you are asked a question for which you do not have an answer, you can opt to say "I don't know, but I will find out." Another option is to defer the question to your attending physician. "Dr. Chen, in your experience with pulmonary embolism, how would you handle this situation?" Avoid at all costs an attempt to bluff or to provide inaccurate information. If you tell someone that you will get back to them with an answer, stay true to your word.

Tips for answering questions at the end of a talk

- Let your listeners know early in the talk when you will answer questions.
- Encourage questions by asking "Do you have any questions?"
- Listen carefully to the question to make sure you understand it.
- Make eye contact with the questioner while the question is being asked.
- Repeat the question, especially in a large group, to make sure it has been heard.
- Make eye contact with the audience as you answer the question.
- If you don't know the answer, don't bluff or lie. You also need not apologize.
- Consider deferring the question to an expert, if one is in the room.

Mistake # 145

Not soliciting feedback

Hopefully, team members will offer you specific feedback after your talk. However, feedback tends to be vague and short on the specifics that you need to improve your performance during future talks. To make the most of this experience, you must solicit specific feedback. Examples of questions you might ask include—

- Was the introduction interesting?
- Was the topic and purpose of my talk clear?
- Did you feel that I made eye contact throughout the talk?

- Did I gesture appropriately? Did my gesturing enhance or detract from my talk's message?
- Was I able to maintain your interest?
- Did I come across as enthusiastic?
- Was the talk well-organized?
- Do you have any other suggestions for improvement?

Take team members' suggestions seriously. Determine how you will use the information you have gathered to improve future talks. What specific steps will you take to improve in these areas? Do not lose sight of the fact that great speakers are not born that way. Speaking well is a learned skill.

In the Outpatient Setting

According to the report "Educational Programs In U.S. Medical Schools, 2003-2004" published by JAMA, students spent varying amounts of time in the ambulatory setting during required third year clerkships, ranging from 20% in surgery to 93% in family medicine (Barzansky). 53 schools had a separate ambulatory care clerkship, during which nearly the entire time was spent in the ambulatory setting. From this data, it is clear that a substantial period of your third year will be spent in the outpatient setting.

If you are like most students, you look forward to outpatient work. In the outpatient world, you will experience medicine as it is practiced by most practitioners. You will have the opportunity to develop your clinical skills in an environment far different from the inpatient setting. While one can argue that the skill set is similar, there are important differences, some of which will present you with unique challenges.

Differences between the inpatient and outpatient setting	
Inpatient setting	**Outpatient setting**
Usually team concept (attending physician, resident, intern, students)	Generally you and your preceptor
Follow up to 3-4 patients at a time	May see as many as 6 patients during a half-day clinic
Luxury of time	Time constraints
Call	No or minimal call
Weekend responsibilities	No weekend responsibilities
Longer hours	Better hours
Schedule often unpredictable	Schedule generally predictable

In order to be successful in the outpatient setting, you will need to adapt to this new world. In this chapter, we focus on the common mistakes that are made in the outpatient setting and offer recommendations to help you meet and overcome the challenges that await.

Mistake # 146

Underestimating the utility of outpatient rotations as preparation for the USMLE Step 2 CS exam

The USMLE Clinical Skills (USMLE Step 2 CS) exam is now required for graduates of U.S. medical schools. The exam simulates a typical day in the outpatient setting, lasting eight hours and requiring focused examinations of patients with a variety of presenting complaints. The absolute best way to prepare for this type of exam is to hone your skills as a physician in the outpatient setting.

Why is this exam now required for graduates of U.S. medical schools? The website www.usmle.org describes the need for a national standard, as medical schools differ in their teaching of clinical skills and their evaluations of those skills. They state that: "During recent field trials, 20 percent of the fourth-year students who completed a survey said they had been observed interacting with a patient by a faculty member two or fewer times. One in 25 said they had never been observed by a faculty member."

The exam utilizes trained individuals that act as the patients. The exam includes a total of twelve patient encounters, and students are given 15 minutes to examine each patient. During this time they must take a history, perform a focused physical examination, and communicate with the patient. They then have 10 minutes to document their findings in the patient note. The cases are chosen to represent the types of problems that would normally be encountered in medical practice. Just as in real life, therefore, the cases may suggest more than one diagnosis, and part of your skill lies in formulating and supporting a differential diagnosis.

Your grade will also be based on your ability to effectively communicate with the patient. The standardized patients are trained in the use of ratings skills to assess communication, interpersonal skills, and English-speaking skills. As in the clinic setting, don't ever be so caught up with the medical issues that you fail to communicate appropriately with your patient. You will also be tested on your documentation, including important positive and negative findings, your differential diagnosis, and your assessment and plan.

The exam is pass/fail, and further information on the exam format, grading, and examples of documentation may be found at www.usmle.org.

Mistake # 147

Forgoing an orientation

Since many third year clerkships are exclusively or largely inpatient rotations, you may be relatively unfamiliar with the outpatient setting. The office setting is very different from the inpatient setting and many students find it difficult to move from one to another. Herein lies the importance of starting your outpatient work with an orientation. An orientation, if done well, can help you transition into this new setting, decreasing your anxiety level and setting the tone for a positive experience.

If you are fortunate, you will work with a preceptor who recognizes the importance of an orientation and has developed one that is highly informative. You may be assigned, however, to a preceptor who provides an orientation that is lacking in the specifics you really need. In the event that you find yourself in such a situation, you must take it upon yourself to gather the essential information. Important questions include the following:

- Who will I be working with?
- What are the office hours? What are my hours?
- What is the dress code?
- Where should I park?
- Is there a space for me to work? Where should I keep my personal belongings?
- What is my schedule? How does the patient schedule operate? How will I know which patients are assigned to me?
- What are your expectations for me?
- What role would you like me to assume in patient care?
- How much time do I have to see an assigned patient?
- What parts of the physical exam can I do without you? What parts of the physical exam would you prefer we do together?
- What are the forms (radiology, lab request) that I need to become familiar with?
- Can you walk me through a typical patient chart? How is the chart organized? Where are charts kept?
- Would you like me to present the patient's case inside or outside the patient's room? Are there any differences in the way you would like me to present in these different settings?
- Would you like me to write or dictate patient notes? How would you like me to do so?

137

- How do I order lab, imaging, and other tests?
- How do I schedule consultations?
- How do I schedule follow-up appointments?
- Can you show me a typical exam room? What instruments are available in the room for use? Where are supplies located (e.g., hemoccult cards, tongue blades)?
- Is there a computer that I can use? Who should I talk to regarding computer access?
- What resources, including textbooks and journals, are available?
- How do I use the phone?
- Do you wish me to write prescriptions? If so, is there a particular way I should write them?
- Who should I contact in the office if I have questions?
- When would be the best time for me to approach you for feedback?
- Will we be able to meet halfway through the rotation, as well as at the end, to go over our experience?

Don't be surprised if your preceptor asks you some questions. He may want to know about your previous clinical rotations, level of experience in the outpatient setting, career goals, and comfort level dealing with certain patients and patient problems.

Tip # 56

I've seen many students rotate in an outpatient clinic and never bother to meet the nurses, medical assistants, and receptionists. In the outpatient setting, they are your team. They participate in patient care, help the clinic run efficiently, and can help you with your responsibilities. Make it a point to introduce yourself on the very first day of the rotation.

Did you know...

In a study comparing the experiences of third-year students in the ambulatory versus inpatient setting, students in the ambulatory rotation "felt more like doctors, more responsible for patients, and more able to know and help their patients." They also reported better relationships with their teachers (Kalet).

Mistake # 148

Lacking an understanding of your responsibilities

Depending on the field of medicine and your particular preceptor, your roles and responsibilities will vary widely. In some primary care settings, for example, you will be given a great deal of responsibility. You may be asked to be an active participant in the care of patients assigned to you. This will generally involve gathering relevant data from the patient's history and physical exam, organizing your thoughts, determining the likely diagnosis, developing a management plan, presenting the case to your preceptor, writing a clinic note, and following up on patient care issues. Unlike the inpatient setting in which time is generally not a constraint, in the outpatient setting you must do all of this in a much shorter period of time.

In other clerkships, your role may be much more limited. You may even function primarily as an observer. Even if your responsibilities are limited, you should make it a point to ask your preceptor if there are any tasks that you may help with. This may include serving as a scribe, in which you write the note in the patient chart while the attending discusses care with the patient. You may write prescriptions as the attending outlines the plan of care with the patient, and then present them for signature. Even if your attending asks you to serve in a very limited capacity, you can still find ways to be helpful. Students can call for the nurse, obtain patient informational material, or fill out lab requisition forms.

Mistake # 149

Walking into the exam room with no information about the patient or reason for the visit

In contrast to the inpatient setting, the time that you have to evaluate a patient's problem in the office will be limited. For this reason, the more you know about the patient before you walk into the exam room, the more you can accomplish. You must do all you can to adhere to the time constraints of the office in order to avoid putting strain on your preceptor's schedule. Keep in mind that while you are seeing your assigned patients, your preceptor will also be seeing patients.

Some preceptors assign specific patients to students. Assignments are often, but not always, made in advance. The day before clinic, ask the scheduling clerk for a list of patients assigned to you along with the reasons for their visit. You can then pull the patient's chart and learn about his active medical problems. It is far easier to do this the day before the visit when you have the luxury of time.

As you review the chart, make note of the following:

- **What is the reason for the visit?**

  For follow-up visits, determine which issues need to be addressed. Review of the previous clinic note will often shed light on this matter.

- **What active issues does the patient have?**

  Many patients will have active issues that need to be reassessed at each appointment. Some of these problems may be in the process of evaluation with a diagnosis not yet established. An example would be anemia. With other problems pertaining to an established diagnosis, such as hypertension, the condition will need to be reassessed.

- **What medications is the patient taking?**

- **What are the results of diagnostic tests (lab, x-ray)?**

  The process of reviewing a chart can take considerable time, especially at the beginning when you are not familiar with the layout of the chart. As you become more familiar with its organization, your speed will increase and it may only take you 5-10 minutes to gather the key information.

Tip # 57

If you are having difficulty obtaining key information from the chart, ask your preceptor to orient you to each section of the chart. Preceptors can provide you with valuable tips on how to review a chart. This can make your patient encounter go more smoothly.

After reviewing the patient's chart, you will be armed with key information that will allow you to make the best use of your time. Before seeing the patient, your preceptor may also provide you with additional patient information that will help you to focus the visit. For example, you may be given a brief medical history and background, including the patient's current problems and concerns, and then asked to proceed with a directed evaluation. In this way, your preceptor may prime you for the patient encounter.

Mistake # 150

Introducing yourself to the patient improperly

Because patients generally expect that they will see their personal physician, it is best to have either the preceptor or a member of the office staff prepare the patient for your role in their care. Some preceptors will meet with the patient to request permission for student involvement in their care. Others may choose to have you accompany them into the patient's exam room while they make the request. You may also encounter the preceptor who would rather have you introduce yourself to the patient.

Never forget that it is the patient's right to refuse such a request. Do not take it personally. Also, don't be surprised if a patient who agreed to a student evaluation changes his mind. If you find yourself in such a situation, do not argue with the patient. Simply respect the patient's wishes.

You must make sure that the patient understands exactly who you are. Well-intentioned preceptors will sometimes introduce a student as "young physician" or "physician-in-training." It is very important that your patient understands that you are not a doctor but a medical student. There should be no ambiguity in this regard.

It also helps to inform the patient of your role in their care. You can simply explain to the patient that you will be performing their history and physical exam. Following this, you will return with your preceptor to complete the evaluation.

Mistake # 151

Focusing on the wrong patient issues

It is always best to ask the patient himself what prompted the visit to the clinic. Although you may have been given a reason for the visit, you would be surprised how often the given reason varies from the actual reason. Start by asking, "What brings you to the office today?" or "What concerns do you have today?" Many patients will visit the clinic with a specific complaint or symptom. Some will present to follow up on a particular issue. For example, a patient may have come for a blood pressure check after having his blood pressure medication adjusted at a previous visit. If the patient does not know the reason for the visit, the previous clinic note will usually shed light on the matter.

141

You should also ask what the patient believes is causing the problem, and what he thinks should be done about it. Patients often have expectations, and they may not share these unless you bring them up.

In the primary care setting, patients commonly present with a number of concerns. In the short period of time that you have, it will not possible to address all issues. Instead, you should aim to tackle two or three of the patient's problems. Which problems should be addressed? Let the severity of the problem and the importance the patient places on it guide you. For problems that are not addressed, inform the patient that another appointment can be scheduled to address them.

After taking the history, excuse yourself while the patient changes into a gown. Return to the patient's room to perform the physical exam. In contrast to the inpatient setting where patients are new to the attending physician, most outpatients will have been seen by your preceptor in the past. As a result, you will usually not be asked to perform a thorough physical exam as you would in a newly hospitalized patient. Instead, you should perform a focused physical exam. If the patient is new to the clinic, on the other hand, you may be asked to perform a thorough examination. When unsure, ask your preceptor.

Did you know...

In a videotaped analysis of histories performed by senior medical students, 24% of all students did not ascertain the patient's main problems (Rutter).

Mistake # 152

Overlooking key aspects of preventive care

Physicians must remain current with preventive care guidelines. These guidelines change regularly as the results of ongoing research become available. Prior recommendations may be debunked, as in the utility of hormonal replacement therapy for post-menopausal women. Others recommendations are found to have utility, and become standard practice in specific populations, such as the administration of the pneumococcal vaccine to individuals $\geq$ 65 years.

Preventive care looms just as large in the management of chronic disease. For patients with diabetes, part of the visit may be spent in titrating medication dosage to ensure optimal control of blood glucose. However, preventive care is a major component of diabetes management. Has the patient had their yearly eye exam? When was a urine test to check for microalbuminuria last performed?

Despite our knowledge of preventive care guidelines, implementation is a different story. Researchers from the Rand Corporation published their findings on implementation of recommended care for acute conditions, chronic conditions, and preventive care. They found that care for medical conditions varied widely. For example, recommended care in hypertension was provided only 64.7% of the time. In patients with diabetes, only 24% had received three or more glycosylated hemoglobin tests over a two-year period. Unfortunately, adherence to guidelines for preventive care was similarly poor. Only 54.9% of the patients studied received the recommended preventive care (McGlynn).

In the inpatient setting, acute care is the entire focus. "Let's get this patient better and get this patient discharged." When students rotate in the outpatient primary care setting, they finally have the opportunity to focus on health maintenance. Do not overlook key aspects of patient health education and preventive care.

Mistake # 153

Documenting poorly

In the hospital setting, you have the time to complete a very thorough and accurate patient write-up. Time constraints in an outpatient clinic means that your note must be written quickly. However, it must still be written with the same attention to detail and accuracy. Harvard researchers looked at the outpatient medical record documentation of internists and pediatricians. Among internists, documentation was 88% for compliance with screening guidelines, and only 61.6% for drug allergies (Soto). Even among practicing physicians, proper documentation is clearly an issue of concern. For medical students, the clinic setting with its need for thoroughness and efficiency along with speed is a major challenge. Despite the challenges, proper documentation is still necessary to ensure the best patient care.

Mistake # 154

Not performing a thorough analysis of the data

After performing the patient's history and physical examination, you are ready to think about the information you have gathered. As you analyze the information, try to answer the following questions:

- **What is the differential diagnosis?**

  The differential diagnosis is a list of conditions that could account for a patient's symptom(s). Note that you will not always be required to develop a differential diagnosis. If the patient is only presenting for a blood pressure check following an adjustment in his antihypertensive therapy, then a differential diagnosis is not needed.

- **What is the most likely diagnosis?**

  From the data you have collected, determine which one of the conditions in the differential diagnosis best accounts for the patient's symptom(s). Be able to offer your preceptor support for your hypothesis. You should also be able to tell your preceptor why other conditions in the differential diagnosis are less likely.

- **What tests are needed?**

  Does any testing (lab, radiology) need to be ordered? You may wish to obtain tests to confirm the diagnosis, exclude other conditions in the differential diagnosis, or assess the severity of the patient's problem. You should be able to explain your rationale for ordering all tests.

- **What is the treatment plan?**

  Be able to offer your preceptor the rationale for your management choices.

Mistake # 155

Wasting your downtime

In some rotations, students may encounter a great deal of downtime. This is particularly common when several students rotate in the clinic at the same time, and then have to wait their turn to present patients. Do not waste this downtime. Some students spend the time loitering in the hallway, talking about their plans for the weekend or the sports game from last night. Remember that conversations in the hallway can be overheard by patients in the examination rooms. They can also be heard by attendings in the examination rooms or walking by. Refrain from unprofessional behavior or casual conversation when in public areas.

Most students also fail to realize that downtime can be an ideal time for learning about your patients. Unlike in the inpatient setting, you don't have the benefit of spending hours reading authoritative texts about your patient's case. Although you may only have a few minutes, that can be enough to significantly improve the quality of your patient presentation and ability to answer attending questions. In every rotation, you should carry a handbook in your lab coat. Make sure you use it.

Mistake # 156
Underutilizing electronic resources

In some hospitals and clinics, particularly ones with electronic medical records, you may have computers in every room along with ready internet access. This means that in the span of just a few minutes, you can complete a preliminary literature search on just about any topic. Internet access means that you can do a Pubmed search, review information in UpToDate, read the chapter in emedicine, or perform a Google search. In many hospitals, you may also be able to access specialized databases or resources. In the Michael E. DeBakey VA Medical Center in Houston, you can access UpToDate, Lexi-Comp Online, and Micromedex, among others. Not familiar with these resources? You should be. These online resources are valuable tools in both inpatient and outpatient settings.

One of your first tasks as a clerk is to learn how to perform a literature search. Many medical center libraries will offer classes in how to maximize your use of Pubmed. You can also take the online tutorial at www.pubmed.org. You should learn how to perform the best possible search. This includes learning how to refine your search efforts. For example, typing in "sarcoidosis" pulls up nearly nineteen thousand references. In contrast, typing in "sarcoidosis and review" pulls up approximately two thousand. You should also learn what databases and journals your institution can access online, and from what computers. This allows you to pull up full-text articles from many journals. An excellent resource to help you navigate these tools is your librarian. I rarely see medical students speak to librarians, but they are experts in retrieving information efficiently. Even though students may ask their residents about useful resources, in my experience residents aren't always aware of the available resources. Also utilize the resources available in your pocket. Many students have access to PDA resources such as Epocrates, but don't use them as often as they should.

Tip # 58

Learn the full extent of online resources available at your institution. Don't just rely on your resident's knowledge of what's available. Many medical center libraries, hospitals, and even outpatient clinics offer access to multiple databases and full-text journals.

Commonly used electronic resources

Resource	Description
PubMed	Service of the U.S. National Library of Medicine offering millions of citations from MEDLINE along with links to full text articles (www.pubmed.com)
UpToDate	Evidence-based clinical information resource available online, CD-ROM, and pocket PC (www.uptodate.com)
emedicine	Evidence-based clinical knowledge base available online and PDA (www.emedicine.com)
Thomson Micromedex	Evidence-based clinical knowledge and drug database (www.micromedex.com)
Lexi-Comp online	Drug/lab test databases available online and PDA (www.lexi.com)
Epocrates	PDA-based drug reference (www.epocrates.com)

Mistake # 157
Taking too much time to present the case

After seeing the patient, your preceptor will expect you to present the case, either inside or outside the exam room. You must be brief, generally taking no more than a few minutes. One study found that teaching a medical student in an internal medicine out-patient clinic added 32.3 minutes to the clinic session (Denton). Even without your presence, many preceptors are under consid-erable time constraints, with a highly scheduled clinic and with patients in the waiting room. Recognize that teaching adds to their time pressures, respect these time constraints, and present in an organized manner with only relevant patient information.

Tip # 59

In the inpatient setting, you will often be asked to make a thorough presentation. In the outpatient setting, however, time limitations require you be as concise as possible. While you should strive to know everything you can about the patient, only present pertinent information.

If you are asked to present inside the exam room, you have addi-tional considerations. It can be very difficult to present in front of the patient. Students often make the mistake of speaking about the patient as if they were not there. In actuality, you should make every effort to include the patient in your discussion. Before you present, invite the patient to chime in during your presentation if the patient feels it is necessary. In this way, the patient can feel comfortable clarifying, correcting, or adding to the history as you relate it to your preceptor. You should also speak in such a way that the patient understands you. You should replace medical terms or jargon, including abbreviations and acronyms, with words that the patient can easily understand. It can be difficult to put this into practice, especially when you have been seasoned to present in a particular way during inpatient rotations. With deli-cate or complex issues, such as a possible diagnosis of cancer, you should bring this up with your preceptor before entering the room together. While you will undoubtedly have questions stem-ming from your patient encounter, you should avoid asking your preceptor esoteric or difficult questions in the company of the patient.

Mistake # 158
Presenting in an informal manner

You must adhere to the time constraints of the outpatient setting. In some clinics, that means very brief, focused presentations. However, don't take that as license to present in an unprofes-sional manner. Even though oral case presentations in the outpatient setting are brief affairs, they should still follow a specific, formal format.

> *"This is an older guy with a lot of AKs we need to treat."*

Versus:

> *"This is a 76-year-old Caucasian man with a history of multiple basal cell and squamous cell skin cancers. This is his six-month skin exam, and I performed a full body skin exam. I saw no lesions suspicious for skin cancer. He has about twelve actinic keratoses on his hands and arms, and two on his nose. I have the liquid nitrogen ready to freeze those."*

Especially given the tendency of most students to think that brief equates to sloppy, your well-structured presentations will stand out in comparison.

Mistake # 159

Being unprepared for your preceptor's questions

After you present your case, expect that your preceptor will ask questions. Some will be clarifying questions to ensure understanding of the patient's clinical presentation. Examples include "Does his chest pain worsen with deep breaths?" and "What's the dose of his lisinopril?" Note that these questions are not asked to gauge your knowledge level.

Contrast this with probing questions, which are asked to assess your fund of knowledge and your understanding of the patient's medical problems. Examples include the following:

• What do you think is going on with this patient?

• What findings support your diagnosis?

• What other conditions did you consider? Why are these conditions less likely?

• What test(s) should we obtain to confirm your diagnosis?

• How should we treat this patient?

Mistake # 160

Presenting the patient without formulating an assessment and plan

Many students will present the patient's history and physical exam and then stop there. Attendings at this point will often ask "What do you think is going on?"

Many students deliberately avoid providing an assessment and plan. They feel they don't have enough experience or information to reach a correct diagnosis, and don't want to be wrong. However, in order to develop your reasoning and problem-solving skills, you should commit to a diagnosis, even if you feel you are going out on a limb.

A diagnosis is not enough, though. Most attendings will continue by asking how you reached your conclusion. For this reason, I recommend that you not only commit to a diagnosis but that you also provide evidence to support your impression. Don't worry if your preceptor doesn't agree with your assessment and plan. You are not expected to be right all the time. The fact that you took it upon yourself to offer an assessment and plan demonstrates initiative, a quality that is highly regarded by preceptors.

Mistake # 161

Failing to follow up on patient issues

In most outpatient rotations, the expectation is that you will follow up on patients you saw in the clinic. After discussing the patient's case with the preceptor, the two of you will decide on a plan of action. A lab test or x-ray may be ordered. An issue may arise that requires research on your part. No matter what it is, it's your responsibility to follow up. For example, if a lab test is ordered, make a note of it and find out when the result will be available. When you do receive the result, determine what it means and report back to your preceptor.

Your follow-up responsibilities may include:
- Arranging for lab work or an imaging test
- Scheduling a follow-up appointment
- Writing or dictating a clinic note
- Educating the patient
- Calling the patient to assess response to therapy

- Updating the patient's problem list in the chart
- Updating the patient's medication list in the chart
- Arranging a referral to a specialist
- Scouring the literature to answer a question related to the evaluation or management of the patient's problem

Following through on these types of issues may not be a stated expectation of the rotation. However, it is still in your best interests to make this one of your responsibilities. You will benefit from the learning value offered. In addition, preceptors are impressed with students who understand that the evaluation and management of patients does not simply end when the patient leaves the clinic.

Tip # 60

Your learning experience should not end when the patient leaves the clinic. Follow through on all issues.

During Attending Rounds

The attending physician is the most senior member of the team. His primary goal is to ensure that the patients assigned to the team receive the best possible care. The attending is also responsible for providing a solid educational experience for the resident, intern, and medical students.

Your interaction with the attending will often be limited to attending rounds. During these rounds, the entire team will meet. What happens during rounds will vary from day to day but, during this time, you will have the opportunity to interact closely with the attending.

Since the attending has considerable input into the determination of your overall grade, one of your goals should be to impress him. You must not only deliver outstanding patient care, you must demonstrate that you are doing so. You can do this by being well read on your patients' problems, delivering solid oral patient presentations, giving terrific talks, and turning in thoughtful and thorough patient write-ups. In this chapter, we discuss mistakes made by students during attending rounds. The mistakes that are made during oral patient presentations, patient write-ups, and talks are discussed in other chapters.

Mistake # 162

Preparing inadequately for attending rounds

Your goals during attending rounds are twofold:
- To learn as much as possible
- To impress the attending physician

Your chances of reaching these goals increase considerably if you prepare for attending rounds. Your preparation should begin the evening before rounds. Since attending rounds usually take place daily, this means you will be preparing almost, if not every, evening. Begin your preparation by giving some thought as to what will happen during the next day's rounds. Will you be post-call? If so, you will present your newly admitted patients. You may also be expected to provide updates on old patients.

If there are no new patients, the entire rounds may focus on the discussion of issues pertaining to old patients on the service. Typically the attending will ask the most junior member of the team (i.e., student or intern) who is following the patient for an update on the patient's hospital course. If there are no new developments in your patient's hospital course, the attending may skip over your patient. Since you will never know this in advance, it is best to be prepared. In general, patients who are severely ill or have complicated issues are almost always discussed, oftentimes before any other issues are tackled. If you happen to be involved in the care of such a patient, rest assured that the attending will want to hear about your patient.

From time to time, team members, including students, may give talks. Other activities may also take place. The key point here is to anticipate what is likely to take place during the next day's rounds. Your next step is to focus your preparation accordingly.

Mistake # 163

Starting off on the wrong foot with the attending physician

You and your attending share a number of qualities, including the desire to provide the best patient care possible. While you may have qualities in common, don't ever lose sight of the fact that the attending is in a position of power. Because of his education, training, and experience, he is your supervisor, having the power and responsibility to direct your work. A few simple rules will help begin this relationship on the right foot:

- **Show proper respect.**

  You must not lose sight of the fact that the attending is in charge. As such, you should show him the proper respect. As simple or as obvious as this may seem, it can sometimes be difficult to put this into practice. You will work with many attending physicians—some of whom you consider excellent, others whom you rate mediocre, and yet others whom you believe are simply bad. Regardless of the type of attending you are working with, you must show him respect that is commensurate with the position.

- **Do your job.**

  If you want to get along, you have to do your job, you have to do it correctly, and you have to do it on time.

- **Do your homework.**

  Always come to rounds prepared. It's not that hard for attendings to determine who is and who isn't doing their homework.

- **Show that you are a team player.**

  Attending physicians value students who put the team ahead of themselves.

- **Display a strong work ethic.**

- **Ask for help when you need it.**

In addition to following the above rules, meet with the attending to learn of his expectations for you during the rotation (see Mistake # 43). Your goal during this meeting is to learn precisely what the attending wants and then proceed to do it.

Tip # 61

Set up an initial meeting with every new attending physician to find out what is most important to him. How does the attending like things to be done? Remember, to do well, you must meet his standards and preferences—not your own.

Tip # 62

The relationship you have with your attending physician will have a significant impact on your clerkship grade. Treat your attending as you would someone who has significant influence over your future—because right now, he does.

Mistake # 164

Being a difficult student

Some of your classmates will be labeled "difficult" by the time your third year draws to a close. Shortly put, that's not a label you want.

What makes a student "difficult?" Researchers reported the results of a study examining faculty members' expectations of student behavior in small group settings (Blue). Nearly 30 faculty members were interviewed to determine how faculty members evaluate student performance in small group settings.

Three types of interaction problems were identified:

- Non-participating, quiet, and passive student
- Disruptive student who is sarcastic, disrespectful, or interrupts discussions
- Student who tries to take over the group and control it

Although the word "difficult" was not used to describe the above behaviors, this study does shed some light on learning behaviors that attending physicians associate with problem students. With this knowledge in mind, you should conduct yourself in a manner that would keep you out of these three types of groups. You should realize that it is possible to be labeled "difficult" with only one instance of unreasonable behavior, especially if the behavior is particularly offensive or has left an indelible mark on the attending physician. Herein lies the importance of being on your best behavior at all times.

Tip # 63

Even one instance of unreasonable behavior, particularly if it is offensive, can taint all your prior positive performance. For example, it can be difficult or even impossible to recover from a disrespectful comment, racist remark, or deceptive act.

In a study looking at problem behaviors in medical students, coordinators of core third year clerkships, including internal medicine, pediatrics, surgery, obstetrics/gynecology, and psychiatry, sent questionnaires to residents and attending physicians at the University of Washington School of Medicine (Hunt DD, Carline J, Tonesk X, Yergan J, Siever M, Loebel JP. Types of problem students encountered by clinical teachers on clerkships. *Medical Education* 1989; 23: 14-18.). Teachers were asked to review a list of 21 types of "problem" students. Residents and attending physicians were asked to comment on how frequently they encountered a particular problem type and the level of difficulty the problem posed for them. Frequent problems included the following:

- Bright but with poor interpersonal skills
- Excessively shy, non-assertive
- Poor integration skills
- Over eager
- Cannot focus on what is important
- Disorganized
- Uninterested
- A poor fund of knowledge

Of these frequent problems, two were consistently identified as the most troubling for teachers: students who were bright but had poor interpersonal skills and students who displayed excessively shy, non-assertive behavior.

Other types of problems were also noted but teachers felt they were less frequent. These less frequent problems included the following:

- Cannot be trusted
- A psychiatric problem
- A substance abuse problem
- "Con artist" (manipulative)
- Hostile
- Rude
- Too casual and informal
- Avoids work
- Does not measure up intellectually
- Avoids patient contact
- Does not show up
- Challenges everything
- "All thumbs"

Of these infrequent problems, teachers were most troubled by students who could not be trusted, had psychiatric or substance abuse problems, or were manipulative. Note that attending physicians and residents have relatively more difficulty dealing with non-cognitive or personality problems than cognitive problems such as poor fund of knowledge. Of course, some non-cognitive issues are easier to address than others. Tardiness on several occasions is easier to address than repeated poor interactions with patients or team members.

Students who are challenging or difficult	Students whom teachers enjoy
Lethargic, listless, lazy	Enthusiastic, energetic, eager
Disorganized (don't use time wisely)	Motivated; have inner drive
Frequently repeats the same mistakes	Learn from mistakes
No initiative (expect to be spoon-fed)	Volunteer for tasks and extra work
Not punctual and ignore rules	Punctual and follow directions
Indifferent (don't appear to care; emotionless)	Put in extra time (arrive early; leave late)
Defensive (hostile when feedback is given)	Ask for feedback on their performance

From Hendricson WD and Kleffner JH. Assessing and helping challenging students: part one, why do some students have difficulty learning? Reprinted by permission of Journal of Dental Education, Volume 66, No. 1, January 2002. Copyright 2002 by the American Dental Education Association.

Mistake # 165

Participating infrequently during rounds

Since your interaction with the attending will largely take place during attending rounds, it is important that you participate and contribute to the discussion. Some students don't participate at all, while others may participate but not to the extent that they should.

Did you know ...

Teaching rounds were observed in a core clerkship at the University of Illinois. Analysis of these teaching sessions showed that medical students often functioned as a passive audience. In teaching rounds, students talked only 4% of the time (Foley).

There are many reasons for this lack of participation. For some students, it's a matter of shyness, timidity, or insecurity. Others may refrain from participating because they are bored, fatigued, or simply indifferent to the topics under discussion. Lack of knowledge, frustration with the rotation experience, dislike of the specialty, cultural norms, and history of passivity in group teaching sessions are other reasons that impede participation. Most often, though, lack of participation stems from fear of criticism or embarrassment.

Students are often hesitant to participate because they feel they have nothing profound to say. You are not expected to offer a breakthrough suggestion or profound comment every time you open your mouth. You are, however, expected to be an active and enthusiastic participant. If you talk to students who have completed a rotation or two, many will describe wanting to make a suggestion during rounds, but holding off because of the fear of looking foolish. Not uncommonly, another team member comes up with the same or similar thought, expresses it, and steals their thunder.

To be an active participant during rounds, you must be assertive. Remind yourself that your thoughts are important and worth communicating. You must have confidence in your ability to contribute to the group.

Tips on increasing participation during attending rounds

- Do your homework. You will feel more comfortable participating if you have prepared for rounds. You cannot speak well unless you have some knowledge of the topic of discussion.

- Sit where you will be noticed, preferably between two team members who are active participants.

- Establish good relationships with team members. If you are comfortable with everyone, you are more likely to share your thoughts.

- Maintain eye contact with the attending physician. If you don't, the attending may conclude that you aren't interested.

- Operate with the philosophy that there are no stupid questions.

- Speak your thoughts. Why let someone else receive recognition for a good idea when you had the same thought?

Mistake # 166

Erring at the bedside

Bedside teaching is any teaching that occurs in the presence of a patient. Over the years, studies have shown that the percentage of time spent in attending rounds at the bedside is on the decline. In fact, some attendings don't conduct any bedside rounds whatsoever, preferring to round solely in the conference room. Most, however, will split teaching time between the conference room, hallway, and the bedside.

Students worry about the impact of bedside rounds on their patients, especially with regards to patient comfort. A patient's comfort level will depend on a number of factors, including what is done at the bedside and how it is done. Keep in mind, however, that several studies have shown that patients generally enjoy bedside visits from the team. As long as team members conduct themselves in the proper manner, displaying respect and sensitivity, you need not be too concerned. These rules should govern your conduct at the bedside:

- Inform your patient, in advance, that you will be returning with the team later for bedside rounds. Let the patient know what will happen during rounds.
- After the team enters the patient's room, close the door to ensure privacy.
- Introduce all team members, including the attending physician, to the patient.
- Before interacting with the patient, wash your hands.
- If the patient is sharing the room with another patient, pull the patient's bedside curtain to ensure privacy.
- If the television or radio is on, ask the patient for permission to turn it off.
- If you are paged during bedside rounds, do not answer using the patient's telephone or other phone in the room.
- Do not carry on side conversations with other team members.
- Do not laugh at the patient or at anything he says, unless it is, without a doubt, a joke.
- Do not bring coffee, soft drinks, or other beverages into the patient's room.
- Do not chew gum while in the patient's room.
- Do not lean against the wall. Stand up straight.

- Do not sit on the patient's bed or place any of your items on the patient's furniture unless you have permission to do so.
- Before leaving the patient's room, ask the patient if he has any questions.

At the bedside, attendings will usually ask the patient questions to clarify and confirm what they have heard from the team. They do so to ensure that they have an understanding of the patient's story, which is essential to patient care. Do not be surprised if the patient's story of his illness differs from your own. Attendings see this all the time, and it doesn't necessarily reflect poorly on your abilities. It has happened to everyone at some point and often on more than one occasion. While this is frustrating, repeated questioning can bring forth new information that has bearing on the diagnosis and management. View this as an opportunity to learn.

During the physical exam, the attending will determine if the physical findings documented by the team are, in fact, present. They may also uncover new findings. If there are aspects of the physical exam that gave you difficulty, inform the attending beforehand so that he can demonstrate the proper exam technique. Be sure to keep the patient appropriately draped during the exam.

You will generally be asked to present the patient before you reach the bedside. From time to time, you may encounter an attending who wishes you to present the patient at the bedside. When asked to do so, you may have to make some changes in the way you present the information:

- Present with sensitivity
- Present in such a way that the patient understands what you are saying.
- Avoid using the words "denies" or "admits" as in "patient denies abdominal pain" or "patient admits to drinking 5 beers a day."
- Avoid detailed discussions of differential diagnosis, which may confuse or even frighten the patient. Save these questions or discussions for the team room.
- Avoid the use of the word "cancer" unless the attending physician has given you permission in advance.

To avoid any trouble, it's always best to know your attending's ground rules for bedside presentations in advance. In particular, you need to know what can and cannot be discussed at the bedside.

Mistake # 167

Losing track of your accomplishments during a rotation

As you progress through the rotation, keep track of your successes. Make an actual written list and a file of your accomplishments. For example, if your attending has written glowing remarks on your write-up, file it carefully. If your talk was particularly well received by the attending, jot down his comments, what he specifically liked about your presentation, and the subject of your talk. If your patient wrote you a thank-you letter, place it in your file.

If you decide later to ask the attending for a letter of recommendation, you will have a record of these accomplishments that can be provided to your letter writer. Remember that attendings work with many students. As the months pass, specific memories may fade. While the attending may remember that you excelled, he may have forgotten the details. The strongest letters of recommendation are those that provide evidence to support their claims. "Aleks is a very compassionate and dedicated student. One of our patients wrote a very heartfelt letter attesting to these qualities."

Mistake # 168

Allowing shyness to affect your evaluation

Every year, there are many excellent students whose evaluations suffer because they are shy. Many attendings find it difficult to evaluate the shy student, and may draw erroneous conclusions. Is the student quiet because of his personality? Or is the student quiet because he lacks interest, motivation, or knowledge? Such students need to make a conscious effort to participate and be heard.

Did you know ...

In a study evaluating problem students, clerkship coordinators, clinical faculty members, and residents were asked to identify the frequency with which certain problem types were encountered (Tonesk). Among 21 types of problem students, the "excessively shy, nonassertive" student was the second most frequently encountered problem type in obstetrics and gynecology, the fourth in surgery, and the fifth in internal medicine, pediatrics, and psychiatry.

Did you know...

The Myers-Briggs type inventory (MBTI), a personality inventory, was administered to medical students during their obstetrics/gynecology clerkship at the University of Arkansas School for Medical Sciences (Davis). The purpose of this study was to determine if a student's personality characteristics could influence the results of medical student clinical performance evaluations. They found a significant correlation between clinical evaluations and MBTI extraversion and introversion. Extraversion was found to correlate positively with clinical evaluations, suggesting that personality characteristics may influence evaluation of student clinical performance.

Mistake # 169

Underestimating the importance of being on time

It is extremely important to arrive on time for attending rounds. Arriving late on just one occasion has been known to negatively impact a student's evaluation. What does arriving late for rounds say about you? It suggests that you are inconsiderate, discourteous, careless, or disrespectful. Lack of respect for the attending physician's time will harm your evaluation.

Unfortunately, this is one of those obvious mistakes that students manage to make time and time again. Many students find themselves becoming complacent as the rotation progresses. Many attendings don't adhere to their own rules, arriving well past their designated start time. If this happens frequently, team members begin to mirror the attending's bad habit. In an effort to take advantage of the time that is available, residents will scurry in and out of the team room instead of waiting for rounds to begin. While it may be tempting to leave the team room to take care of a task on your to-do list, I urge you to refrain from doing so. Some attendings operate with the idea that rounds begin when they arrive, in which case your absence will surely be noticed. Be punctual not only at the beginning, but also throughout, the rotation. You will be seen as a reliable and dependable student.

Mistake # 170
Offering no reason for your tardiness

While attendings expect the entire team to arrive on time for rounds, considerably more leeway is afforded to interns and residents. They have many more demands on their time, some of which may arise just before rounds, making it difficult for them to arrive on time. Students are also responsible for the care of their patients, but it is felt that these responsibilities are seldom pressing enough to interfere with the start of attending rounds. Exceptions to this rule include the following:

- There may be a time when a patient problem prevents you from being on time (i.e., Mr. Smith develops chest pain five minutes before starting rounds). In these cases, patient care takes precedence.

- The resident may realize that he forgot to check out patient films from the radiology file room for the attending physician's review. If he realizes this five minutes before rounds begin, he may send you in his place, making it impossible for you to be on time.

- It is common for a conference or lecture to extend past its scheduled time. This leads to problems when rounds immediately follow the end of the conference. Students can either leave the conference early or inform their attending of the conference schedule, allowing the attending an opportunity to adjust the start time of rounds. Once informed of the schedule, some attendings will simply ask students to join rounds after the conference has ended.

In these situations, your attending will understand your reasons for being late. Do not, however, assume that a team member has informed the attending of the reason for your tardiness. It is best to take the attending aside at the end of rounds to make sure the two of you are on the same page. If you may be delayed because of a conference, it is always better to inform the attending before it happens rather than after.

Tip # 64

On the first day of the clerkship, inform your attending physician of your conference schedule, especially mandatory lectures. Often, attendings are not familiar with the schedule, let alone which conferences are mandatory.

In the event you are late for rounds, you should offer an apology. Too often students say nothing, which leaves the attending feeling that you lack respect for his time.

Mistake # 171
Leaving rounds early

As a general rule, you should not leave rounds early. Sometimes, however, it can't be avoided. Your clerkship director may have informed you that certain conferences or lectures are mandatory, even taking precedence over attending rounds. If this is the case, you should inform your attending ahead of time. To avoid any potential problems, I recommend that you discuss your conference schedule with the attending on the first day of the rotation. If it seems likely that rounds will extend into mandatory lecture time, tell the attending, preferably before rounds, that you have to leave at a specific time. Also apologize for any inconvenience this may cause.

Tip # 65

If you must leave rounds because of a conference, be sure to return immediately after the conference ends in case rounds are still in progress.

Mistake # 172
Being seen and not heard during rounds

Students *should* be asking questions during attending rounds. Asking questions is one way to demonstrate interest in the subject matter under discussion. However, some students never ask questions, and others don't ask nearly as many as they would like. What holds students back? A major factor is fear or embarrassment. They are often concerned that their question is too basic, and that by asking it, they will only embarrass themselves.

Don't worry about what your team members think of your question. Other students may have the same question as well. They will respect you for being comfortable enough to ask the question in the first place. Students are often surprised to learn that their questions can also benefit interns and residents. Remember that house officers don't always have answers to questions raised by students. Attendings expect students to ask them questions. They welcome questions because they often stimulate discussion that can enrich the entire team's educational experience.

Should you be concerned that your questions will take valuable time away from other tasks that need to be done during rounds? Attending rounds may certainly be busy, but a good teacher always responds favorably to questions. He may either answer them immediately, choose to answer them after rounds, or set aside time during the next day's rounds. If your question is not answered immediately, it doesn't imply that the question is unimportant. The attending may simply be waiting for a more appropriate time to answer.

If you are still hesitant to ask questions, consider developing a list of potential questions before rounds. You may do so as you read about your patients' problems. Then, at the appropriate time, be sure to ask.

Mistake # 173

Asking questions without permission

While it's not necessary to always seek permission before asking a question, sometimes it can be difficult to know if the time is right. You must take into account all sorts of factors, ranging from your superior's frame of mind to any time pressures he is under. For example, questions should not be asked when a patient's condition has taken a sudden turn for the worse or during a delicate moment in the operating room.

If the time is not right, the chance of obtaining useful information is low. A poorly timed question may not be answered accurately or as completely as it would have been otherwise. By seeking permission to ask questions, you demonstrate respect. "Dr. Gonzalez, I wanted to ask you about testing for pulmonary embolism. Would now be a good time, or should I wait until later in the week?" This simple courtesy demonstrates respect for your team members.

Mistake # 174

Listening passively

You should demonstrate to the attending that you take his teaching seriously. Asking questions is one way to do so. Another is to take notes after asking questions. While not necessary after every question, it can be helpful to do so when the information is complex or very detailed. Jotting down the main points is usually sufficient. The act of writing down information improves recall, another benefit.

Mistake # 175

Underestimating the importance of displaying enthusiasm

Some students demonstrate a passion for learning. It doesn't matter what rotation they're on. They are excited to be learning about this particular field and are thrilled to have the chance to finally take care of real-life patients with these diseases. Attendings are always impressed with students who demonstrate a passion for learning and enthusiasm for their work, their fellow team members, the rotation, and the specialty.

How important is enthusiasm? One measure of its importance is the frequency with which the word "enthusiasm" appears on clerkship websites. At the website for the Michael E. DeBakey Department of Surgery (www.debakeydepartmentofsurgery.org) at the Baylor College of Medicine, it is stated that "avid interest and enthusiasm exhibited by students is also strongly recommended" during the core surgery clerkship. In their Orientation to the Surgery Clerkship document, the University of Virginia Health System writes that "most of the evaluation that occurs from the interaction between the faculty and residents with the student as far as grades are concerned has to do with the enthusiasm, interest, and energy displayed by the student on the wards and not by their exact fund of knowledge during the clerkship." At the website for the University of Washington School of Medicine Department of Obstetrics and Gynecology Education and Training, there is a statement that reads "preparation, interest, enthusiasm, and availability will maximize your opportunity to have one-on-one interaction with faculty and staff, to develop problem-solving techniques, and to participate in hands-on-activities in the wards, clinics, and operating suites."

I have yet to meet an attending physician who doesn't think enthusiasm is important. If given two students with equal ability, attendings will almost certainly give a better evaluation to the enthusiastic one.

Tip # 66

Displaying enthusiasm regularly can have a "halo effect" on your work. People will tend to view all aspects of your work in a more positive light.

165

Mistake # 176

Waiting for a spark

Too often, students wait to be inspired before exhibiting enthusiasm. They may wait for an interesting patient case or may look to their attending for a teaching point that sparks their enthusiasm. "This was a boring week in the emergency room—there was no trauma, only heart attacks and asthma attacks." Students such as these, who rely on external forces, are subject to highs and lows in the rotation. Such students are typically labeled as unenthusiastic, especially when their spark arrives late in the rotation.

The key is to take responsibility for your own enthusiasm. You must choose to be passionate about your education during this rotation. As some of you read this, you may think, "I just don't have an enthusiastic personality." You don't need to have an effervescent or extroverted personality to demonstrate enthusiasm during attending rounds.

As one attending remarked, "If a student takes her education seriously, gives me her complete attention, values rounds, and essentially carries an attitude that there is nothing else she would rather be doing," she is demonstrating enthusiasm. Attendings measure enthusiasm and interest in many ways. They take note of how students speak, how they sit, their facial expressions, their body language, and their questions.

Your level of enthusiasm can wane during attending rounds, especially if you become too relaxed or if rounds stretch on and on. In some specialties, rounds may last two, three, or even four hours. To guard against a loss of enthusiasm, perform a self-check at twenty minute intervals. If your interest has waned, you can take steps to correct it. It's not necessary to make dramatic changes. Simple actions such as sitting straighter in your chair, leaning slightly forward towards the attending, and occasionally nodding when the attending makes eye contact with you demonstrate your continued interest.

Mistake # 177

Dispensing with the greeting

Early in my career, I was surprised how infrequently my team members, including students, would greet me when I arrived for attending rounds. Upon entering the team's conference room, I would usually find students, interns, and residents busily working. It was a rare team member who would stop what he was doing to acknowledge me with a smile, friendly gesture, or a greeting. Having attended on the wards many times since then and seen this same scenario repeat time and time again, I am now surprised when a student does actually greet me or acknowledge my presence. It is simply polite to greet your colleagues and superiors respectfully each and every day.

It is common for attendings to visit the team outside of rounds. The attending may simply want to be available to answer any questions or check on the progress of a patient. Irrespective of the reason for the visit, make it a point to acknowledge his presence. Don't be the student who just keeps his head down and continues to work until the attending physician leaves.

Mistake # 178

Dreading pimp questions

Wear defined pimping "as the clinical practice where persons in power ask questions of their junior colleagues" (Wear). In this study, eleven fourth-year medical students were interviewed to determine their views on pimping. All, except for one, divided pimping into two groups—malignant or bad versus benign or good. Any question that was asked to embarrass or humiliate students was viewed as malignant pimping. Although the entire group of students had witnessed such behavior, they all felt that it was the exception rather than the rule. It seemed that, in most cases, pimping had been of the good variety.

As a third year medical student, you will be pimped. Students generally view pimping as a means for attendings to evaluate their knowledge base. They feel that pimping is a way for attendings to ensure that they are, in fact, reading about their patients' problems and are knowledgeable about these problems. While pimping has an evaluative function, there are other reasons why attendings ask questions. Pimping allows the attending to determine your learning needs to enable teaching to your level. Attendings also ask questions to stimulate students, keep them engaged, and monitor their progress.

Embrace these teaching sessions. While you may be anxious, recognize that these sessions are a great opportunity to demonstrate your knowledge and capabilities.

Mistake # 179

Allowing the audience to prevent you from performing up to your capabilities

You will be asked questions during attending rounds. Since the entire team is required to be present during rounds, you will have an audience. In some cases, students who know the answer to a question can't come up with it when put on the spot in front of the entire team. This is akin to stage fright—some students have difficulty thinking properly when others are present, listening, and watching.

You must not let the presence of others affect your ability to answer the attending's questions. Remind yourself that your team members want you to succeed. When a team member does well, it reflects well on the entire group.

Mistake # 180

Inappropriately preparing for attending round questions

Your chances of answering questions correctly increase considerably with proper preparation. Preparation should begin the evening before rounds by anticipating the next day's questions. If you will be responsible for presenting a newly admitted patient, then naturally you can expect to be asked questions about the patient's illness. Questions will generally fall into one of the following two categories:

- **Clarifying questions**

    A clarifying question is one an attending asks to ensure his understanding of the patient's clinical presentation. Examples include "How did he describe his pain?" and "How has the serum creatinine changed from his last visit to his primary care physician?" Your odds of answering clarifying questions increase significantly if you perform a thorough history and physical examination, organize the data, and have it readily accessible.

- **Probing questions**

    A probing question is one that an attending may ask to gauge your knowledge and understanding of the patient's medical problems. Examples include "What are the physical exam findings of aortic stenosis?" and "What does S3 indicate to you?" To field these questions you must be well read about your patient's medical problems.

Mistake # 181
Answering questions with hesitation

When answering the attending's questions, your goal is to answer them confidently. It's not possible to have answers to every potential question that could be asked, so you may not always be confident in your replies. However, many students deliver a correct response to a question but do so in a way that suggests that they are not confident about their response. They do this even when they are sure of the answer. A classic example is the student who phrases his response in the form of a question:

> *Attending physician: What are the two major causes of acute pancreatitis in the United States?*
>
> *Student: Aren't alcohol and gallstones the two major causes?*

Some students will preface their response with the words "I think" when, in fact, they know.

> *Attending physician: What are the two major causes of acute pancreatitis in the United States?*
>
> *Student: I think alcohol and gallstones are the two major causes.*

Don't diminish the strength of your responses with the words "I think." Also, avoid responses that begin with the following:

> *"I may be wrong but..."*
>
> *"I'm not sure but..."*

Both are examples of how students discount their response before they ever provide it. In her book "Thinking on Your Feet," Marian Woodall said that when asked questions "Many people give mediocre responses with superb delivery; they generally fare better than those with good responses and mediocre delivery skills" (Woodall, MK. Thinking on your feet, how to communicate under pressure. Lake Oswego, Oregon Professional Business Communications, 1996).

Mistake # 182

Answering questions incorrectly

Of course, it's not enough to answer questions confidently—you must also answer them correctly. How can you maximize your chances of answering questions correctly? First, you must learn about your patient and his problems using multiple sources of information. Too often, students rely heavily or entirely on handbooks. While you should definitely use handbooks, you should also utilize the larger, more authoritative texts. Remember that handbooks are often geared to students and residents. However, your attending will have a deeper working knowledge of the patient's problems based on his reading of larger texts, the literature and years of practical experience.

Tip # 67

Among students, small handbooks are popular because they are concise and relatively inexpensive. However, many handbooks lack the depth and breadth of information required to take care of patients on a day-to-day basis. For this reason, it is important that you use one of the larger textbooks of that field, recognizing that it too, at times, may fail to provide you with the information you seek. If you need the most current information, then you need to perform a Medline search.

An attending physician's initial questions may not be all that difficult. Many attending physicians will begin with questions that they would expect an average student to answer. These questions generally require students to simply recall factual information. In fact, some data indicates that 70% of questions asked by teachers involve simple recall (Williamson). You will find that handbooks are particularly useful in helping you answer these questions. As you field these initial questions successfully, the attending may then ask more difficult questions. Although these may be questions that he would expect an intern or resident to answer, they may be posed to you first. These questions generally require students to offer an explanation and cannot be answered by simply recalling a fact. You can increase your chances of answering these questions correctly if you turn to the larger texts and the recent literature. Especially useful are recent review articles on the patient's illness, which will have up-to-date information. These resources will help you develop a deeper level of understanding.

Many attending questions deal with different aspects of the patient's diagnosis. For example, if your patient has acute pancreatitis, you should be prepared to answer questions about the incidence, epidemiology, pathogenesis, risk factors, differential diagnosis, clinical features (symptoms and signs), laboratory studies, imaging/other diagnostic tests, prognosis, complications, and therapy of this condition.

While you may be tempted to focus your reading only on the illness that prompted the patient's hospitalization, you should read about the patient's other medical problems as well. Your goal is to become knowledgeable about these problems too. If asked about them, you will be in a better position to answer. Reading about these other problems will also aid patient care if and when they become active. For example, a patient may come in with asthma exacerbation. The past medical history reveals a history of diabetes mellitus. What often happens in such a case is that the student becomes well read about asthma exacerbation but spends little or no time reading about diabetes. When the patient is placed on corticosteroids for the treatment of the asthma exacerbation, the blood sugar may increase. The student is then at a loss because he didn't review the management of diabetes.

As you read, try to anticipate the questions that the attending physician may ask. It is particularly useful to make a list of possible questions and prepare answers to those questions. Practice by feeding questions to yourself or having someone else do so. Anticipating possible questions, preparing answers to these questions, and then practicing your responses can yield fantastic results. Unlike standardized exams or basic science exams, you won't be given a choice of five different answers. Too often, students remember reading about something but aren't able to retrieve the information and express it properly. When the attending answers the question, students often kick themselves, saying "Oh, yeah. I do remember reading about that" or "I wish I had said that better."

Understand that the same questions may come up again later in your rotation. For example, your attending may ask you a number of questions about the patient you just admitted for acute renal failure. One week later, another patient admitted with pneumonia develops acute renal failure while in the hospital. The same questions may arise again, and you have no excuse for answering them incorrectly this time around. For this reason, after rounds, spend some time making a list of the questions you were asked. Make sure you know the answers to each and every question, and if you don't, find them.

Tip # 68

If another student is unable to answer a question, refrain from jumping in, no matter how tempting it may be. Wait until you are asked the question or it is thrown out to the entire group. Never make a colleague look bad.

Mistake # 183

Having diarrhea of the mouth

Your goal in answering questions during attending rounds is to deliver your responses concisely. How concisely? As concisely as possible. If you are asked a question but you have no idea what the correct answer is, you should simply say, "I don't know but I will find out." Not uncommonly, students will ramble on in a variety of directions, in the hope that they will stumble upon the right answer. In doing so, students end up providing a long-winded response that is usually incorrect. If you don't know the answer to a question, say so. Your attending doesn't expect you to know everything. In fact, part of being a good physician is recognizing limitations in your knowledge and having the confidence to say "I don't know."

While many questions are open-ended, others can be answered with either a "yes" or "no." When asked such a question, respond appropriately. If further information is needed from you, the attending can ask you for it. It is particularly important to answer questions concisely when you are in the operating room. Surgical attendings, at some point in the case, will ask their students questions about the patient and his problems. If questions are met with long-winded responses, he may cease to ask further questions. As one attending physician told me, "students must avoid diarrhea of the mouth."

Mistake # 184

Sitting too far away from the attending physician

Attending rounds may take place at the patient's bedside or in the team room. If in the team room, you should sit somewhere where the attending can easily see you. Many team rooms are not conducive to teaching. If you are sitting in a corner of the room, you may send a nonverbal message that you are not interested in participating. Even if you have been assigned to a workstation in the corner, you should plan on moving to a better location, one which sends the message that you want to learn and be involved.

Mistake # 185
Not modeling yourself after a "with it" team member

Is there someone on the team who really impresses the attending? Students are often surprised to learn that faculty members choose future chief residents early on in their residency. Even as interns, some individuals are able to clearly excel and attract notice due to their abilities. What is it about these individuals that makes them so impressive? Is it their fund of knowledge? Do they present patients well? Do they give outstanding talks? Once you have identified the specifics of why such individuals excel, model yourself after them.

Tip # 69
You will come across team members that are highly regarded. What is it that makes these people stars? Listen to what others say about them, observe how they work and interact with colleagues, and pattern yourself after them.

Mistake # 186
Lacking appreciation

Don't hesitate to show the attending physician your appreciation. He will be involved in your training, supporting you in different ways and offering feedback essential to your growth. Let your attending know how much you appreciate his help by saying, "thank you." You need not wait until the end of the rotation to do so.

As studies have demonstrated, working with an excellent clinical teacher can improve a student's overall performance in the rotation. If you have found that your attending was particularly helpful, you can reinforce the specific behavior by showing your appreciation, thereby increasing the chance that it will be repeated. "Dr. Huang, I really found it helpful when you went over the cardiac exam with me at the patient's bedside. Thank you for taking the time to do so."

When showing appreciation, it is best to speak directly to the recipient. Praising the attending to the rest of the team doesn't mean that he'll hear about it. In order for the compliment to be as meaningful as possible, deliver the message directly. You should be careful not to sound insincere, and avoid giving a compliment just before you make a request. Excessive praise may arouse suspicion of a hidden agenda.

Mistake # 187

Reading only about your own patients

Although you won't be directly involved in the care of all patients assigned to your team, realize that these other patients will be discussed during attending rounds. You stand to learn much more from these discussions if you have had a chance to read about these patients' problems beforehand. Reading about your own patients is, of course, most important. However, the smart student will also set aside some time to read about the other patients on the service. Also realize that during a two month clerkship you are not likely to personally encounter all of the medical issues that may be included on the clerkship examination.

When other team members are presenting patients, pay close attention. This is not the time to let your mind wander—you never know when the attending may involve you in the discussion. It is common for attendings to ask students questions about patients they are not following. You may just be able to answer correctly if you have taken the time to read about their medical issues and have listened closely to the discussion.

Mistake # 188

Preparing inadequately for an attending physician's talk

From time to time, an attending may give a talk to the team. In some cases, this will be announced in advance. If you learn that the attending will be speaking on a particular topic, you should read about it carefully before the day of the talk. This will help you become more familiar with the subject matter and you'll gain much more from the talk. In the event that the talk is interactive and the attending asks questions, your preparation will help you field any questions sent your way.

Mistake # 189

Using humor inappropriately

Let's face it. Taking care of sick patients is a serious business. To alleviate the stress, it's helpful to introduce some humor. Humor can be especially useful when you find yourself in an awkward situation, diffusing tension and even building rapport.

Although humor can be a terrific stress reliever, it must be used properly. It's easy to inadvertently offend others and incite conflict. You must avoid any ethnic, religious, racial, or sexist jokes. Jokes involving sarcasm also have the potential to offend, particularly when used with people you do not know well. Never make jokes at the expense of other people, including patients, no matter how tempting.

It's also important not to overdo it. As a student and future physician, you want people to take you seriously. Inappropriate or excessive humor will not put you in a good light.

Tip # 70

It is never acceptable to make fun of your patients. Even if other team members are making jokes at a patient's expense, do not join them. You never know when a patient or family member may be within earshot of your conversation. It may also diminish your standing with team members.

Mistake # 190

Accepting praise poorly

There will be times when an attending will praise you for a job well done. When accepting praise, do so graciously. A smile and a simple "Thank you" is all that is needed. Too often, students respond to a compliment with a self-deprecating statement. "I just wish I hadn't gotten so flustered during my talk and gone over the time limit, but thanks." This only serves to diminish your accomplishment. After receiving a compliment, don't feel compelled to offer one in return. Save the praise for later when it will be more meaningful and sincere.

Mistake # 191

Being unable to recover from a poor performance

During attending rounds, there may be times when you find your-self in a difficult situation. For example, you might lose your train of thought during an oral case presentation, causing you to become flustered and leading to a less than polished presenta-tion. You will always encounter difficulties during rounds in some way, shape, or form. When faced with difficult situations, you can either obsess over the negative or bounce back quickly. Over the years, I have seen many students become dejected during rounds when they feel that their performance has been subopti-mal. It may have been due to a question they were unable to answer or a talk that did not go as well as anticipated. When such situations arise, some students focus so much on the negative that they cease to be fully engaged in rounds. In many cases, this has negatively impacted their performance.

Tip # 71

No matter how well you prepare, there will be times when things don't go as well as you had hoped. You can't win them all. Just do your best and get ready for the next challenge.

Students who consistently do well during their clerkship years are able to maintain a positive attitude when faced with adversity. While it may seem difficult, remember that you do have complete control over your attitude. If you find yourself displaying a nega-tive attitude, take a deep breath and let it go, so that you can con-tinue to be a fully active and engaged participant during rounds.

Mistake # 192

Letting your dislike of the rotation affect your relationship with the attending physician

There may come a time when you find yourself on a rotation that you simply don't like—not because of your team members, but because you dislike the specialty. Realize that your dislike of the specialty has the potential to affect your working relationship with the attending physician. If you tune out the attending, you may miss out on some valuable learning opportunities. Even though you may not want anything to do with the specialty, the knowledge that you gain may prove helpful in the future. As I tell students rotating in the dermatology clerkship, it really doesn't matter what field of medicine they choose. Everyone, eventually, will have a dermatology question, either for themselves, a patient, or a relative at a party. As a physician, some knowledge of every field of medicine may ultimately prove helpful.

Do not lose sight of the fact that your attending will also be evaluating your performance, and that his evaluation has considerable bearing on your overall clerkship grade. This grade will be part of your transcript. The attending physician's comments may find their way, often word for word, into your Dean's letter. "Stacy rotated on our Obstetrics service, where she received a grade of Pass. She is interested in a future career in dermatology, and in evaluating her work ethic, we found that lifestyle issues did appear to be of importance to her." Such a grade, and such a comment, will definitely have the potential to weaken your residency application.

Mistake # 193

Letting your dislike of the attending physician affect your rotation performance or working relationship

You don't get to choose your attending most of the time. Therefore, be ready to encounter attendings with a variety of personalities and work styles. Be ready to encounter individuals whom you don't like or with whom you find it difficult to work. How do you deal with such attendings?

Realize that this won't be the last time you'll have to work with someone you don't like. In our professional lives, there are many times when we have to work with or deal with such people. Learning how to do so is a valuable skill that will serve you well. First and foremost, in your interactions with these individuals, remember to be polite, courteous, and respectful. Liking someone is not a prerequisite for displaying good manners. Also ask yourself what you can learn from your attending. You can still learn useful facets of medicine from attendings whom you don't like. Also evaluate your interactions with this person. You are going to encounter similar personalities in the future, and you need to learn the best way to work with such individuals.

Tip # 72

You don't have to like your attending physician but you do need to give them the respect that is commensurate with their position. Appreciate what they have to offer. Even "bad" attending physicians have something to offer. If nothing else, you'll learn what not do when you become an attending.

Mistake # 194

Dealing poorly with a rude attending physician

A few attendings may frequently display rude behavior. However, such behavior is more commonly an isolated event, often the result of stress. The stress may stem from a personal or professional issue. After all, attending physicians have their own lives and are subject to the same stressors as the rest of us. Work-related stress, family issues, and health problems are just some of the factors that can lead to rudeness and irritability.

When you encounter such an attending, you may be tempted to be rude in response. It's only natural to feel this way, but rather than lashing out, consider handling the situation in a more productive manner. One option is to pretend the rude behavior didn't happen. Another option involves acknowledging the behavior. With this approach, however, you must be careful to do so in a polite manner. If you caught your attending at a particularly busy time, they may snap at you. A polite way to acknowledge the rudeness: "You seem to be really busy. I'm sorry I interrupted you. I'll speak with you at a better time."

Mistake # 195

Destroying your credibility

In every interaction with your team, you have the opportunity to establish your credibility. From day one of the rotation, your team will be listening to what you say and how you perform. They'll want to know if you are a person of your word. It is impossible to have a successful rotation experience if you do not engender trust. Students run into trouble when they say things they don't mean or make promises they don't keep. If you tell your intern that you'll finish the patient's progress note by 10:30, then do so. You can establish your credibility by consistently saying what you mean, doing what you say, resisting the temptation to stretch the truth, and admitting mistakes.

Tip # 73

Don't lie. Once you are found out, it will be difficult, if not impossible, to restore the trust you have lost. Everyone will always wonder "What else you are lying about?"

Did you know ...

Questionnaires were sent to the deans of student affairs at U.S. and Canadian medical schools, inquiring about the use of noncognitive criteria for student evaluation. Of the noncognitive criteria cited, honesty was mentioned most often followed by professional behavior, dedication to learning, appearance, and respect for others (Miller).

Did you know ...

In a survey of interns and residents in a university-based internal medicine residency program, researchers sought to determine the frequency and type of unprofessional behavior among students, residents, and faculty over a one-year period (Shea). Unprofessional behaviors that were noted included breaching patient confidentiality in public places, documenting history and physical examinations not actually performed, lying to patients, and signing others' names.

Being credible also involves the willingness to admit to mistakes. The credible student admits the error in a forthright manner rather than ignoring, minimizing, or covering it up. If need be, he apologizes for his error but does so without justifying. By taking responsibility for the mistake, he is able to demonstrate strength of character. He then corrects the mistake right away or, if not possible, takes action to better the situation.

Credibility is something that is earned and requires effort to maintain. As many students have learned, it is easily destroyed, and once destroyed, can be difficult to restore.

Mistake # 196

Doing only what's expected

Team A was on call and getting slammed with new patient admissions.

Julie had finally finished her work evaluating two new patients.

Niko, her resident, asked, "Can you help us evaluate and write orders on this next patient with pyelonephritis? I really want to get the antibiotics started."

"I've already worked up two patients, and the clerkship director made it clear that we were only required to pick up two patients on call."

"I realize that, Julie, but we could really use your help."

"All right, I'll do it" replied Julie abruptly.

As in this true story, not all students go the extra mile. In fact, most students do only what they need to do to get by. Why would some students go beyond what's expected while others won't? In my experience, many students don't realize the benefits of going the extra mile. They operate with the idea that if they do something beyond what they are asked or expected to do, it should result in some immediate, tangible return. If you, in an effort to be helpful, retrieved all of the patients' films from the file room, you expect a show of immediate gratitude. However, what students fail to realize is that the benefits are not often immediate. They need to be patient to see the returns, which may include more teaching, better teaching, gratitude, and a more favorable evaluation.

Mistake # 197

Succumbing to the pressure

Attending rounds can be stressful. Your goal is to maintain a professional image at all times. You wish to be seen as a student who can handle stressful situations with poise.

Although you may be feeling stressed, recognize that those around you won't often recognize that fact. Do not call attention to yourself and your stress level. Avoid saying things like "I'm sorry. I'm just nervous." Let others reach their own conclusions. Also avoid gestures and mannerisms that indicate anxiety. Remember that your knowledge, abilities, and overall performance will all be assessed in the context of how confident you appear.

Mistake # 198

Listening poorly

More errors are made during clerkships because of poor listening habits than anything else. The costs of not listening can be quite high, including missing vital information, failing to follow-up on important issues, turning off team members, and even negatively impacting patient care.

As a team member, your goal is to establish a solid working relationship with others. In order to reach this goal, you must truly listen to others. During attending rounds, you must give the attending your undivided attention. As simple or obvious as this seems, you would be surprised how often this piece of advice is not followed.

What are the factors that lead to poor listening on the part of students? In some cases, it may be something as simple as an external distraction. You may be sitting close to an open door and find yourself distracted by activity occurring just outside. Internal distractions such as hunger may also prove a problem. Emotions such as fear, stress, and anger can also interfere with effective listening.

Rounds are not always fascinating. During boring times, it can be especially difficult to maintain interest. Many students tend to focus on what interests them during rounds, such as discussions regarding their own patients. They may tune out the rest. As hard as it can be, don't let your mind wander. Enter rounds with the proper attitude and motivation, recognizing that all of the discussion is ultimately relevant to your education.

Also recognize that some attendings are more difficult to listen to. Some are more disorganized, speak at an awkward pace, or have distracting speech patterns. Make a concerted effort to focus on the message rather than the delivery.

While listening, be sure that your body language is congruent. In other words, you may be listening but may not look as if you are. An attending may assume that you are not listening if you are engaged in any of the following actions:
- Not looking at him
- Looking through papers or working on the computer (unless it pertains to what is happening during rounds)
- Looking at the clock or your watch
- Leaning away

- Slouched in your seat
- Repeatedly shifting your position in the chair
- Talking to others
- Sitting with your feet up on the table or chair
- Doodling, playing with your hair, tapping or clicking your pen, drumming your fingers, tapping your feet, or twisting paperclips

As you read through the above list, you may be thinking that you yourself would never be caught doing any of these things. Keep in mind, however, that most students have no awareness of these habits and that attendings commonly catch students doing one or more of the above.

Students who are good listeners maintain an interested expression, make eye contact with the attending, and nod their head occasionally while listening. They may take notes to help them focus on the material being presented. They also ask questions which demonstrate that they are interested in what the attending physician is saying. Occasionally, they may paraphrase by saying "If I understand you correctly ..." or "So what you are saying is..."

Tip # 74

You would be surprised how often students fall asleep during attending rounds. Don't think it won't happen to you. The combination of fatigue, long hours, lack of sleep, and boredom can easily cause you to nod off. To prevent it from happening with absolute certainty, take notes during rounds. It does work.

Tip # 75

If the attending physician stops by to see how the team is faring, stop whatever it is you are doing and give him your full attention. Greet the attending, listen to what he has to say, and take notes, if necessary. Whatever you are doing can usually wait.

Mistake # 199

Being unable to read people

One of the most common complaints students have about their rotation experience is the lack of feedback. Clearly, team members can and should do a better job of providing their students with feedback. However, you can learn a lot about your performance by observing your colleagues and how they respond to you. In other words, you can learn a lot from reading people.

Many attendings and residents dislike giving negative feedback. Therefore, they may give you a lower evaluation without specifying the reasons. Students who pay close attention to nonverbal behaviors can pick up on dissatisfaction or disapproval before it is ever voiced, and even if it is never voiced.

Did you know ...

To highlight the importance of reading those around you, consider the results of a study performed to determine how attending physicians respond to students and residents who behave in a manner that conveys a negative attitude toward a patient (Burack). Three types of problematic behaviors were identified by attending physicians. These included showing disrespect for patients, cutting corners, and outright hostility or rudeness. However, it was noted that attending physicians often did not respond to these behaviors. When they did, they often responded subtly with nonverbal gestures such as rigid posture, failing to smile, or remaining silent.

Mistake # 200
Compromising your integrity

In your efforts to be a successful student, you will often have opportunities to choose paths that may compromise your ethics and values. While such paths may lead to outward success, they don't make you a better physician, your ultimate and overriding goal. The guilt and regret you will experience just serve to highlight this important fact. Always maintain your integrity.

Opportunities to compromise your integrity arise almost on a daily basis. A student is asked to order a serum TSH level, but forgets to do so. The student only remembers when asked during the next day's rounds. Not wanting to look bad, he says the result isn't back yet, knowing fully the test was never ordered. Such situations arise frequently, and many students choose to lie rather than admit the truth. The correct way to handle this situation would be to admit the mistake, apologize, assure the attending it won't happen again, and then proceed to correct the situation.

Did you know ...

In a survey of students at The Johns Hopkins University School of Medicine, 13 to 24% admitted to cheating during the clinical years of medical school (Dans). Examples included "recording tasks not performed" and "lying about having ordered tests."

Did you know ...

In a study performed at the University of New Mexico School of Medicine, students were asked whether certain behaviors were ethical or unethical (Anderson). Survey participants were also asked if they had heard of or witnessed these behaviors on the part of their student colleagues. In response, 21% had personal knowledge of students "reporting a pelvic examination as 'normal' during rounds when it had been inadvertently omitted from the physical examination." Another 35% had personal knowledge of students "reporting a lab test or x-ray as 'normal' when in actual fact there had been no attempt to obtain the information."

Mistake # 201

Not taking initiative

Initiative is a characteristic that all successful students possess. Without initiative as a driving force, you yourself would not have reached this point today. Students with initiative are prized by their teammates because they get things done. During clinical rotations, opportunities to demonstrate initiative arise every day. It's up to you to recognize and seize these opportunities. The best way to demonstrate initiative is to begin a task and follow it through to completion. The task may be one assigned to you or one that you seek out yourself. Accept your responsibility readily and with enthusiasm.

Volunteering to give a talk or to perform a procedure is a perfect example of displaying initiative. Attendings commonly ask for volunteers to give talks. Often, team members remain silent and deliberately avoid eye contact. This demonstrates a lack of initiative on the part of the entire team. When the opportunity arises, always be the first to volunteer, even if it's an assignment that neither you nor anyone else wants.

Also realize that you don't have to wait to be asked. Make it a point to recognize tasks that need to be completed. Realize that you can accomplish the task, inform your team members that you will take responsibility for it, and then proceed to get it done. "I know Mr. Sapolsky has been hesitant to get the bone marrow biopsy done. I went to the library and pulled some patient information booklets. Would it be alright if I sat down with him and went over the information?"

Tip # 76

Look for opportunities to demonstrate initiative. Don't wait for other team members to invite you to observe a procedure or perform one. If a procedure is to be performed, ask if you can do it. If not, ask if you can observe. Better yet, ask if you can help get everything ready for the procedure.

Mistake # 202

Reacting rather than anticipating

Edgar and his team admit Mrs. Motumbo, a patient with pyelonephritis.

After a full evaluation, intravenous antibiotics are ordered.

Edgar completes his work, heads home, and retires for the night.

The next day, however, the patient's symptoms have not changed despite 24 hours of antibiotic therapy.

During rounds, the attending turns to Edgar and asks "What do you suggest we do now?"

"I'm really not sure. The intravenous antibiotics should have worked. Maybe we just need more time?"

This is a common scenario, with most students unsure of the next step. However, when admitting any patient and reading about their issues, you should always anticipate the possible outcomes. After starting treatment, one of three outcomes will occur: the patient's condition will be better, the same, or worse. You should always plan in advance on the course of action required with these different outcomes.

You should approach rounds by anticipating issues on the team's other patients as well. Most students approach attending rounds with the "let me play it by ear" attitude. They react to situations as they arise in rounds. Students who anticipate can better prepare. If your intern admits a patient with diabetic ketoacidosis, he will present the patient during rounds the following day. After the presentation, the attending will likely engage the team in a discussion about the topic. Although the patient isn't yours, anticipating the discussion and reading about the condition means that you can contribute to the discussion. You can ask intelligent questions and respond intelligently to any questions.

Mistake # 203
Showing no diplomacy

Dr. Greco took Albert aside halfway through the rotation to ask him about his rotation experience.

"Is there anything I can do to make your experience better?"

"What about shorter rounds?" replied Albert.

While actual names were not used in this real-life example, the message is clear. Diplomacy is not just useful in politics. It is helpful in everyday life, including the life of a third year medical student. To thrive in a team environment, you must use tact and sensitivity when dealing with your fellow team members. The diplomatic student considers others' feelings before speaking or acting.

Tip # 77

If your attending physician asks you how the rotation is going, be very positive, unless of course you have a major concern. Answer with a "Great," "I'm really enjoying it," or "I really appreciate all the teaching."

Mistake # 204
Talking too much

Overly talkative students have a tendency to dominate rounds. While this may be done unknowingly, at other times it is done in a deliberate attempt to flaunt knowledge. While you should be an active and enthusiastic participant during rounds, don't take it to an extreme by talking too much and dominating rounds. Give others the opportunity to speak as well.

Students who dominate rounds may be reined in by the attending. In some cases, the attending may be quite direct, asking you to speak less. In other cases, the cues may be more subtle. He may interrupt you or re-direct questions to other team members. Pay careful attention to any signals, either verbal or nonverbal.

Mistake # 205
Not showing compassion

As a physician, you will have the opportunity to observe compassion or the lack of it among your colleagues. While you will work with physicians who exhibit compassion in every aspect of patient care, you'll also encounter some physicians who, for a variety of reasons, have forgotten that compassion is an essential component of care.

Caring for patients can be challenging. As a student, there will be times when the intensity of the work along with the long hours leaves you feeling exhausted and stressed. At these times, it can be difficult to be compassionate.

There are also many times when patients are unpleasant or downright hostile. You must not take this personally. Realize that being ill is a stressful and emotional experience. In addition, patients must deal with a hospital setting that strips them of their privacy and sense of control. They may yell or lash out at you, even blaming you for their current condition. Although you may find it difficult to remain compassionate, remember to place the needs of your patient first.

Mistake # 206
Putting your foot in your mouth

Before you speak, carefully consider what you plan to say and the effects it will have on others. Too often, students speak in haste, later regretting the words that came out of their mouths. A colleague of mine told me about a mid-rotation meeting she had with her student during the Internal Medicine rotation. After providing the student with feedback, she asked the student how the rotation was going and whether there was anything she could do to make the experience better. The student replied, "Well, I really don't like medicine. I'm going into ophthalmology."

The attending asked the question with the goal of improving the student's experience. The student certainly had every right to dislike the specialty. However, what purpose did such a statement serve? This was a situation that clearly required the student to think before she opened her mouth.

Mistake # 207

Lacking confidence

To be a good medical student, you must first believe that you *are* a good medical student. This is easier said than done, especially when everyone else on the team seems to know exactly what they're doing, with the exception of yourself. However, remember that new rotations are trying times for all team members. The resident wonders whether he is ready to be a team leader. The attending ponders how best to teach team members at different educational levels. The bottom line is that everyone has doubts.

I have seen some very smart medical students who fail to impress their attendings because they lacked self-confidence. I've also seen medical students, not as smart perhaps, but who are able to project a positive self-image and carry themselves with confidence. These students appear more impressive.

Tip # 78

If you appear and act more confident than you feel, those you work with will have more confidence in you.

Mistake # 208

Making the resident or intern look bad in front of the attending physician

On occasion, your attending will ask the intern or resident a question that they can't answer, but that you can. No matter how much you want to answer that question, refrain from doing so. Blurting out the answer to a question not directed to you is considered bad form—your residents may feel that you are showing them up. If, however, the attending turns to you and asks you the same question, then feel free to answer. Try, however, to answer the question with some humility: "I was just reading about this yesterday and I found out that..."

Mistake # 209

Functioning at the lowest student level

Within the past few years, a new method of evaluating students has gained popularity in clerkships across the country. This system is called the RIME method and stands for—

Reporter
Interpreter
Manager
Educator

Dr. Pangaro, who developed the RIME method, describes four stages in a student's development.

In the first or lowest stage, students are reporters. Students are said to have mastered this stage if they:

- Consistently and reliably take an excellent history and physical exam
- Present patients or report patient data consistently, reliably, concisely, and in an organized manner, clearly communicating the key issues (oral and written communication)

Note that you have already been introduced to your function as a reporter during your basic science years. Your physical diagnosis course focused on developing your ability to perform a history and physical exam. Now, in your clerkships, your goal is to master this role and then proceed to the next stage, that of an interpreter.

It is vital that you master the reporter stage because educators believe that by the end of a clerkship, at the very least, students should reach this level. Students who have mastered their role as a reporter but have not mastered the next stage (interpreter) are generally given a pass for the rotation, assuming that there are no problems with their professionalism.

If simply passing the rotation is your goal, then mastering the role of reporter may be sufficient for most rotations. However, most students have higher aspirations. In order to earn a better evaluation, you must show the attending that you have not only mastered the reporter role but are also functioning as an interpreter.

For most students, making the transition from reporter to interpreter is quite difficult. In order to be an interpreter, you must be able to:

- Identify problems (requires the ability to recognize normal and abnormal). Problems can include symptoms, physical exam findings, abnormal lab tests, and so on
- Prioritize among these identified problems
- Create a differential diagnosis for each problem

189

- Rank the entities in the differential diagnosis in terms of likelihood

As an example, consider the student who learns that his patient's platelet count is low. He must recognize that thrombocytopenia is a problem. Then he must develop a differential diagnosis for the thrombocytopenia. The term "differential diagnosis" refers to a list of conditions that could account for the problem.

With this example in mind, the student who is functioning only as a reporter might make the following statement:

I just checked to see if today's lab test results came back for Mr. Kim. His platelet count is 110. Yesterday it was 250.

Contrast this with the statement made by a student functioning as an interpreter:

I just checked to see if today's lab test results came back for Mr. Kim. His platelet count is 110. Yesterday it was 250. There are many causes of thrombocytopenia but the most likely causes, in Mr. Kim's case, are heparin-induced thrombocytopenia, bone marrow depression due to the effects of alcohol, and splenomegaly. Since a spleen tip was not palpated on exam, I believe that bone marrow depression due to alcohol and heparin-induced thrombocytopenia are more likely. I believe that heparin is the cause—he didn't have thrombocytopenia when he was first admitted and it developed five days after starting heparin therapy.

Provided that there are no problems with professionalism, students who consistently perform as an "interpreter" are generally given a high pass evaluation.

By the end of a clerkship, most students will either be in the reporter or interpreter stage. Some students, however, are able to move past these two stages to reach the "manager" level. These students generally receive the highest evaluation, usually honors.

Students who are at the "manager" level are able to recommend a particular diagnostic test or course of treatment tailored to their patient's clinical situation. Below is an example of a student who is functioning as a manager:

I just checked to see if today's lab test results came back for Mr. Kim. His platelet count is 110. Yesterday it was 250. There are many causes of thrombocytopenia but the most likely causes, in Mr. Kim's case, are heparin-

induced thrombocytopenia, bone marrow depression due to the effects of alcohol, and splenomegaly. Since a spleen tip was not palpated on exam, I believe that bone marrow depression due to alcohol and heparin-induced thrombocytopenia are more likely. I believe that heparin is the cause since he didn't have thrombocytopenia when he was first admitted and it developed five days after starting heparin therapy. ***I propose that we discontinue the heparin and switch to another form of therapy for DVT prophylaxis. If the platelet count returns to normal after stopping the heparin, then we will have confirmed the diagnosis.***

Please note that the student's statements before the bolded portion show us that he is reporting and interpreting the information. In the bolded portion, he takes it a step further by demonstrating that he is also managing the patient.

Functioning as a manager is not easy for students. Part of this difficulty has to do with inexperience. As a student, you simply haven't seen a condition as often as the rest of the team. Your lack of experience, however, should not prevent you from making efforts to manage your patient's problems. Always try to come up with a plan. Ask yourself, "What should I do next?" Once you have decided on a plan, share it with your team. Your team won't expect that your plan will always be correct, but they will be pleased with your efforts to manage the patient. Since many students stop at the reporter or interpreter stage, your attempts to manage the patient will set you apart from these other students.

Tip # 79

Even when unsure, outstanding students will offer a plan. Team members are impressed with students who have given a problem considerable thought and are brave enough to recommend a course of action.

Tip # 80

After presenting the plan, listen carefully to how the team receives it. Don't be dismayed if the plan is modified. Instead, ask questions to understand why a particular course of action is recommended. Making decisions is difficult for students, but only through active participation can you develop this skill.

It is the rare student who reaches the educator stage during a clerkship. At the "educator" level, students show that they are the team's expert in the area in the following ways:

- Being able to not only identify knowledge gaps but also address them

- Reading deeply and sharing new information with others

- Probing the literature to find the evidence that backs up a particular course of therapy, diagnostic test, or other action

Do not be afraid to share what you learn with the team. Never lose sight of the fact that all team members, including the attending physician, are learners.

While it is gaining in popularity, the RIME method of evaluation may not be officially used in your clerkship. However, many attendings, even if they have never heard of the RIME method, use the same principles in the evaluation of their students. (Pangaro L. A new vocabulary and other innovations for improving descriptive in-training evaluations. *Academic Medicine* 1999: 74: 1203-1207.)

Mistake # 210

Not knowing how to interpret an EKG or chest film

EKGs and chest x-rays are commonly obtained both in the inpatient and outpatient setting. To avoid missing important findings, it is essential to analyze every EKG and chest film systematically. During your clerkships, you will find that your attending can make rapid EKG and chest film diagnoses without the need for systematic inspection. With time and experience, physicians become more adept, decreasing the time needed for interpretation. For now, however, it is best to approach every EKG and chest film systematically.

If you have not been introduced to a system, check with your intern or resident, who will be happy to share their system with you. Remember to always follow the same sequence of analysis. Consider the following system for EKG interpretation:

Systematic Approach to EKG Interpretation

Rate

Rhythm

Intervals (PR, QRS, QT)

Blocks

Axis

Hypertrophy

Conduction disturbances

Myocardial injury/infarction

ST-segment changes

T-wave changes

Q waves

Changes from previous EKG

Consider the following system for chest film interpretation:

Systematic Approach to Chest Film Interpretation (PA or AP film)

Patient name

Date of study

Comment on whether it is a PA or AP film

Comment on rotation of the patient

Comment on penetration of the film

Bones

Breasts

Soft tissue

Costophrenic angle

Lung markings/fields

Mediastinum

Cardiac shadow

Cardiac chambers

Comparison with previous chest film

Don't be surprised if the attending asks you to interpret an EKG or chest film during rounds, especially with your own patients. Prepare for this in advance by doing the following:

- Interpret the study on your own in a systematic manner.
- Review the EKG or imaging study with your resident or intern. Ask them to comment on your interpretation.
- Review all imaging studies with the radiologist.
- Know the criteria for any EKG abnormalities that are present (e.g., left bundle branch block), as well as the clinical significance of the findings.

You may also be asked to interpret a study of a patient you are not following. Many students lose their composure when asked to interpret an unfamiliar study. To maintain composure, just remember that you are not expected to be proficient with EKG or chest film interpretation. The attending has asked you to interpret the study because you can only become comfortable with time, experience, and practice. When asked to interpret a study, allow yourself 15 to 20 seconds to simply look at the study. This pause will also help you regain your composure. Then proceed to describe the findings using a systematic approach.

Tip # 81

If you don't know how to interpret an EKG or chest x-ray, have your resident introduce you to his system of analysis. Do this early in the rotation so that you'll be ready when the attending physician calls on you.

Mistake # 211

Differential diagnosis of an abnormal lab test is not known

Lab tests can be used to confirm or exclude a diagnosis, provide information regarding severity of a disease, monitor the course of a disease, monitor the response to therapy, and offer prognostic information.

It has become standard practice to obtain basic laboratory tests in every hospitalized patient. Other tests may also be ordered depending upon your patient's illness. Although an occasional patient may have completely normal laboratory test results, most have one or more abnormalities. It is important to not only make note of these abnormalities but also to develop a differential diagnosis for each. Every abnormal lab test result has its own differential. Attendings commonly ask for the differential diagnosis of abnormal lab test results.

Some Important Tips about Lab Tests

- On a daily basis, keep track of all lab tests that have been ordered. Check the computer periodically to see if results have become available.

- While some test results return in just an hour or two, others, such as blood or urine culture, may take days to become available. Have a system in place to keep track of all pending lab test results.

- Always check the computer for results just before attending rounds. Remember that you want to convey the most up-to-date information to your attending.

- Students, residents, and attendings are in the habit of ordering multiple lab tests every day. Not uncommonly, indications for these tests are lacking. While phlebotomy is not associated with major risk to the patient, the procedure does subject patients to pain and inconvenience. Obtaining unnecessary lab tests is also expensive. Before ordering any lab test, consider how the result will affect your management of the patient's illness. Tests that will not affect patient management should not be ordered.

- If a lab test is abnormal, develop a differential diagnosis. Attendings commonly ask students for the differential diagnosis of abnormal lab test results.

- When working up the symptom(s) that prompted a patient's hospitalization, always ask yourself if the abnormal lab test result supports any of the conditions in the differential diagnosis of the symptom(s).

- While offering a differential diagnosis is important, it's even better if you're able to answer this question: "What work-up should we do to determine the etiology of this abnormal lab test result?" Attendings are impressed with students who offer an approach to establishing the cause of the abnormality.

Mistake # 212

Letting unanswered questions in rounds remain unanswered

During rounds, a question may arise for which no one has the answer. In some cases the attending may turn to a team member and ask him to research the issue. If no one is asked to look into the issue, you need to do so yourself. You don't need to wait until you're asked—take the initiative to explore the issue on your own. Share what you find with the team at the appropriate time, along with a copy of a relevant article.

Mistake # 213

Letting favoritism affect your performance

Ideally, all attendings would treat their students in the same manner, and favoritism would not be an issue. Unfortunately, attendings aren't always consistent in their interactions with students. When students are favored for reasons other than work performance, problems may occur. You may become cynical or jealous, and find that these emotions affect your work performance and professionalism. Despite your attending's behavior, continue working hard. Positive reinforcement from your attending is not your only motivating factor for performing at a high level.

Mistake # 214

Relying too heavily on self-assessment

As a physician you will have few, if any, formal evaluations of your performance. Therefore, you will need to rely on your self-assessment skills. Unfortunately, studies have demonstrated that the self-assessment skills of medical students are lacking. Students need to improve in this area, and you can begin by asking yourself the following questions:

- What did I learn?
- Was I an engaged listener during rounds?
- Did I ask enough questions?
- Was I on time? dependable? enthusiastic?
- What questions was I unable to answer?
- What feedback did I receive about my oral case presentation, write-up, progress note, etc.?

Even though educators emphasize the importance of self-assessment, several studies have cast doubt on the accuracy of students' self-assessment. In a study examining the accuracy of self-assessment among 130 medical students, students were asked to complete a self-assessment form at the end of their anesthesiology rotation (Sclabassi). Their self-assssed grades were then compared to their teachers' evaluations to determine the degree of agreement. The results showed that only 4.6% were in general agreement.

In another study, 47 medical students at the Lehigh Valley Hospital were asked to assess themselves at the end of their Obstetrics/Gynecology rotation in the following areas (Weiss):

- Fund of knowledge
- Personal attitude
- Clinical problem-solving skills
- Written/verbal skills
- Technical skills

These self-assessments were then compared to their final clerkship grades in each of the above areas. The results demonstrated poor agreement between students' self-assessment and teacher assessment in the areas of global fund of knowledge, personal attitudes, and clinical problem-solving skills.

The results of these two studies suggest that students' self-assessment during a clerkship is not accurate in predicting how residents and faculty will evaluate them. Therefore, students should not rely on self-assessment alone. Rather, they should solicit feedback from their evaluators to more accurately determine their own strengths and weaknesses.

Tip # 82

While self-assessment is important, do not rely on it alone. It is critical that you supplement self-assessment with feedback from others.

Mistake # 215

Not asking for feedback

Eliciting feedback from your attending physician is crucial to the learning process. One of the most common complaints students have about their rotation experience is the lack of feedback. Many students, if they don't hear otherwise, assume that they are performing well. This assumption can be misleading. If an attending is displeased with some aspect of a student's performance, he may not yell or take the student aside for a discussion. Instead, he may demonstrate his displeasure in subtle ways, which may or may not be recognized by the student. Students in this situation often receive a poor evaluation at the end of the rotation, and are surprised to find that they were performing poorly or not meeting expectations.

Herein lies the importance of eliciting feedback. In a perfect world, the attending would sit down with you periodically to give you feedback. In reality, this often doesn't happen unless you are proactive in seeking it. Don't be afraid to ask for feedback because it seems like an imposition. It is not. It is one of the many responsibilities that attendings have as educators, and is important for your growth. Ask for feedback in an appropriate manner, paying close attention to timing. If the attending is hard to approach or always seems busy, ask your resident for advice on the best way to solicit feedback.

Ask for feedback early in the rotation. If any areas of improvement are suggested, you want to have enough time to demonstrate improvement. You should be receiving specific and timely feedback on an ongoing basis, including after an oral case presentation or talk. A formal one-on-one session should take place halfway through the rotation, although this usually serves as a general summary of your performance.

Tip # 83

To perform at a high level, it is critical that you receive frequent feedback. Without it, you can't know for sure whether your performance is better or worse than you believe. If you are not receiving feedback, you must take the initiative to obtain it.

Mistake # 216

Settling for nonspecific feedback

Consider the following statements made by attendings to their students:

"Your presentation was too long."

"Your progress note is too disorganized."

"Your write-up needs to be more detailed."

All are examples of feedback, but note that the comments are not specific. What part of the presentation was too long? Is there a particular section of the write-up that requires more detail? Without specific feedback, it can be difficult to determine what changes are needed.

When you ask for feedback, make your request as specific as possible. Too often, students ask general questions such as "How am I doing?" or "How do you find my progress notes?" More often than not, attendings respond to these general questions with general responses. "You're doing just fine." By asking specific questions, you increase your chances of receiving useful feedback.

Mistake # 217

Receiving feedback poorly

Feedback is an important component of growth. Dealing with positive feedback is fairly easy—we all like to hear about things we're doing well. Negative feedback is more of an issue for students. Some individuals have a difficult time handling negative feedback. They may become defensive, shift the blame elsewhere, or deny that any problem exists. Some students view any suggestions for improvement as a personal attack. These responses leave your evaluator with the impression that you are not receptive to feedback and are unwilling to alter your behavior.

There are correct ways to react to and respond to negative feedback. Always allow the person to finish before you respond. As obvious as this seems, you'd be surprised how often evaluators are interrupted by students. Especially with negative feedback, you need to stay in control of your emotions, because you may experience feelings of shame, embarrassment, frustration, or even anger. If you disagree with an attending's feedback, your goal is to determine why the attending feels differently. Do not, under any circumstances, allow the conversation to turn into an argument. After unfavorable feedback, students have been known to react in all sorts of ways, including outbursts of anger and crying. Do not lose sight of the fact that negative feedback is not a personal attack, but rather one individual's opinion of your performance. It is definitely possible that the evaluator reached his conclusion in error, but reacting with anger or tears is not likely to lead to a change in opinion. A more productive approach is to engage in a collegial discussion to ascertain why you received this type of evaluation.

After listening, ask for clarification if any items are unclear. Summarize what has been said before you respond. This is a good way to make sure you have interpreted the feedback correctly. If you have erred, take responsibility for the mistake, take action to correct the situation, inform your superior that it won't happen again, and stay true to your word. If you think the feedback is unfair or unfounded, you can, of course, express your opinion and defend yourself. Be sure that you do so in a friendly and collegial manner.

Tip # 84

Attending physicians commonly sandwich their feedback, starting with positives, followed by areas needing improvement, and ending with positives. With this approach, students sometimes only hear the positives. To avoid this, always summarize the feedback you receive so that you are clear on the positives as well as the areas needing improvement.

Tip # 85

As you summarize feedback to ensure your understanding, be sure to speak in a neutral tone. This is particularly important with negative feedback, especially if you don't agree with it. If you are feeling angry or depressed, you may have to consciously change your tone of voice to avoid communicating these emotions.

Mistake # 218

Not acting on feedback

With some feedback, students aren't sure how to proceed. The attending may inform you that your oral case presentations on newly admitted patients are taking up too much time during rounds. How do you shorten your presentation? Do you shorten the history of present illness, the review of systems, or some other section? Start by asking the person who identified the problem. In this situation, the attending probably has a solution, or at least some suggestions. While you can ask others on your team, recognize that the attending may prefer that you correct the problem in a particular way. As you make changes in your behavior, check back with your evaluator to see if you're progressing satisfactorily.

Tip # 86

It's never too late to make changes. If you have performed poorly overall or in some specific regard, don't assume that you can't change the way others view you and your abilities. Avoid thinking that things are hopeless—this is precisely the type of thinking that can prevent you from moving forward. Recognize that things can improve, consistently show team members that they have improved, and watch your image change for the better.

Mistake # 219

Completing the rotation without a final meeting with the attending physician

Ideally, before leaving a clerkship, you will have a face-to-face final meeting with your attending. During this meeting, you will hear his thoughts regarding your clinical performance along with suggestions for improvement. Unfortunately, attendings don't always initiate an end-of-clerkship meeting, even though clerkships typically require it. If so, don't be afraid to ask for a meeting to discuss your performance. "Dr. Parsi, since Friday's my last day, would it be possible for us to meet to discuss our month together and any suggestions you might have for me?" In order to learn and improve during your next clerkship, it is essential that you have such meetings before moving on to your next rotation.

For more information about attending rounds, see also …	Chapter	Mistakes
Psychiatry Clerkship: 150 Biggest Mistakes And How To Avoid Them	8	101 – 105
Internal Medicine Clerkship: 150 Biggest Mistakes And How To Avoid Them	7	134 – 150
Surgery Clerkship: 150 Biggest Mistakes And How To Avoid Them	8	106 – 110
Pediatrics Clerkship: 101 Biggest Mistakes And How To Avoid Them	7, 18	53 – 60 101

Commonly Made Mistakes

With Residents and Interns

In most, if not all of your rotations, you will be a member of a team. As a third year medical student, you will be the most junior member of the team. Above you on this totem pole are the intern, resident, and attending physician. You'll spend most of your time with the intern and resident. Since both often have significant input into the determination of your grade, it is in your best interests to develop a solid working relationship with these individuals. In fact, rotation success often hinges on the relationship you build with these team members.

Every patient on the team is assigned to an intern, who functions as the patient's primary caregiver. When issues arise during the patient's hospitalization, it is the intern who is often the first to be notified by the nurse or other healthcare professional. Interns work hard to make sure the things that need to be done for their patients are, in fact, done. Among other activities, they order lab tests, write progress notes, call consultants, write orders, and even draw blood. Interns work hard to provide the best possible care for their patients.

Interns usually turn to their resident for advice. Residents supervise interns, providing them with guidance in matters that they are not yet comfortable with. The resident is responsible for conducting morning or work rounds. During these rounds, the interns and medical students tell the resident about what has happened with the patient since the previous day's rounds. The resident then helps make decisions as to what needs to be done for the patient on that particular day. It is the resident's responsibility to make sure that the interns and medical students carry out these activities.

Residents and interns are busy individuals with many demands placed on them. As a student, you can make their lives easier in many ways. The best way is to take on as much responsibility for your patients as you can. Essentially, you should strive to function as your patient's intern. By being a productive team member who improves team efficiency, you will go a long way towards impressing the resident and intern. In this chapter, we will discuss mistakes students make with residents and interns.

Mistake # 220
Not being a team player

As a future physician, you will not care for patients alone. In order to deliver quality care to your patients, you will rely on a team of caregivers. This team may include nurses, social workers, pharmacists, physical therapists, and other physicians. Your success as a physician depends on how well you work with members of your team.

Your introduction to this team approach will occur during your clinical years of medical school. From the first day of your new rotation, you are part of a team. Your nuclear team typically consists of an attending physician, resident, interns, and students. You will also be a part of a larger team that includes other healthcare professionals. Even though every person on the team has different roles and responsibilities, you all share the same goal— to provide your patients with the best care possible. Dedicated students look out for the best interests of the team rather than themselves. This involves thinking about the needs of your team by being observant and making inquiries. Learn about their standards for high quality work, the best way you can support them, and how you can increase their efficiency.

Did you know...

In a study in which interviews were conducted with residents and attending physicians to ascertain the behaviors that make students "good" or "bad" clerks, it was learned that supervisors viewed behavior as positive when students acted "for the sake of patient care, for the sake of their own learning, or for the sake of their own team" (Lavine). Behavior was considered negative if students were thought to be shirking responsibility or "acting for the sake of appearance."

Mistake # 221
Being disorganized

Organization is a skill that will serve you well, not only in rotations and residency but also throughout your entire career as a physician. With every new patient assigned, you are responsible for performing a thorough history and physical exam. You also need to gather the results of laboratory and imaging test data. After your evaluation, you will have collected a considerable amount of information which may seem overwhelming. Take the example of a patient who comes in with diabetic ketoacidosis. A major part of the management of these patients is frequent laboratory testing, sometimes as often as every hour. The only way you can properly manage these patients is to stay organized.

There are many methods of staying organized, and you'll often hear others proclaim their method as the best. In the end, you must decide on a system that will work for you. Common methods include the following:

- Clipboard
- Blank or pre-made note cards/sheets
- Pocket-sized notebooks
- Personal digital assistants (PDA)

There are advantages and disadvantages to each method. Clipboards, for example, are often lost because you have to put them down so many times a day. Note cards are popular with residents and interns because they are more portable. Mark them with your name and beeper number so that if lost, they may be returned. In recent years, PDAs have become popular. Now available are PDA programs that can help you stay organized. Regardless of which method you choose, try to have your system in place on day one of the rotation.

The benefits of staying organized abound. The organized student is readily able to relay important information to team members within seconds. Key information you should have at your fingertips includes:

- Patient name
- Medical record or social security number
- Room number
- Date of birth
- Admission date
- Chief complaint
- History of present illness
- Medications, including frequency, route, and dosage as well as start and end dates
- Daily vital signs and I/O (input/output)
- Pertinent physical exam findings
- Results of lab/diagnostic studies

- Problem list (patient's active problems) along with management plan

Understand that the record that you keep is not static but will change on a daily basis as your patient's condition changes, new tests are ordered, and medications are started or stopped. No matter what system you have chosen, you must be able to add information to your record and keep it organized in such a way that it is readily accessible.

Strive to be the organized student who has patient data at his fingertips. Do not be the disorganized student who fumbles around, flipping page after page looking for data. Without superb organization skills, you may lose track of important patient information or even mix up patient information. Not only will this make you look unprofessional, it may affect the quality of care your patients receive.

If you are a disorganized student, you will undoubtedly annoy and frustrate your team members. On the other hand, the organized student will come across as efficient, competent, and thorough, making fewer mistakes than his disorganized counterpart. Which student would you rather be?

Did you know ...

In a study evaluating problem students, clerkship coordinators, clinical faculty members, and residents were asked to identify the frequency with which certain problem types were encountered. Among 21 types of problem students, the disorganized student was the second most frequently encountered problem type in internal medicine and pediatrics. It was the third most frequently encountered problem type in surgery (Tonesk).

Mistake # 222

Taking care of patients without a to-do list

Early in your day, you will confer with the team to determine the day's plan for each of your patients. During this discussion, your intern and resident will ask you to take care of a number of tasks. Write each and every task down. The only exception to this rule is when you are assigned a task that requires your immediate attention, in which case you should drop everything and attend to it.

Making a to-do list can be particularly helpful when you are following many patients. Even with one patient it's a smart idea. Don't try to memorize the tasks that need to be completed—that's a recipe for disaster. As you complete tasks on your list, cross them off. At the end of the day, review your list. You may not be lauded for getting everything done. However, if you forget even a single task, your residents will be upset. You will appear unprofessional, and you may harm your patient.

I've seen some students take a haphazard approach to keeping track of tasks. One action item may be written on a note card, another on a progress note, and yet another on a hand. When action items are scribbled in a variety of places, problems often arise. Something may be forgotten or even lost amidst a sea of papers. For these reasons, keep your to-do list in one location.

Mistake # 223

Taking care of patients without prioritizing the tasks that need to be completed

After seeing your patients every morning, the team will decide on a plan of action for the day. This plan may involve a variety of tasks, including ordering laboratory tests, performing studies, and requesting consultations. Some of these tasks are clearly more important than others. The importance of each is something you have to ascertain from talking with your team. Tasks of higher priority should be tackled first. Some tasks won't be done that day unless you tackle them early. For example, at some hospitals, if a CT scan is not ordered early in the day, it may not be done until the next day. This may prolong the patient's hospitalization.

Tip # 87

Do as much of your work as you can in the morning. If orders are written, tests are scheduled, and consults are placed in the morning, they are more likely to be done. If something is particularly important, speak with the appropriate person to make sure it gets done.

It can be difficult for students to determine which tasks on the list are of higher priority. Interns and residents often don't make this clear, mistakenly assuming that their students are on the same page. If you aren't sure, you need to ask. Avoid making your own judgments about what's most important, and remember that priorities are to be set by the intern and resident.

Tip # 88

What tasks are most important? Which should be tackled first? Which can be delayed until later in the day? If your resident doesn't make this clear, you need to ask. It is imperative that you have this information.

Mistake # 224

Assuming that others believe you are working hard

Most students describe themselves as hard workers. In fact, it's unlikely that you would find yourself in the position you are in today—as a junior medical student—if you were not a hard worker. You will want to bring this strong work ethic with you to your clinical rotations. You will need it because caring for patients requires considerable effort, energy, and stamina. However, just because you're working hard, that doesn't mean that others view you as a hard worker. Seek input about your work ethic from your residents.

Mistake # 225

Thinking that certain work is beneath you

As a student, it sometimes seems as though all you ever do is grunt work. No one would argue that tasks such as filling out forms, calling for laboratory test results, or pulling radiology films are exciting. Students often label this menial work "scut" or "scut work." The Wikipedia dictionary defines scut as "menial work, especially in the medical profession, to describe the work that medical students are required to do for residents and attending physicians."

In the American Medical Student Association (AMSA) document titled "Principles regarding wellness of medical students and housestaff," AMSA maintains "that the performance of repetitive scut work, past the point where such work is a learning experience, is an infringement upon the medical student's educational time and should not be required of the student." Note that AMSA states that scut work does have educational value. This important point is often forgotten by students. Even mundane tasks have learning value. You will be asked to perform scut work as an intern. An introduction to it now, as a student, will teach you how to manage your time.

Most students do not have any problem doing scut work for their own patients. Problems sometimes arise when students have to do scut work for other patients. How often this occurs varies from one resident to another. While some residents don't scut their students at all, others have a reputation for it. Most students aren't troubled by infrequent requests to pitch in and help out with other patients. If you are asked to perform occasional scut work for another patient, embrace the opportunity with the same level of enthusiasm and professionalism you have brought to other aspects of the rotation. While you may not be excited about the work, your assistance will solidify your standing as a team player. Team players are often rewarded with increased teaching, chances to participate in procedures, and other exciting opportunities.

What should you do if the scut work is excessive or inappropriate? One option would be to simply comply with the requests. Many students would choose this option, declining to make it an issue for fear that it may affect their clerkship grade. Another option would be to bring it up directly with your resident. You may prefer to discuss it first, however, with a more neutral party such as your mentor or clerkship director.

Mistake # 226
Making the intern and resident look bad

As a student, you need to make your intern and resident look good. This will help them score points with the attending physician. If you help them look good, you'll also look good. You can help in the following ways:

- Understand their goals, priorities, pressures, and work styles.
- Anticipate their needs.
- Keep your intern and resident informed of any new developments with your patients. Do not surprise them in front of the attending.
- Never criticize your intern and resident to others.
- Do not show up or correct your intern or resident in front of others, unless your silence may compromise patient care.
- Pay attention to what makes their lives more difficult. Volunteer to help in these areas.
- When the opportunity arises, praise them to the attending. For example, if your intern is going above and beyond in his teaching role, let the attending know.

Tip # 89

If you learn of a new patient development just before attending rounds, you may not have the chance to inform the intern or resident. If this happens, you will have to present the information delicately so that you do not inadvertently show up your intern or resident. You might say, "Right before rounds, I learned that..." Although your intern or resident may be surprised by the information, your approach will save them from any embarrassment.

Mistake # 227

Not updating your intern and resident

Some interns and residents are very hands-on. They will want to have frequent updates on the status of your patients. They will also want to know about your progress in accomplishing the day's work. Others are more hands-off, checking in with you less often. When you update them, inform them of the following:

- The tasks you have completed, the results of your efforts, and any new information that has been learned
- The tasks you have yet to finish
- What you are currently working on

Tip # 90

Keep your intern and resident well informed of your progress. Contact them when you have finished a task, if you are not sure how to complete a task, or if a problem arises that makes it difficult for you to follow through with the task.

Mistake # 228

Being inaccessible

You are expected to participate fully in the care of your patients. Team members would like to have you involved as much as possible. To keep you involved, they need you to be easily accessible. They only have a short time in which to reach you before they take care of any issues on their own.

Keep your resident and intern informed of where you will be at all times, check with them before you leave for a conference, and respond to pages quickly. If you follow this advice, you will avoid having to hear "Where have you been?" or "I've been looking all over for you." Suffice it to say that if you ever hear these words, you have annoyed your intern or resident.

Mistake # 229
Missing deadlines

On a daily basis, you will have a list of tasks that have varying deadlines. With so many tasks on your "to do" list, you must stay on track, especially with your limited time. Avoid gossip, politics, and other distractions. Remain focused on the responsibilities of your job. If you tell your intern or resident that something will be finished by a certain time, then be sure to meet that deadline. Keep in mind that unforeseen situations may prevent you from meeting a deadline. If so, notify your superior right away. If you can consistently meet deadlines, you will be seen as a reliable student.

Tip # 91

The best students don't surprise their intern. If a deadline can't be met, they inform their intern well in advance. This allows the intern to step in and help you complete the task. When team members are informed late in the game, the task may not be completed and the team will have to answer to the attending physician.

Mistake # 230
Dropping the ball

As you tackle the tasks on your "to-do" list, do not cross off a task until it is truly completed. With some tasks, you will need the cooperation of others. If someone tells you that he will help you finish a task, do not assume that it has been done. Wait until you have confirmation.

I recall one student who was asked by his attending to check out films from the radiology department and have them ready for afternoon rounds. This student called the radiology department, spoke with the radiology file clerk, arranged for the clerk to pull the films and to have them delivered to the team's conference room just before rounds. He crossed the task off his list. When the team gathered for rounds, the films were not available. Needless to say, the attending was not pleased.

Mistake # 231

Not maximizing teaching from your resident and intern

If you are fortunate, you will be on a team where the resident and intern enjoy teaching and make it a priority. Even with the best teachers, the amount of teaching you receive will vary from day to day depending on the workload. On some days, the team will be so busy they hardly have time to breathe, let alone teach. On other days, the workload may be lighter, allowing for more teaching.

What can you do if you aren't receiving enough teaching? Don't do what many students would—that is, whine or become frustrated. These are not productive responses. Instead, consider the following:

- The best way to increase teaching is to help create some time in the residents' day for teaching.

> Offer to help your residents, even with tasks not involving your patients. This will free up time for teaching and demonstrate that you are a team player. Residents often reward such students with increased teaching.

- Determine your residents' interests and strengths.

> If your resident is particularly strong in EKG interpretation, then bring him your patient's EKG and engage him in a discussion about EKG interpretation.

- Be visible and accessible.

> You never know when a lull in the action might occur. The resident might take advantage of this time to teach, but if he can't find you, the opportunity may quickly be lost.

- Express your appreciation.

> After a teaching session, always thank your resident. Your goal is to reinforce the behavior by showing your appreciation.

Students often don't realize how much teaching they do receive. They tend to think of teaching only in the traditional sense. A block of time is set aside and a prepared talk on a particular topic is given. On the wards, teaching often doesn't occur in this form. Consider the following examples:

- An intern instructing the student on how to organize patient data
- An intern reviewing the student's progress note and suggesting ways in which the note can be improved
- An intern showing the student how to prioritize, use time wisely, and accomplish work efficiently
- A resident demonstrating a procedure and then supervising the student

All are examples of teaching, although not in the traditional sense.

Mistake # 232

Handling conflict poorly

Stress among medical students, not surprisingly, is common, and the issue has been studied by researchers. Lloyd and Gartrell found frequent stressful interactions between students and their attending physicians and residents during the junior year of medical school (Lloyd). Researchers at the University of Illinois College of Medicine examined the nature of conflict situations that students encountered (Spiegel). They found that conflict situations were common, occurring, on average, every other day. While one may assume that stressful interactions would decrease as students become more familiar with the clinical arena, the literature does not support this assumption. Researchers at the University of Miami found that while some stresses did decrease as the junior year progressed, stresses due to conflict with superiors and peers did not (Linn).

The results of these studies demonstrate that conflict is common. The question, then, is not if it will occur, but rather when. With this in mind, it is best to have a strategy in place to manage conflict.

What type of conflict situation might you find yourself in? In the University of Illinois study, the majority of the conflict situations (57/99) involved problems with residents, attending physicians, or others in positions of authority. The nature of these situations varied considerably and included problems as minor as asking for clarification of a responsibility or making small talk, to as major as handling public criticism.

In many cases, the conflict will be minor, in which case you need not do anything. Even if you were right and the resident was wrong, it is best to let go of trivial matters. Most have no lasting impact.

However, the time may come when you find yourself in a particularly sticky situation with a team member. You must learn how to handle these situations with poise. When faced with major conflict, many students tend to retreat, choosing to avoid all efforts to address the conflict directly with the other person. These students hope that the issue will simply resolve if they leave things alone. However, avoidance generally does not lead to the resolution of major conflict. In some cases, it may worsen it.

The preferred way of handling major conflict is to address the issue directly and quickly with the other person. This should always be handled face to face. If done otherwise, there is potential for misunderstanding, which may make a difficult situation even worse. It takes courage to have a face to face discussion but it is, by far, the best way. Arrange a proper time and location for this meeting. It should not take place in a public place like a hallway.

Before the meeting, examine the issue carefully. Have you done something wrong? Did you step on someone's toes? If it's your mistake, then you have to acknowledge your error and apologize. In your apology, let the other person know that you understand the problems that have resulted from your words or actions. Do not make excuses or offer explanations. Simply take full responsibility for your error and inform the other party of your intent to resolve the situation. If you are not sure how to rectify the situation, consider several options, present them, and come to some agreement on which is best. A sincere apology is often all that is needed to put most issues of this sort to rest.

During the meeting, listen carefully. Conflict often arises from miscommunication, incorrect assumptions or incomplete information. For example, we may assign motives for someone's behavior based on incorrect assumptions. By listening carefully, you are better able to understand where the other person is coming from. Don't be afraid to ask questions to better understand the other person's perspective.

As you discuss the situation, don't overreact. If the other person is angry, allow him to vent his anger. Even if you feel angry, remain poised and calm. As difficult as it may be, you must keep your emotions in check. When you let your emotions escalate, you may say things that you will later regret. Choose your words carefully, avoiding any language that may inflame the situation further. Remember that your goals are to resolve this conflict by finding a fair solution. Since you must continue to work with this individual, you must do what you can to preserve the relationship.

If you are unable to reach a resolution, then you may wish to discuss the issue with your clerkship director. It's far better to bring up an issue earlier, rather than later, in the rotation. Informing the clerkship director of a problem two days before the end of the clerkship doesn't give him any chance to improve the situation.

If you sense that you will need to discuss the situation with the clerkship director, I recommend that you begin documenting your problems. You might want to keep a daily diary of events. Keep a record of the date and time of any incidents, a factual description of the behavior, names of witnesses, impact of the behavior on patient care, and the effects of any actions taken to resolve the problem. This will be particularly helpful if you have to recount the details of the situation later. It is very easy to lose track of details, especially when you are so busy on the wards.

Tip # 92

You should not be harassed, discriminated against, or belittled. Unfortunately, the literature shows that such behavior does occur. Should it happen to you, consider discussing it with the clerkship director. Often, students don't bring these issues to light, which prevents the clerkship director from taking corrective action.

Mistake # 233

Mishandling the toxic colleague

While most medical students are collegial, some are difficult to work with because of their competitiveness. Their goal is to impress team members with a "whatever it takes" attitude. These students may use a variety of underhanded and unscrupulous tactics in an effort to put themselves in a better light while diminishing their colleagues. Examples of such toxic behaviors include lying, cheating, blaming their mistakes on fellow students, rounding on other students' patients, or writing progress notes on other patients without permission.

What do you do if you find yourself in this type of situation? First and foremost, maintain your own professionalism. Do not pursue a "don't get mad, get even" approach. This type of approach may damage your reputation and erode your self-respect. Instead, meet with your fellow student to discuss the situation. Take care in your choice of words. Rather than aggressively saying, "You are way out of line. I demand that you stop ..." say, "We've had a good working relationship but, over the last few days, I've noticed that something has changed. Yesterday, during rounds, I felt that you ..." As you discuss the situation, be sure to emphasize cooperation rather than competition. Some students will respond with a change in their behavior while others may not. When change doesn't occur, you may need to involve other team members, especially if your colleague's behavior is interfering with your ability to work or is damaging your reputation. If you must meet with one of your superiors, present the facts of the situation, how it has affected your ability to do your work, and what you have done to resolve it. End with "I would like to get your thoughts on what else I can do."

Tip # 93

When dealing with an overly competitive student colleague, consider his past actions. If his behavior is out of the ordinary, it may be because of extenuating circumstances. Illness, family issues, and other stressors can cause otherwise decent people to behave in negative ways.

Lighten your colleague's load if he is having a tough time or if you are aware of personal circumstances that are weighing heavily. When students work well together, the service runs smoothly, there is camaraderie among team members, learning opportunities increase, and the clerkship is more enjoyable. Also, remember that your superiors will be observing your interactions with other students. Most evaluation forms ask evaluators to rate students on how well they interact with their peers.

Tip # 94

Assume that everyone you work with, including a fellow student, has the ability to influence your grade. Never make a classmate look bad in an effort to make yourself look better.

Mistake # 234

Complaining

Demanding attendings. Difficult patients. Lengthy rounding. Not enough time to read. These are just a few of the issues that students complain of. While it is entirely reasonable to complain, save your complaints for your fellow students, family, or friends outside of work hours. Don't subject your team members to these gripes no matter how comfortable you feel with them.

When should you complain to your resident or attending? If the problem is persistent or serious enough that it is affecting your performance, then it would be in your best interests to discuss your concerns. If it's a minor issue, ask yourself whether it's even worthwhile to bring it up. If you complain about minor issues, you may be labeled a whiner. If you aren't sure whether the problem is minor or major, or simply don't feel comfortable broaching the issue with your resident or attending, don't hesitate to approach your advisor or clerkship director for guidance.

Tip # 95

Complaining about work generally doesn't help. As one resident once told me, "Everyone has to do some grunt work, including students. Nobody likes complainers." If you need to complain or vent, save it for someone you don't work with.

Mistake # 235
Dating team members

Dating a team member will present a variety of challenges. It will be distracting. It has the potential to affect your performance, as well as your partner's performance, to the detriment of patient care. If you receive recognition for your work, others may attribute it to the relationship rather than your skills. For these reasons, I strongly advise you to keep your personal life separate from your work life.

If you do decide to date a fellow team member, then you need to do everything possible to keep it private. Don't share details of your relationship with others on the team or with anyone else that you might encounter in the hospital. Although it should go without saying, I feel obligated to say it: Do not, under any circumstances, have any physical contact with this person while in the hospital. I know of such situations. Students have been caught being physically intimate with their partners while at the hospital or clinic. This may lead to disciplinary action.

Did you know ...

In a study of 154 residents at hospitals affiliated with the Brown University Medical School, over 25% reported that a supervisor had dated a fellow trainee (Recupero). Over 7% had been asked on a date by a supervisor.

216

Mistake # 236
Letting your guard down

You should never lose track of the fact that your team members are your superiors and not your friends. They can be your friends later. During the rotation, consider them your bosses. Not uncommonly, students who were on their best behavior at the start of the rotation let their guard down as the clerkship progresses. As their comfort level increases during a rotation, their behavior often changes. Once you've gotten to know team members, you may start to act chummy with them. You may even reach a point where you feel comfortable making inappropriate comments or crude jokes. You may not realize that your behavior is offensive to one or more people on the team. You may only realize it when you look at your evaluation and realize that the team didn't find you very professional.

Tip # 96

Be friends with your resident and intern after the rotation. Until then, treat them as you would any other person who has considerable influence over your grade and career—because right now, they do.

Mistake # 237
Not paying attention during work rounds

During work rounds, the resident, interns, and students walk and see each patient together. Before seeing each patient, the intern or student will inform the resident about any significant events that may have occurred overnight. A diagnostic and therapeutic plan is then formulated and it is the responsibility of the intern and student to implement the plan.

Work rounds is an ideal time for teaching. Many residents take this opportunity to demonstrate interesting physical findings, discuss lab test results, go over imaging test results, and make management decisions. Because residents can often predict what an attending will ask during rounds, it's important to pay close attention during work rounds (on all of the patients—not just your own). The pearls of information, tips, and questions that come up during work rounds are likely to come up again during attending rounds.

Mistake # 238

Knowing a lot about your patient

Knowing a lot isn't enough. You need to know **everything** about your patient. Team members are impressed with students who know everything about their patients. Strive to be the team's expert on your own patients. This is easier said than done, due to a variety of factors.

As an example, your patient's condition deteriorates while you are away at a mandatory conference. Your intern then changes the management. You return from conference, but not having touched base with your team or reviewed the chart, you are unaware of the change. The attending sees you and asks you about this change in patient status. You inform him that you are unaware of this new development. Needless to say, the attending is not impressed.

As a student, you will often find yourself out of the loop. Important patient information may bypass you. You may be off the floor when there is a change in your patient's hospital course. Your intern, being busy with work, may forget to inform you of what has happened. Every day, situations of this sort leave students frustrated.

As frustrating as it may be, it is up to you to stay current. To stay current, you must be proactive. Do so by—

- Keeping in touch with your intern and resident throughout the day
- Reading the chart frequently for new progress notes, consultants' notes, and new orders
- Being aware of changes in vital signs, lab test results, and so on

Mistake # 239

Letting your intern write orders on your patients

Unless the clerkship forbids it, you should write orders for all of your patients. Orders are essentially instructions communicated from the physician to other members of the healthcare team regarding the care of a patient.

Order writing begins on the first day of the patient's hospitalization with the admission orders. On each subsequent day, the patient is reassessed and new orders are written based on changes in the patient's condition. If the team wishes to start a new medication, then an order must be written. If the team wants the phlebotomist to draw blood at 8 AM for measurement of the blood glucose, an order must be written. Unless the hospital forbids it, there is simply no reason why you shouldn't be writing all of the orders.

Mistake # 240

Being arrogant

Team members would like their students to be confident but not arrogant. Since the difference can be subtle, how can you be sure that you are displaying confidence rather than arrogance?

While the confident student believes in himself, the arrogant student considers himself superior. The confident student is not afraid to admit a mistake while the arrogant student never owns up to a mistake. These are just a few examples to highlight the differences between confidence and arrogance.

Of course, in the end, it is those around you who will decide if you have healthy self-esteem or an arrogant manner. If you ever receive feedback saying that you are overconfident, cocky, or arrogant, do not take it lightly. Make inquiries to determine what it is about your manner, language, or attitude that made the person feel that way. If you aren't sure what type of attitude you project, don't be afraid to ask those around you.

Did you know ...

In one report, arrogance was one of the top 10 examples of unprofessional behavior. Others include the following:

Dishonesty	Lack of due diligence (i.e.
Arrogance and disrespectfulness	carelessness, laziness, and not
Prejudices	following through)
Negative interactions with colleagues	Personal excesses (i.e.
Lack of accountability for medical errors	substance abuse, gambling, and
No or lack of commitment to lifelong	reckless behavior)
learning	Sexual misconduct

From Hicks PJ, Cox SM, Espey EL, Goepfert AR, Bienstock JL, Erickson SS, Hammoud MM, Katz NT, Krueger PM, Neutens JJ, Peskin E, and Puscheck EE. To the point: medical education reviews—dealing with student difficulties in the clinical setting. *Am J Obstet Gynecol* 2005; 193(6): 1915-1922.

Mistake # 241

Not eliciting feedback from the resident and intern

One of the most common complaints students have about their rotation experience is the lack of feedback. Eliciting feedback from your intern and resident is crucial. You need to know what you are doing well and what you need to work on. Ideally, the intern and resident would meet with you periodically to give you feedback on your performance. In reality, this often doesn't happen unless you are proactive in seeking feedback.

A formal one-on-one feedback session should definitely take place halfway through the rotation. This meeting will give you a good feel for how you are performing. Ask about the items you are doing well and the areas that need improvement. You can then focus on turning your weaknesses into strengths during the remainder of the rotation. If your intern and resident do not initiate this meeting, you should do so.

Did you know ...

In one study, the teaching behaviors of fourteen internal medicine residents were observed during work rounds (Wilkerson). Residents offered feedback to team members in only 11% of 158 patient encounters.

Mistake # 242

Leaving the rotation without having a final feedback meeting with your intern and resident

In Mistake # 219, we discussed the importance of a final meeting with the attending physician. It is equally important to have an end of the rotation meeting with your intern and resident. You will generally work much more closely with the intern and resident than with the attending. Having worked up patients with you, they will be able to readily comment on your ability to perform a history and physical exam. They have also observed your performance of simple procedures such as phlebotomy and can evaluate your proficiency in these areas.

Commonly Made Mistakes

With the Written Exam

Most, if not all, of your third year clerkships will end with a written examination. Between 1993 and 1998, the Liaison Committee on Medical Education (LCME) performed full accreditation surveys at 97 medical schools. From this data, it was learned that the written exam was the second most common method of student evaluation in core clinical clerkships, just behind faculty/resident ratings of student performance.

For many years, the faculty at each school was responsible for the development of the written exam. In recent years, however, an increasing number of clerkships have adopted the National Board of Medical Examiners (NBME) subject examination as their end-of-clerkship examination. In their accreditation survey, the LCME also sought to determine the percentage of clinical clerkships using NBME subject examinations. The results are shown in the following table

Percentage of 97 U.S. medical schools Using NBME Subject Examinations for the Evaluation of Students During 1997-1998	
Clerkship	**% of medical schools**
Family Medicine	25.6
Internal Medicine	84.8
Obstetrics and Gynecology	77.6
Pediatrics	68.0
Psychiatry	64.0
Surgery	68.8
From LCME Medical Education Databases for 97 U.S. medical schools that underwent full accreditation surveys between July 1993 and June 1998. Also from Kassebaum DG, Eaglen RH. Shortcomings in the evaluation of students' clinical skills and behaviors in medical school. *Academic Medicine* 1999; 74: 841-849.	

Clerkships use written exams to assess students' factual knowledge and their ability to apply it. The commonly used NBME subject examinations are carefully constructed to ensure their reliability, validity, and objectivity. Because these exams are easy to administer and they provide data comparing performance to national norms, these examinations have been adopted by many clerkships nationwide.

These are difficult exams. While you are undoubtedly a good test taker, clerkships pose challenges that can affect your performance. In this chapter, we offer practical and specific strategies that will help you maximize your examination performance.

Before the exam

Mistake # 243

Underestimating the importance of the written exam

The weight that the written examination score carries in the determination of the overall clerkship grade varies from clerkship to clerkship, even at the same school. Typically, the written exam accounts for 20 to 40% of a student's clerkship grade.

Median Contribution of the Written Examination to a Student's Grade

Clerkship	% of grade
Family Medicine	20.0
Internal Medicine	25.0
Obstetrics and Gynecology	40.0
Pediatrics	25.0
Psychiatry	33.3
Surgery	30.0

From LCME Medical Education Databases for 97 U.S. medical schools that underwent full accreditation surveys between July 1993 and June 1998. Also from Kassebaum DG, Eaglen RH. Shortcomings in the evaluation of students' clinical skills and behaviors in medical school. *Academic Medicine* 1999; 74: 841-849.

While evaluations of your clinical performance are generally more important than your written examination score, it is important that you understand your clerkship's grading policy. Some important points to consider:

- In most rotations, a superb performance on the written examination will generally not make up for a poor performance on the wards.

- A passing examination score may not be sufficient to achieve a clerkship grade of honors, even if you have secured outstanding clinical evaluations. In some rotations, you must exceed a certain exam score or percentile to be considered for an overall clerkship grade of honors.

- If you fail the examination, you will usually have to retake it. In some cases, students are asked to repeat the entire clerkship.

Mistake # 244
Preparing for the exam without knowledge of the exam format

In order to prepare effectively, you need to know the format of the exam. As obvious as this may seem, I have encountered many students who are unaware of the exam format, not just at the start of a rotation but also well into it. Since studying for the end-of-clerkship exam begins with the first day of the rotation, it is essential that you know particulars about your exam right from the start. Your method of preparation and study will differ depending on whether it is a multiple-choice or essay exam.

Mistake # 245
Delaying examination preparation

Studying for the written examination should begin on Day # 1 of the rotation, especially with short rotations that may last only a few weeks. In these rotations, you cannot delay your preparation. With longer clerkships, it can be tempting to delay exam preparation. Keep in mind, however, that clerkship days often start early and end late, leaving students with little time to study. In the basic sciences, students get used to coasting in the first few weeks, and then doing their heavy studying closer to exam time. Clinical rotations do not allow for that type of preparation, as the workload is heavy throughout the rotation. An early start to preparation is the key to not only getting through the material, but also in providing the time needed to properly review the subject matter.

Tip # 97

One of the best ways to prepare for the exam is to read actively about your patients. A particularly effective approach is to read about each problem on the patient's problem list. Then, for each problem, ask yourself the following questions:

> What are the symptoms of the disease?
>
> What are the signs of the disease?
>
> What is the differential diagnosis?
>
> How are these diagnoses differentiated from one another?
>
> How do you work-up or evaluate the disease?
>
> What test(s) are available to confirm the diagnosis?
>
> What are the treatment options?
>
> What is the prognosis?
>
> What is the pathogenesis?

Mistake # 246

Preparing for the exam without setting up a schedule

Savvy students create a schedule to help them stay on track. Create a reasonable schedule—one that doesn't force you to do too much on a daily basis but that does allow for coverage of all topics before the examination. If a busy day prevents you from reading about your scheduled topic, your schedule should afford you enough flexibility to catch up on a subsequent day.

Take advantage of downtime during the day. Since you never know when time may present itself, it's best to be prepared for these blocks of time, having reading material handy. At the end of the day, you'll find that these short blocks of time can add up. Many students are able to complete their scheduled reading during the workday while waiting for a lecture to begin, waiting for rounds to begin, or while on the bus ride home.

Tip # 98

Carry with you copies of the chapters you are scheduled to read. It's easier to carry copies of chapters rather than the book itself. Again, you never know when a short block of time may present itself. Be prepared to use this time to your advantage.

Mistake # 247

Preparing for the exam without taking the time to review the content of the exam

If your clerkship uses the NBME subject examination as the end-of-clerkship exam, take the time to review the content of the exam at www.nbme.org. At their website, the NBME has made available the content of each subject examination, including the percentage of questions that will come from various areas. If your clerkship uses its own exam, refer to the orientation syllabus for information about exam content. If you aren't able to find this information, ask the clerkship director. This is clearly information you need in order to focus your preparation.

Clerkships often recommend that students use comprehensive textbooks such as *Harrison's Principles of Medicine, Cecil's Textbook of Medicine,* or *Nelson's Textbook of Pediatrics* as their primary resource. Because of their length and level of detail, these books are not ideal for exam preparation. A better approach is to use these books for patient-directed reading and to rely on shorter books for exam preparation. You will find that opinions vary widely among students regarding "the book" you should use. Solicit input from a number of colleagues, review the recommended titles, and select one that you feel is a good fit for you and your learning style.

Did you know ...

A number of studies have shown that student performance on NBME subject examinations improves with increasing clerkship experience (Manley) (Reteguiz) (Hampton) (Cho). This gives students taking the exam at the end of the third year an advantage, especially over students who take it early in the year.

During the exam

Mistake # 248

Taking the exam without pacing yourself

Students are given two hours and ten minutes to complete an NBME subject examination consisting of 100 questions. Essentially, you have a little over a minute per question. While this at

225

first may seem like a reasonable amount of time, many students have had difficulty answering all questions in the time allotted.

What can you do to make sure you finish the examination in the allotted time? First, realize that you have 1 minute 18 seconds per question. It isn't practical to time yourself as you read and answer every question. A better practice is to determine where you need to be at one quarter, one half, and three quarters of the time allotted to finish. Do not rely on the proctor to keep you abreast of the time—it is your own responsibility. You may or may not receive updates on how much time is remaining.

Mistake # 249
Reading the clinical vignette first

The NBME states that questions on clinical science subject examinations are "framed in the context of clinical vignettes." These vignettes are often long and students have to read a considerable amount of information before they reach the actual question. A better approach is to read the question before the vignette. This helps you focus on the pertinent information in the vignette. As you consider the answer choices, read each and every option. Many students err by picking the first choice that seems like the best answer. Instead, consider each option carefully.

Mistake # 250
Reacting emotionally to questions

NBME subject examination questions tend to be as difficult as USMLE Step 2 questions. On such a difficult exam, you will come across questions to which you don't know the answer. Make an educated guess and then move on to the next question. Frustration or discouragement will negatively affect your concentration. I recommend that you—

- Not spend too much time on a difficult question. This will cut down on the time you have to answer the remaining questions. You don't want to miss easy questions located at the end of the exam because you spent too much time on questions at the beginning.

- Make an educated guess rather than leaving it blank. When question(s) are left unanswered, they may weigh heavily on your mind. Will you have enough time to return to them? Preoccupation with these thoughts can affect your performance on the rest of the exam.

Tip # 99

Leave some time to review questions that gave you difficulty. Information you read in one question might jog your memory or provide a clue to help you answer a previous question.

Tip # 100

There is no penalty for guessing on the NBME subject examination. Don't forget to answer all questions.

For more information about clerkship exams, see also...	Chapter	Mistakes
Psychiatry Clerkship: 150 Biggest Mistakes And How To Avoid Them	9	136 – 150
Surgery Clerkship: 150 Biggest Mistakes And How To Avoid Them	10, 11	126 – 150

References

1) Anderson RE and Obenshain SS. Cheating by students: findings, reflections, and remedies. *Acad Med* 1994; 69(5): 323-332.

2) Arond-Thomas M. Understanding emotional intelligence can help alter problem behavior. *Physician Exec* 2004; 30(5): 36-9.

3) Barzansky B and Etzel SI. Educational Programs In US Medical Schools, 2003-2004. *JAMA* 2004; 292(9): 1025-1031.

4) Bates DW, Cullen DJ, Laird N, et al. Incidence of adverse drug events and potential adverse drug events. Implications for prevention. *JAMA* 1995; 274(1):29-34.

5) Beckman HB, Markakis KM, Suchman AL, Frankel RM. The doctor-patient relationship and malpractice. Lessons from plaintiff depositions. *Arch Intern Med* 1994; 154(12):1365-1370.

6) Beers MH, Munekata M, and Storrie M. The accuracy of medication histories in the hospital medical records of elderly persons. *J Am Geriatr Soc* 1990; 38(11): 1183-7.

7) Benadapudi NM, Berry LL, Frey KA, Parish JT, and Rayburn WL. Patients' perspectives on ideal physician behaviors. *Mayo Clin Proc* 2006; 81(3): 338-344.

8) Bikowski RM, Ripsin CM, Lorraine VL. Physician-patient congruence regarding medication regimens. *J Am Geriatr Soc* 2001; 49(10):1353-1357.

9) Blendon RJ, DesRoches CM, Brodie M, Benson JM, Rosen AB, Schneider E, Altman DE, Zapert K, Hermann MJ, and Steffenson AE. Views of practicing physicians and the public on medical errors. *New Engl J Med* 2002; 347(24):1933-1940.

10) Blue AV, Elam C, Fosson S, Bonaminio G. Faculty members' expectations of student behavior in the small-group setting. *Med Educ Online* [serial online] 1998; 3:5.

11) Blue AV, Griffith CH, Wilson J, Sloan DA, and Schwartz RW. Surgical teaching quality makes a difference. *Am J Surg* 1999; 177(1): 86-9.

12) Bosk CL. Forgive and remember: managing medical failure. Chicago: University of Chicago Press, 1979.

13) Brown G and Manogue M. Refreshing Lecturing: a guide for lecturers. *Med Teach* 2001; 23(3): 231-244.

14) Burack JH, Irby DM, Carline JD, Root RK, Larson EB. Teaching compassion and respect. Attending physicians' responses to problematic behaviors. *J Gen Intern Med* 1999; 14(1): 49-55.

15) Cho JE, Belmont JM, and Cho CT. Correcting the bias of clerkship timing on academic performance. *Arch Pediatr Adolesc Med* 1998; 152: 1015-1018.

16) Colletti LM. Difficulty with negative feedback: face-to-face evaluation of junior medical student clinical performance results in grade inflation. *J Surg Res* 2000; 90(1): 82-87.

17) Copeland HL, Longworth DL, Hewson MG, and Stoller JK. Successful lecturing: a prospective study to validate attributes of the effective medical lecture. *J Gen Intern Med* 2000; 15(6): 366- 371.

18) Cox JL, Zitner D, Courtney KD, MacDonald DL, Paterson G, Cochrane B, Maters J, Merry H, Flowerdew G, and Johnstone DE. Undocumented patient information: an impediment to quality of care. *Am J Med* 2003; 114(3): 211-216.

19) Dans P. Self-repeated cheating by students at one medical school. *Acad Med* 1996; 71(1 Suppl): S70-72.

20) Davis KR and Banken JA. Personality type and clinical evaluations in an obstetrics/gynecology medical student clerkship. *Am J Obstet Gynecol* 2003; 193(5): 1807-1810.

21) Denton GD, Durning SJ, Hemmer PA, and Pangaro LN. A time and motion study of the effect of ambulatory medical students on the duration of general internal medicine clinics. *Teach Learn Med* 2005; 17(3):285-289.

22) Edwards MJ, McMasters KM, Acland RD, Papp KK, and Garrision RN. Oral presentations for surgical meetings. *J Surg Res* 1997; 68(1): 87-90.

23) Elliott DL, Hickam DH. How do faculty evaluate students' case presentations? *Teach Learn Med* 1997; 9(4):261-3.

24) Foley R, Smilansky J, and Yonke A. Teacher-student interaction in a medical clerkship. *J Med Educ* 1979; 54(8): 622-626.

25) Garbutt JM, Highstein G, Jeffe DB, Dunagan WC, Fraser VJ. Safe medication prescribing: training and experience of medical students and housestaff at a large teaching hospital. *Acad Med* 2005; 80(6):594-599.

26) Greenberg LW and Getson PR. Assessing student performance on a pediatric clerkship. *Arch Pediatr Adolesc Med* 1996: 150(11); 1209-1212.

27) Gupta A, Della-Latta P, Todd B, San Gabriel P, Haas J, Wu F, Rubenstein D, Saiman L. Outbreak of extended-spectrum beta-lactamase-producing Klebsiella pneumoniae in a neonatal intensive care unit linked to artificial nails. *Infect Control Hosp Epidemiol* 2004; 25(3):210-5.

28) Hampton HL, Collins BJ, Perry KG, Meydrech EF, Wiser WL, and Morrison JC. Order of rotation in third year clerkships: influence on academic performance. *J Reprod Med* 1996; 41: 337-340.

29) Hendricson WD and Kleffner JH. Assessing and helping challenging students: part one, why do some students have difficulty earning? *J Dent Educ* 2002; 66: 43- 61.

30) Hicks PJ, Cox SM, Espey EL, Goepfert AR, Bienstock JL, Erickson SS, Hammoud MM, Katz NT, Krueger PM, Neutens JJ, Peskin E, and Puscheck EE. To the point: medical education reviews—dealing with student difficulties in the clinical setting. *Am Obstet Gynecol* 2005; 193(6): 1915-1922.

31) Hoffman M and Mittelman M. Presentations at professional meetings: notes, suggestions and tips for speakers. *Eur J Int Med* 2004; 15(6): 358-363.

32) *How-to Guide: Improving Hand Hygiene.* From CDC and Society of Healthcare Epidemiology of America. http://www.shea-online.org

33) Howley LD and Wilson WG. Direct observation of students during clerkship rotations: a multiyear descriptive study. *Acad Med* 2004 (3); 79: 276-280.

34) Hu S, Bostow TR, Lipman DA, Bell SK, Klein S. Positive thinking reduces heart rate and fear responses to speech-phobic imagery. *Percept Mot Skills* 1992; 75 (3 Pt 2):1067-73.

35) Hunt DD, Carline J, Tonesk X, Yergan J, Siever M, Loebel JP. Types of problem students encountered by clinical teachers on clerkships. *Medical Education* 1989; 23: 14-18.

36) Hunt DD. Functional and dysfunctional characteristics of the prevailing model of clinical evaluation systems in North American medical schools. *Acad Med.* 1992; 67(4): 254-259.

37) Institute of Medicine. *To Err is Human: Building a Safer Health System.* Washington, DC:National Academy Press; 2000.

38) Kaboli PJ, Hoth AB, McClimon BJ, and Schnipper JL. Clinical pharmacists and inpatient medical care. *Arch Int Med* 2006; 166(9):955-964.

39) Kalet A, Earp JA, Kowlowitz V. How well do faculty evaluate the interviewing skills of medical students? *Journal of General Internal Medicine* 1992; 7(5): 499-505.

40) Kassebaum DG, Eaglen RH. Shortcomings in the evaluation of students' clinical skills and behaviors in medical school. *Academic Medicine* 1999; 74(7): 841-849.

41) Kernan WN, Quagliarello V, and Green ML. Student faculty rounds: a peer-mediated learning activity for internal medicine clerkships. *Med Teach* 2005; 27(2): 140-144.

42) Kogan JR, Shea JA. Psychometric Characteristics of a Write-Up Assessment Form in a Medicine Core Clerkship. *Teach Learn Med* 2005; 17(2): 101-6.

43) Lang NP, Rowland-Morin, PA, and Coe N. Identification of Communication Apprehension in Medical Students Starting a Surgery Rotation. *Am J Surg* 1998; 176(1): 41-45.

44) Lankford MG, Zembower TR, Trick WE, Hacek DM, Noskin GA, Peterson LR. Influence of role models and hsopital design on the hand hygiene of health-care workers. Emerg Infect Dis [serial online] 2003 Feb. Available from: URL: http://www.cdc.gov/ncidod/EID/vol9no2/02-0249.htm.

45) Lavine E, Regehr G, Garwood K, Ginsbury S. The Role of Attribution to Clerk Factors and Contextual Factors in Supervisors' Perceptions of Clerks' Behaviors. *Teach Learn Med.* 2004; 16(4): 317-22.

46) Levine, DM. Communicating with chronic disease patients. Comment: A Newsletter from the Miles Council for Physician-Patient communication, 1989, 3(3), 1.

47) Linn BS, Zeppa R. Stress in junior medical students: relationship to personality and performance. *J Med Educ*, 1984; 59(1): 7-12.

48) Linney BJ. Presentations that hold you spellbound. *Physician Exec* 2000; 3: 72-75.

49) Littlefield JH, DaRosa DA, Anderson KD, Bell RM, Nicholas GG, Wolfson PJ. Accuracy of surgery clerkship performance raters. *Academic Medicine* 1991; 66 (9 Suppl): S16-18.

50) Lloyd C, Gartrell NK. A further assessment of medical school stress. *J Med Educ*, 1983; 58(12): 964-67.

51) Makaryus AN and Friedman EA. Patients' understanding of their treatment plans and diagnosis at discharge. *Mayo Clin Proc* 005; 80(8): 991-994.

52) Manley M and Heiss G. Timing Bias in the Psychiatry Examination of the National Board of Medical Examiners. *Acad Psych* 006; 30: 116-119.

53) Marinella M. Residents and Medical Students Noting the Chief Complaint during Verbal Presentations. *Acad Med* 2000; 75(3): 89.

54) Marinella MA, Pierson C, Chenoweth C. The stethoscope. A potential source of nosocomial infection? *Arch Intern Med* 1997; 157(7):786-90.

55) McGlynn EA, Asch SM, Adams J, Keesey J, Hicks J, DeCristofaro A, Kerr EA. The quality of health care delivered to adults in he United States. *N Engl J Med* 2003; 348(26): 2635-45.

56) McLeod PJ. Faculty Assessment of Case Reports of Medical Students. *J Med Educ* 1987; 62(8): 673-677.

57) Medalie JH, Zyzanski SJ, Langa D, Stange KC. The family in family practice: is it a reality? *J Fam Pract* 1998: 46(5): 390-6.

58) Mehrabian A and Ferris, SR. Inference of Attitudes from Nonverbal Communication in Two Channels. *Journal of Consulting Psychology* 1967; 31(3): 248-258.

59) Metheny WP. Limitations of physician ratings in the assessment of student clinical performance in an obstetrics and gynecology clerkship. *Obstet Gynecol* 1991; 78 (1): 136-141.

60) Miller GD, Frank D, Franks RD, and Getto CJ. Noncognitive criteria for assessing students in North American medical schools. *Acad Med* 1989; 64(1): 42- 45.

61) Moran MT, Wiser TH, Nanda J, and Gross H. Measuring medical residents' chart-documentation practices. *J Med Educ* 1988; 63(11): 859-65.

62) Moser KM: Venous thromboembolism. *Am Rev Respir Dis* 1990; 141: 235-49.

63) Noel GL, Herbers, JEJ, Caplow MP, Cooper GS, Pangaro LN, Harvey J. How well do internal medicine faculty members evaluate the clinical skills of residents? *Annals of Internal Medicine* 1992; 117 (9): 757-65.

64) Pangaro L. A new vocabulary and other innovations for improving descriptive in-training evaluations. *Academic Medicine* 1999: 74: 1203-1207.

65) Parenti CM and Harris I. Faculty evaluation of student performance: a step toward improving the process. *Med Teach* 1992; 14(2-3): 185-188.

66) Pau AK, Morgan JE, Terlingo A. Drug allergy documentation by physicians, nurses, and medical students. *Am J Hosp Pharm* 1989; 46(3):570-3.

67) Pittet D. Improving adherence to hand hygiene practice: a multidisciplinary approach. www.cdc.gov. Special issue Vol 7, No. 2.

68) Pulito AR, Donnelly MB, Plymale M, and Mentzer RM. What do faculty observe of medical students' clinical performance? *Teach Learn Med* 2006; 18 (2): 99-104.

69) Recupero PR, Cooney MC, Rayner C, Heru AM, and Price M. Supervisor-trainee relationship boundaries in medical education. *Med Teach* 2005; 27(6): 484-488.

70) Rennie SC and Crosby JR. Are "tomorrow's doctors" honest? Questionnaire study exploring medical students' attitudes and reported behavior on academic misconduct. *BMJ* 2001; 322: 274-275.

71) Reteguiz J and Crosson J. Clerkship order and performance on Family Medicine and Internal Medicine National Board of Medical Examiners exams. *Fam Med* 2002; 34: 604-608.

72) Rosenblum ND, Wetzel M, Platt O, Daniels S, Crawford J, and Rosenthal R.

231

Predicting medical student success in a clinical clerkship by rating students' nonverbal behavior. *Arch Pediatr Adolesc Med* 1994; 148(2): 213-219.

73) Rosenstein AH and O'Daniel M. Disruptive behavior and clinical outcomes: perceptions of nurses and physicians. *Am J Nurs* 2005; 105(1): 54-64.

74) Rutter DR and Maguire GP. History-taking for medical stuents. *Lancet* 1976; 2(7985): 558-560.

75) Saloojee H, Steenhoff A. The health professional's role in preventing nosocomial infections. *Postgrad Med J* 2001;77 (903):16-.

76) Sclabassi SE, Woelfel SK. Development of self-assessment kills in medical students. *Medical Education* 1984; 18(4): 226-231

77) Shea JA, Bellini LM, and Reynolds EE. Assessing and changing unprofessional behavior among faculty, residents, and students. *Acad Med* 2000; 75(5): 512.

78) Soto CM, Kleinman KP, Simon SR. Quality and correlates of medical record documentation in the ambulatory care setting. *BMC Health Serv Res* 2002; 2(1):22.

79) Speer AJ, Solomon DJ, and Fincher RM. Grade Inflation in Internal Medicine Clerkships: Results of a National Survey. *Teach Learn Med* 2000; 12 (3): 112-6.

80) Spiegel DA, Smolen RC, Jonas CK. Interpersonal conflicts involving students in clinical medical education. *Journal of Medical Education*, 1985; 60(11): 819-829.

81) Spinler SA. How to prepare and deliver pharmacy presentations. *Am J Hosp Pharm* 1991; 48(8): 1730-8.

82) Starver KD and Shellenbarger R. Professional presentations made simple. *Clin Nurse Spec* 2004; 18(1): 16-20.

83) Stern DT, Williams BC, Gill A, Gruppen LD, Woolliscroft JO, and Grum CM. Is there relationship between attending physicians' and residents' teaching skills and students' examination scores? *Acad Med* 2000; 75(11): 1144-1146.

84) Tonesk X, Buchanan RG. An AAMC pilot study by 10 medical schools of clinical evaluation of students. *J Med Educ* 1987; 62(9): 707-718.

85) Walling A, Montello M, Moser SE, Menikoff JA, and Brink M. Which patients are most challenging for second-year medical students? *Fam Med* 2004: 36(10): 710-714.

86) Wear D, Kokinova M, Keck-McNulty C, Aultman J. Pimping: perspectives of 4th year medical students. *Teach Learn Med* 2005; 17(2): 184-191.

87) Weiss PM, Koller CA, Hess LW, Wasser T. How do medical students self-assessments compare with their final clerkship grades. *Med Teach* 2005; 27(5): 445-449.

88) Wigton RS. The effects of student personal characteristics on the evaluation of clinical performance. *J Med Educ* 1980; 55 (5): 423-427.

89) Wilkerson L, Lesky L, and Medio FJ. The resident as teacher during work rounds. *J Med Educ* 1986; 61(10); 823-829.

90) Williamson KB, Ya-Ping K, Steele JL, Gunderman RB. The art of asking: teaching through questioning. *Academic Radiology* 2002; 9(12): 1419-1422.

91) Woodall, MK. Thinking on your feet, how to communicate under pressure. Lake Oswego, *Oregon Professional Business Communications,* 1996.

Clinician's Guide to Diagnosis:
A Practical Approach

ISBN # 1930598513

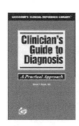

Many medical students have wondered if there was a book that could lead from symptom to diagnosis through a series of steps. We are pleased to inform you that there is. It's called the *Clinician's Guide to Diagnosis*, and it provides you with practical approaches to commonly encountered symptoms. These approaches have been designed to mimic the logical thought processes of seasoned clinicians like your attending physician. Let the *Clinician's Guide to Diagnosis* become your companion, providing you with the tools necessary to tackle even the most challenging symptoms.

"This book serves as a worthy guide to a stepwise approach to common diagnoses. The information is presented in a simple to follow manner. It is intended to provide a practical approach to commonly encountered symptoms, a worthy objective that the book meets. The author provides a unique step-by-step approach to the diagnosis of common problems. Tables and flowcharts are very well done. Medical students and house officers are the intended audience but I would add primary care physicians. As a primary care physician, I am impressed with how easy it is to use this quick reference during a busy schedule."

—Doody Health Science Review written by Peter M. Daher, M.D., Assistant Professor of Medicine at Creighton University Medical School

Clinician's Guide to Laboratory Medicine: A Practical Approach

ISBN # 1591950627

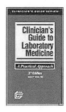

This is the only book that can lead you from abnormal lab test to diagnosis through a series of logical steps. That's right—a step-by-step approach to lab test interpretation. The approaches have been designed to mimic the thought processes of seasoned clinicians like your attending physician. There's simply no easier way of interpreting abnormal lab tests.

"In our Medicine Clerkship, the *Clinician's Guide to Lab Medicine* has quickly become one of the two most popular paperback books that our students purchase for our clerkship. They also use it for other clerkships. Our students have praised the algorithms, tables, and ease of pursuit of clinical problems through better understanding of the utilization of tests appropriate to the problem at hand."—Greg Magarian, M.D., Director, 3rd Year Medicine Clerkship at Oregon Health Sciences University

"I was recently confronted on rounds with a clinical question in an area with which I was not familiar. I quickly pulled the pocket companion out and was able to inform the primary team of the best tests to order to help narrow their differential diagnoses. Needless to say, I was very pleased with the ready availability and accessibility of the information in this book; I may have also unknowingly increased the market for this book as the residents closely observed my choice of quick reference material. I think this is an incredibly useful book for anyone in healthcare. I'm keeping my companion pocket guide in my lab coat for daily use."

—Doody Health Science Review written by Valerie L. Ng, M.D., Ph.D. (Alameda County Medical Center/Highland Hospital)

"I've looked over the book ... It's excellent! ... Great job ... I wish I had this for the past year ... I'm going to recommend it to my class! ... It was the primary source I used on my magnesium presentation and I got some smiles from the director of the internal medicine residency (my first choice), who said it's the best magnesium presentation she has ever heard!"

—Niraj, 4th year medical student at Texas College of Osteopathic Medicine

The Residency Match: 101 Biggest Mistakes And How To Avoid Them

ISBN # 0972556117

Are there any steps you can take to maximize your chances of matching with the residency program of your choice? One of the keys is to become familiar with the major mistakes that students make during the residency application process. These are mistakes that are well known to residency program directors but are not familiar to many applicants. In this book we not only show you these mistakes but also help you avoid them, placing you in a position for match success.

"This book cuts down on the amount of necessary reading that you must do in order to match well. It has tips about subjects I had not thought about (for example, you should have a case ready to present to your interviewer), as well as questions you will be asked in interviews and questions you should ask the interviewer. Overall, this is an easy-to-read book that I would definitely recommend because it contains all the essentials to matching in your ideal residency spot."

—Review posted by Jonathan Welch on amazon.com

Internal Medicine Clerkship: 150 Biggest Mistakes And How To Avoid Them

ISBN # 0972556125

Did you know that most medical students begin doing their best work at the end of the Internal Medicine clerkship? Wouldn't it be great if there was a book available that could speed up the learning curve so that students were performing at a high level right from the start? Now with this book, there's absolutely no reason to save your best for last.

"This manual, published by MD2B in 2004, contains information about many aspects of the clerkship that are not 'taught' but certainly need to be 'learned.'"

—Taken from the University of Iowa Department of Medicine Orientation Syllabus 2005 - 2006 for the Inpatient Medicine Clerkship

"I read the book cover to cover prior to starting the rotation, and it helped me get off to a good start. I feel the book had a great influence on my performance as a clinical student and my evaluation by my teammates. Overall, an extremely helpful and eye opening text. I attribute much of my success to the wisdom I gathered from this book."

—Brian Broaddus, after completing his Internal Medicine clerkship at the Baylor College of Medicine

Surgery Clerkship: 150 Biggest Mistakes And How To Avoid Them

ISBN # 0972556133

At most medical schools, the surgery clerkship is considered to be the most difficult rotation. Days start early, end late, and, from start to finish, the work is intense and demanding, often leading to physical and mental exhaustion. Of course, this can negatively impact your learning, enjoyment, and performance during the clerkship. To prevent this, turn to this book, a resource that will help you overcome the challenges that await you. Lessen your anxiety, alleviate your fears, and position yourself for success by turning to the only book that will help you with every aspect of the rotation, including not only your day to day patient care responsibilities but also your preparation for the oral and NBME clerkship exams.

"This new book will not only prepare the student for the tasks and responsibilities of the surgical clerkship, but will also provide a head start that is sure to impress."

—F. Charles Brunicardi, M.D., F.A.C.S., DeBakey/Bard Professor, Chairman, Michael E. DeBakey Department of Surgery, Baylor College of Medicine

Pediatrics Clerkship: 101 Biggest Mistakes And How To Avoid Them

ISBN # 0972556141

The Pediatrics Clerkship is different in many respects from every other core clerkship, and many students are uncertain of how to success-fully navigate the transition from adult care to the care of children. Students are often unsure of how to take a pediatric history, perform a physical exam, produce a comprehensive pediatric write-up, see patients in the outpatient setting, and take care of patients in the nursery. This book will ease the transition by introducing you to the all-too-common mistakes that are made during the clerkship. With this knowledge in hand, you will become a more productive team member at an earlier point in the rotation, ready to fully focus on learning the fundamentals of pediatric medicine.

"This book is worth the attention of every medical student who wants to optimize time spent on the pediatrics clerkship. It covers all the bases on how a medical student should approach clinical roles, responsibilities, and education during every aspect of the pediatric experience—in the inpatient setting, the ambulatory setting, or the nursery."

—Melanie S. Kim, M.D., Associate Professor, Boston University School of Medicine, Department of Pediatrics, Associate Director of Residency Training, Boston Combined Residency Program in Pediatrics, Deputy Editor, *UpToDate in Pediatrics*

"This book should be entitled, *Success on the Wards*. It gives advice specific to a pediatrics clerkship, as well as helpful do's and don'ts that apply to any rotation. The lessions are clear and concise. They will save any medical student time and energy—plus the ability to impress attendings and residents."

—Samira L. Brown, 4th year Medical Student, Harvard Medical School

Psychiatry Clerkship: 150 Biggest Mistakes And How To Avoid Them

ISBN # 097255615X

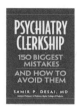

Many medical students find the psychiatry clerkship formidable, not because of a lack of knowledge about psychiatry, but because of a lack of preparation for actually doing the rotation. This "insider's guide" can help you shave weeks off the learning curve by identifying the most common and deleterious mistakes that medical students make, as well as the best approaches to avoiding them. Plus, the "must know" information contained in the appendices will be an invaluable resource in answering questions during rounds and preparing for your exam.

"A student who reads this prior to starting the psychiatry clerkship will be primed for an excellent experience."

—Timothy K. Wolff, M.D., Psychiatry Clerkship Coordinator and Associate Professor of Psychiatry, University of Texas Southwestern Medical School

"This is a very useful and straightforward book that will successfully guide medical students through not only the psychiatry rotation, but many other clerkships as well."

—Anita Afzali, third year medical student, University of Washington School of Medicine

"The authors provide an astonishing amount of practical wisdom in easily understandable and readable prose. It deserves a place alongside the Washington manual in the pocket of every white coat in the halls of every medical school."

—Glenn O. Gabbard, M.D., Brown Foundation Chair of Psychoanalysis, Professor of Psychiatry, Baylor College of Medicine

MD2B TITLES

250 Biggest Mistakes 3rd Year Medical Students Make And How To Avoid Them

The Residency Match: 101 Biggest Mistakes And How To Avoid Them

Internal Medicine Clerkship: 150 Biggest Mistakes And How To Avoid Them

Surgery Clerkship: 150 Biggest Mistakes And How To Avoid Them

Psychiatry Clerkship: 150 Biggest Mistakes And How To Avoid Them

Pediatrics Clerkship: 101 Biggest Mistakes And How To Avoid Them

Clinician's Guide to Laboratory Medicine: A Practical Approach (published by Lexi-Comp)

Clinician's Guide to Diagnosis: A Practical Approach (published by Lexi-Comp)

Clinician's Guide to Internal Medicine: A Practical Approach (published by Lexi-Comp)

ABOUT MD2B.NET

Our website, md2b.net, is committed to helping today's medical student become tomorrow's doctor. The site is dedicated to providing students with the tools needed to tackle the challenges of medical school. The website provides the following information:

Survival guides for 3rd Year Clerkships

Success tips

Residency match information/tips

And much more…